Reforms and Policy

Adult education research in
Nordic countries

Reforms and Policy
Adult education research in Nordic countries

Editorial comittee
Sigvart Tøsse, Norway. Chief editor
Pia Falkencrone, Denmark
Arja Puurula, Finland
Bosse Bergstedt, Sweden

© Tapir Academic Press, Trondheim 2000

ISBN 82-519-1588-0
ISSN 1502-3796

Front-page illustration:
Bertil Hansson: «Berøring» ("Touch")

Printed by Tapir

Secretariat
Bodil Blom and Margit Lea Myklebust,
Norwegian Institute of Adult Education

Previous publications in the series
Adult education research in Nordic Countries 1990/91. Linköping, 1992.
Adult education research in Nordic Countries 1991/92. Copenhagen, 1993.
Adult education research in Nordic Countries 1992/93. Trondheim, 1994.
Adult education research in Nordic Countries 1994. Linköping, 1995.
Adult education research in Nordic Countries 1996. University of Jyväskylä, 1997.
Corporate and nonformal learning. Trondheim: Tapir Akademisk Forlag, 1998.
Challenges and development. Trondheim: Tapir Academic Press, 1999.

TAPIR ACADEMIC PRESS
N–7005 TRONDHEIM, Norway

Tel: 73 59 32 10
Fax: 73 59 32 04
E-mail: forlag@tapir.no
http://www.tapir.no/forlag

PREFACE

The present book is a continuation of the series *Social Changes and Adult Education Research* first published in 1992, and subsequently yearly 1993 – 1999. The aim of these Nordic yearbooks is to present the most recent, on-going research into adult education in the Nordic countries to an international audience. The yearbook is a joint enterprise by educational institutions in Denmark, Finland, Norway and Sweden, with one person from each country constituting the editorial staff.

A main focus in this book is on recent reforms and policy, especially in Finland, Norway and Sweden. Other themes are also included representing current trends of research and areas of interest in the field of adult education research. All are new articles which have not previously been published.

The editorial committee

Content

INTRODUCTION
  Sigvart Tøsse --- 1

ADULT EDUCATION TRENDS AND REFORMS
  Sigvart Tøsse --- 5

NEW DIRECTIONS OF ADULT EDUCATION POLICY IN FINLAND
  Risto Rinne and Markku Vanttaja --- 23

INTEREST AND MOTIVATION TO PARTICIPATE IN ADULT EDUCATION. A STUDY WITHIN THE ADULT EDUCATION INITIATIVE
  Per-Olof Thång and Gun-Britt Wärwik --- 39

FACTORS BEHIND THE FINNISH HIGHER EDUCATION REFORM - THE ESTABLISHMENT OF AMK-INSTITUTIONS
  Hannele Salminen --- 59

REFORM 94 – CONSEQUENCES FOR ADULTS
  Heidi Engesbak --- 79

DISTANCE EDUCATION AT THE TURN OF THE CENTURY – HISTORICAL BACKGROUND AND NEW DEVELOPMENTS ILLUSTRATED BY A CASE STUDY OF AN INSTITUTION IN CHANGE
  Torstein Rekkedal --- 99

WORKING LIFE AND NON-FORMAL EDUCATION
  Bjarne Wahlgren --- 123

MANAGEMENT EDUCATION AND ORGANIZATION DEVELOPMENT
  Juha Kettunen --- 143

EXPERIENCING THE CHANGES BROUGHT BY IT AND THEIR CONSEQUENCES IN SMES
  Tarja Tikkanen --- 161

THE LIFE-STORY IN ADULT EDUCATION
  Marianne Horsdal --- 183

IDENTITIES IN TRANSITION: KEY INTERVIEWS AS A WAY TO ANALYSE THE TRANSFORMATION OF THE PUBLIC SECTOR
  Karin Filander --- 197

AUTONOMY AND COMMUNALITY IN SELF-DIRECTED OPEN LEARNING
  Leena Ahteenmäki-Pelkonen --- 221

GRUNDTVIG´S EDUCATIONAL IDEAS
  Ove Korsgaard --- 237

SOCIAL PARTICIPATION AS A CHALLENGE TO LIFE-LONG LEARNING IN EUROPE
Anja Heikkinen and Kristiina Laiho------ 255

A FUTURE FOR LIFELONG LEARNING? SOME COMMENTS ON A NORDIC SCENARIO PROJECT
Gunnar Grepperud and Odd Einar Johansen ------ 279

Contributors------295

INTRODUCTION

Sigvart Tøsse

In recent years, governments in all the Nordic countries have implemented new adult education initiatives and reforms. A lot of research therefore concerns trends, reforms and state policy and much of this research is paid for by the state authorities. In this presentation of recent and ongoing research in the Nordic countries reforms and policy is thus selected as a main theme.

Sigvart Tøsse analyses recent trends that he characterizes as a transformation of adult education from being dominantly conceptualized as something cultural into education related to the world of work. This development is most clearly demonstrated in the competence reform which is now at the top of the agenda for adult education policy in Norway. What appear to be the emergent, dominant and residual trends are discussed in terms of rhetoric, resources and participation.

Risto Rinne and Markku Vanttaja support this analysis with results from Finland. On the basis of an observed increase in vocational adult education they conclude that adult education has become a tool of labour policy and that the former declaration of educational equality has almost disappeared from official educational planning documents. The authors are highly critical to the development which according to their views does not satisfy the hopes and needs of people.

In Sweden, due to a rapid increase in unemployment in the 1990s, the government launched an Adult Education Initiative which followed the extended education for youth. The target groups are the unemployed and people with low levels of education. *Per-Olof Thång* and *Gunn-Britt Wärwik* discuss the crucial issues of motivation and also find that the new Adult Education Initiative is proof of the dissociation of the humanistic aspects of adult education from the 1970s and places a new focus on economic growth and employment.

Hannele Salminen looks into the factors behind the Finnish higher education reform and the establishment of new institutions of vocational higher education (AMK). These AMKs evolved from the former vocational institutions which were upgraded and merged in the 1990s into new, multi-field higher education institutions offering vocational postgraduate studies and new degrees. The reasons for this reform are found both in the problems in the education system and changes in society. In spite of the severe economic depression, which hit Finland in the early 1990s, there seems to be widespread educational optimism and a strong belief in steady economic growth.

One of the recent education reforms in Norway is Reform 94 giving all youth aged 16 – 19 a statutory right to three years of upper secondary education. In her article *Heidi Engesbak* analyses the consequences for adults, i.e. how Reform 94 has influenced adults' accessibility and chances of participation in higher secondary education in the period 1994 –1997.

Torstein Rekkedal gives a short history of distance education in Norway, and discusses recent developments and the research carried out. As a researcher and director of research and development in one of the largest distance education institutions in Norway he has a firm belief in the new technologies, claiming that the Internet is changing the whole concept of distance teaching and learning. However, he is also critical and emphasizes that the providers have to learn to adopt the technologies to achieve optimal outcomes for different kinds of learners. The medium itself does not solve any problems.

A joint research project, started in 1996, between four research institutions in the Nordic countries focused on the relationship between working life and non-formal education. *Bjarne Wahlgren* presents the results from the case studies in the four countries. He concludes that it is difficult to find evidence that the collaboration between non-formal education and working life has been mutually promotive. There are, however, interesting differences between the four countries, and the experience from the case studies will hopefully stimulate further research.

As part of the vocational trend in adult education management education has come to the fore. Employers pay most willingly for management education and regard this as investment in human capital. It is also an investment from the participants's side. Finland is probably the leading Nordic country in this kind of education, and the universities, business schools and other institutions have a great number of Professional Development programmes and Master of Business Administration programmes. *Juha Kettunen* discusses and compares management education in the USA, Japan, Germany and Finland.

Tarja Tikkanen addresses the issue of how information technology is changing work and the work environment in small and medium-sized companies. Her study considers the effects of age and occupational sector and provides a mutual comparison of two age groups (-45/45+) and two occupational sectors (services and information). The study shows interesting differences regarding age and sector but the findings also suggest that the role that chronological age plays in managing new technology varies from one occupational sector to another.

In Denmark, a state-supported research project *Adult Education and Democracy* aims to clarify the complex changes in the relationship between adult education ("folkeoplysning") and democracy in post-modern society. *Marianne Horsdal* advocates the life-story approach and presents new challenges for adult education towards a stimulation of reflexivity and narrative competencies.

Karin Filander's article refers to a key interview with a professional person in the public sector, Petra, thus constructing a life story in which the narrator switches to different forms of self-definition. In the present analysis multiple identities are an aspect of a social transformation where single exhaustive stories about stable identities do not exist anymore. Filander claims that identities may be seen as socially structured and socially changing subject positions. Thus narrative and construction are open to repeated redefinitions. According to the author, this life-story indicates that the new market-oriented discourse that is increasingly used by public servants has given rise to a kind of identity crisis both at the individual and group levels.

A key concept in adult education, self-directed learning, may be understood as a concept consisting of four categories, according to *Leena Ahteenmäki-Pelkonen*: autonomy, communality, critical reflection, and integration to reality. However, only the two first ones are discussed in her article. Autonomy comprises three subconcepts: self-initiative learning, emotional independence and authenticity. Communality refers to solidarity and dialogue. Ahteenmäki-Pelkonen discusses these concepts in relation to the theories of Jack Mezirov.

No educational reform or educational enterprise in Denmark can omit references to Grundtvig and his influence on Danish society, and few Nordic educators have been studied more thoroughly. This research has mostly concentrated on his pedagogical ideas and the folk high school. *Ove Korsgaard* claims, however, that a third category must be added, namely Grundtvig's ideas regarding enlightenment. He gives a short presentation and analysis of this and also argues for the relevance of these ideas in a time of growing individualization and globalization.

From 1998 to 1999 a research group at the University of Tampere participated in a Socrates studies and analysis project "Effective Processes for the Acquisition of Qualifications for Life-long Learning" (Lifequal). *Anja Heikkinen* and *Kristiina Laiho* have used this project to discuss social participation as an educational category, why it should be a challenge for lifelong learning and for whom it is a challenge.

The perspective in the concluding article is the future for lifelong learning looking 20 years ahead. The scenario outlined by *Gunnar Grepperud* and *Odd Einar Johansen* is based on interviews with 15 selected experts from the field of adult education practice, policy and research. The authors address eleven main themes which are discussed in the article. Although this is speculative, the assumptions hopefully will offer some inspiration for reflection on lifelong learning in coming years. More than providing accurate answers, the scenario aims to inspire the necessary questions that need to be asked for further development.

ADULT EDUCATION TRENDS AND REFORMS

Sigvart Tøsse

Abstract

The article traces the development of adult education from being dominantly conceptualized as culture into education and the world of work. Adult education as formal education, vocational training and labour market policy appeared in the 1960s while culture remained a residual element. Through analysis of rhetoric, resources and participation the development towards this dominant vocational trend is confirmed. The latest emergent trend however seems to be a transformation of adult education beyond the division between culture, education and work as is indicated by a new learning paradigm and the extended use of concepts such as qualification and competence. The new competence reform in Norway is also an indication of an internationally observed transformation of adult education into further and continuing education.

Introduction

In a cultural process some trends are dominant, others are residual and new elements appearing as emergent (Williams, 1977). The dominant ones are the main structures and trends. The residual ones are elements from the past which may turn up and be activated through reinterpretations, reformulation or accentuation. Emergent trends are the shaping of new values, practices and conditions.

Trends have often been linked to socio-economic structures. Researchers associated with the new sociology in the 1970s claimed that the norms, values and skills prevailing in the world of production and manufacturing are reflected and reproduced in the educational system. Bowles and Gintis stated for instance that

> "The educational system helps integrate youth into the economic system, ... through a structural correspondence between its social relations and those of production " (Bowles and Gintis, 1976:131).

This structural correspondence, however, is not unambiguous. Education may have a relative autonomy, the educational system is claimed to have a certain slowness and is influenced by personal intentions, values and ideologies. There is always a complicated dialectic between economic structures, power and hegemony on the one hand and resistance, critics and social actions on the other. My assumption is that in the field of adult education trends are the result of the interplay of national policies, individual choices and demands, and socio-economic structures. National policy and structures are again increasingly influenced by processes of globalization. The focus here is on the state policy, recent reforms in adult education and analysis of the dominant, emergent and residual trends in terms of rhetoric, resources, and participation.

Adult education as part of the culture policy

In a previous article (Goderham and Tøsse, 1996) it is claimed that adult education in Norway has passed through three overlapping yet distinctive phases labelled the philantrophic, the socio-cultural and the institutional phase. Adult education originated in a Nordic tradition of popular enlightenment in which philanthropists and social movements became the main responsible bodies of adult education. From the 1880s state support could be given to lectures, worker's academy and evening schools, later (1930s) also to study circles. After 1945 the socio-cultural phase gradually turned into the institutional phase, i.e. the incorporation of adult education into the state's sphere of legitimate interest so that adult education is included in public policy. The transformation of an office into a permanent state advisory body on adult education in the 1960s and the implementation of an Adult Education Act in 1976 indicate its full institutionalization.

In the socio-cultural phase the main aims of adult education were personal development, the democratization of culture and social change. Education or enlightenment had only slight references to practical work, economic utility and growth as these were regarded as chiefly indirect benefits. There were significant arguments for state support to adult education from voluntary organizations in the 1930s – the formative period (cf. Hake, 1994). In their eyes the severe prevailing economic crisis was not only "financial and materialistic but spiritual and moral" and the aim of adult education was henceforth to lay the basis of the human spiritual and intellectual development. This had to take place in spare time, not in work time, and the organization urged for using spare time, which in the 1930s was expanded by enforced unemployment, to study work and the acquirement of culture (Statens folkeopplysningsråd, 1959).

Still in the post-war years facing the problems of economic recovery adult education was largely a spare time activity and discussed as part of the cultural policy. Becoming aware of the "leisure time problem" the Government increasingly supported libraries, folk academies, sports and youth associations in their efforts to give all opportunities for "sound recreation". State subsidies were managed by an office for art and culture within the Department of Education and in the political party programmes we find adult education (by that time named *folkeopplysning*, i.e. popular enlightenment) under the heading culture.

In the 1950s increasing state subsidies were given to study circles, evening schools, lecturing, amateur arts (i.e. song, music, theatre) and cultural efforts in new industrial centres. State interventions into the field of voluntary associations were however opposed from the beginning by the non-socialist parties fearing that subsidies could hurt voluntarism, idealism and curtail autonomy. Nevertheless the non-governmental organizations welcomed – and urged – state support and joined a public committee in 1958 to consider how their work could be better organized and supported. The aims of adult education (*folkeopplysning*) were defined by the committee to be:
- making the cultural benefits available to all,
- developing the individual as a person and citizen, and
- releasing human capabilities and aptitudes such that everyone can participate in the creation of cultural values (Innstilling, 1960).

As in the 1930s adult education in this Report still was far away from the world of formal schooling, the world of work and economic utility. State commitment was required to give individuals "extended possibilities to obtain a better use of their spare time". Since the popular enlightenment had stronger links to culture than to education the Report advised that separate cultural committees in municipalities and counties should administer the field of adult education.

Even research identified adult education with cultural work. The largest research project in the 1950s was a historical inquiry into popular education and published under the title Popular Cultural Work (*Folkelig kulturarbeid*, 1958). One of the few academic researchers, Egil Nilsen, devoted himself to a mapping of leisure time interests among the adult population (Nilsen, 1958).

Adult education as general education

Conceptions of adult education changed rapidly in the 1960s. The concept of popular enlightenment (*folkeopplysning*) now became declared antiquated, associated with education from above and accused of not having any current interest for people who demanded "real useful and skilled knowledge" (Studienytt, no. 7, 1960). The term itself changed from enlightenment (*folkeopplysning*) to education and training (*voksenoplæring*).

In midst of the 1960s the Minister of Education (Helge Sivertsen) was responsible for a parliamentary bill on adult education (St. prp. no. 92, 1964 – 65). His main idea was to involve the educational system in adult education and incorporate adult education in the state reform education policy. The bill emphasized general education as the main task of a state supported education of adults. On the one hand general education was increasingly important for working life, on the other it could counterweight the strain caused by specialization of work. "Therefore in their leisure-time people must try to achieve their potential and use the abilities and power which they do not make use of in their daily work", the bill declared. As we see adult education was still to be confirmed as a leisure-time activity.[2]

An important statement was that adult education and the school system should have equal status. The schools were given the responsibility for all certified education (i.e. formal education) while the voluntary organizations should take care of studies without examinations, cultural and leisure-time activities (i.e. non-formal education). As a consequence adult education was removed from the cultural office to a new division in the Department of Education and subsidies to amateur arts were transferred to cultural budgets.

The main reason for this transformation from culture to education is the extension of youth education. In 1959 a law on compulsory 9-year schooling was implemented. Moreover greater shares of the age groups took secondary education and thus widened the educational gap between the young and the elderly. Adult education became the solution for giving the adults a second chance for education and giving delayed justice for the older generations. Even the voluntary organizations were admitted to play a role in this development despite of being principally restricted to non-formal education. After 1969, when adults were allowed to take the equivalent of one A-level subject at a time, the organizations engaged themselves in upper secondary education and increasingly in higher education too.

---

[2] We also find the same conception of adult education as a leisure-time activity in Denmark and confirmed there by the Act on Leisure-time Instruction in 1968.

Adult education as vocational training and labour market policy

Already in the 1950s the labour unions and the labour party argued for the education of adults as an important part of vocational training, readjustment to new conditions and jobs and further education. Due to rapid technological development and restructuring these aims became even more obvious in the 1960s. Adult education, now also encompassing further and continuing education, was considered increasingly instrumental to economic development. At the end of the 1960s state founded regional colleges were built up to accommodate the demand for higher and tertiary education.

The Parliamentary bill of 1965 divided the field of adult education in two parts; 1) the traditional educational and cultural work provided by schools and voluntary organizations, and 2) vocational and work-related education and training arranged by the employers, trade unions, professional bodies and labour market boards. In addition to transferring adult education from the cultural to the educational sphere, the Minister of Education moved parts of the field to labour market policy. Influenced by the human capital theory the bill considered adult education as an important means of improving the productivity of the labour force, solving economic and social problems, promoting the mobility of the work force and counteracting unemployment in rural districts. The labour unions even argued for a separate directorate of adult education associated with the Ministry of Labour. The non-Socialist parties, that were in government in the second half of the 1960s, ensured, however, that adult education remained under the Ministry of Education.

Dominant, emergent and residual

In the dominant conception prevailing till the end of the 1950s adult education meant the acquirement of culture, personal refinement and transmission of traditions and values. As main agents the voluntary organizations provided membership education (sometimes with strong appeal to group or class commitment) and offered cultural and social education, some even political education, as well as recreation to the public at large. Their activities were valued by state authorities as enlightenment of the people and contributions to democracy and citizenship. Learning was non-formal or informal.

An emergent meaning of adult education in the 1960s was formal education to make up for lost education, pass an examination in order to gain entrance into higher education or better paid jobs. These aims involved in addition to the voluntary organizations the school system and distance institutions and required special arrangements for adults. In 1959 – 60 the first courses in adult education were offered at the universities in order to provide a more professional and educated staff of teachers, instructors and managers. This trend put more emphasis on formal learning in a classroom setting.

A second emergent meaning of adult education in the 1960s was vocational training to qualify oneself for new tasks, jobs and the use of new technology. On-the-job training, public financed labour market training and further training were all included in the concept of adult education and regulated by the law of 1976. This trend included experience learning in a workplace setting.

Partly due to a more outspoken opposition to the human capital thinking and the growth economy the meaning of adult education as culture had a revival in the 1970s. A new cultural policy emphasized decentralized administration, people's own active involvement, local identity and the non-economic qualities of life. The labour movement revitalized ideas of a worker culture, arranged "cultural days/weeks" and a lot of cultural activities. Left-wing radicals engaged themselves in political and ideological education and accentuated emancipation and social change as the most important aims. The advocates of adult education also believed that more education would promote sexual, geographical and social equality. Spokespersons from the voluntary organizations reminded politicians that adult education was linked to culture as their domain was general cultural work, transmission of knowledge and training of skills with no other aim than personal development. These advocates therefore opposed that adult education should be administered on the local level by the Municipal School Board and advised a reorganization into a common board for education and culture (NOU 1972:41; St. prp. no. 7, 1975 – 76). Adult education as culture became – and continued to be - a residual element in adult education.

This trend is also observed internationally. The UNESCO world conference in Tokyo, 1972, declared for instance that adult education and culture are intertwined. This world-wide organization has probably played a supporting role to organizations (and Folk High Schools in Nordic countries) in framing adult education in terms of a cultural humanization of development (Wildemeersch, Finger & Jansen, 2000:10).

The revitalization of adult education as culture may also be seen as an alliance between the socialist's aim of cultural democracy and the liberal's aim of personal development. The Norwegian Adult Education Act of 1976 stated among other values that the "purpose of adult education is to help the individual to attain a more meaningful life ... and help in their personal development".

Adult education policy and new reforms

The 1980s lead to economic, political and ideological change. The right-wing wave in Norway brought the non-socialist parties to power with the Conservatives (Høyre) as the leading party. The conservative and liberal success was however staggered by economic recession and increasing unemployment and the Labour party recaptured power in 1986. In a White Paper (St. melding 43, 1988 – 89) the Labour government announced that they would make a strong bid for education. In the following years the social democrats carried out a reform policy at all level of the educational system; teacher training and higher education, upper secondary education (see Engesbak), basic education and turned finely to adult education at the end of the 1990s. A main architect of this policy was professor in sociology and Minister of Education 1990 – 1995, Gudmund Hernes. His ambitious aim was to increase both the quantity and quality of education. "A main element of a long-range policy for economic development", the white paper declared, "is to provide knowledge to more people". Moreover it stated that the

> "development and progress of knowledge is a prerequisite for a strengthening of the Norwegian economy, provide full employment, readjustment and lay the basis for new business in working life ...Education, in economic terms, is of strategic importance for our formation of values".

The labour policy restored the human capital thinking, now with competence and qualification as the core concepts. The adult education reform programme was presented in a public report called *New competence* in 1997 (NOU, 1997:25). It was followed by a White Paper (St. melding no. 42, 1997 – 98) which the Norwegian parliament debated on 19 January 1999.[3] "The basis for the reform is the need for competence in the workplace, in society and by the individual" the parliament stated - with workplace, society and individual in that order of preference. Generally the educational reforms changed the focus from the individual to the requirements of society. A basic argument for the adult education initiative was the need for a more qualified workforce, caused

---

[3] Abridged version in English will be found on
http://odin.dep.no/kuf/publ/1999/competence and
http://odin.dep.no/repub/97-98/stmld/42/engelsk/index.html

by a "widening gap between the need for and the availability of new knowledge at the workplace". Accordingly the reform presented itself as a working life reform, not a matter of common welfare as was usually underpinning educational reforms. It stated, however, that "the reform will embrace all adults in and outside the labour market" and be based on a broad conception of knowledge. It will be "implemented as a process in which employers, employees and the government will have to make an active contribution". The main elements of the reforms are:

- *Documentation of adults' non-formal learning:* A project has been started to establish a system for documentation and recognition of non-formal learning related to upper secondary education. A governmental committee is also considering admitting students to courses in higher education based on their work experience, non-formal learning or combinations of work experience, training and education.[4]
- *Right to leave of absence*: From 2001, employees who have been working at least 3 years will have an individual right to study leave. The expense of subsistence during study leave is a matter of negotiation between the employer and the employees. The government will however adapt the rules of the State Educational Loan Fund more closely to continuing education and training for adults. Tax on education paid by the employer has been removed.
- *Right to education*: The Norwegian Parliament has given adults the individual right to primary and lower secondary education and will even extend such a right even to upper secondary education.
- *Support to programmes and projects*: A lot of money is put into a competence-building programme which will finance projects and development programme. The government especially recommends exploiting the huge potential that lies in the workplace as a place of learning and encouraging greater use of information and communications technology. As Rekkedal comments, this will stimulate universities and higher educational institutions to develop strategies for distance education.

The rhetoric of the new adult education initiatives indicate that the vocational trend with emphasis on the need of the working life have become dominant. However, the new policy is not exclusively committed to the world of work. It is also characterized as strongly idealistic (Telhaug, 1997). Adult education is still aiming at cultural development, democracy and the promotion of equality

---

[4] Two reports from the committee are: NOU 1999:17 *Realkompetanse i høgre utdanning.* NOU 2000:14 *Frihet med ansvar.*

and will serve the participants as total human beings, as citizens and as employees. As in the Swedish Adult Education Initiative (see Thång and Warvik) an important aim in the competence reform is to give all adult opportunities to upper secondary education – which also indicates that adult education as proper education still is a predominant trend.

We will now look to what analysis of resources and participation will tell us.

Resources

Up to 1960s adult education - conceptualized as culture - received modest state support. The main providers were the voluntary organizations which based their activities largely on unpaid and voluntary work.

As adult education gradually became second-chance and work-related education state subsidies rose rapidly. From the end of the 1960s support to adult education in the school system was introduced in the public budget and this item rose more rapidly than any other. In the 1970s subsidies to adult higher education were added. State subsidies were also given to shop steward training (St. prp. no. 1, 1945; Tøsse, 1996).

The bulk of the state subsidies went however to the study work, i.e. evening schools, study circles and a wide range of different courses, arranged by the voluntary organizations. In principle, every activity carried out, regardless of aims and content, received subsidies, in fact a strong acknowledgement of their societal utility. As subsidies also increased from 50 % to 80 % of approved costs the state funding increased from NOK 15 million in 1970 to NOK 264 million in 1979. Then an upper limit was put on state subsidies and public expenditure was pressed downwards. From 1980 to 1985, the Government reduced subsidies to adult education from 4.2 % to 3.3 % of the total public expenses to education granted from the Department of Education (St.prp. no. 1).

Table 1. States subsidies to adult education from the Department of Education

	1970	1974	1980	1985
State subsidies	NOK 15 million	NOK 44 million	NOK 283 million	NOK 235 million
% of budget to education	-	1.2 %	4.2 %	3.3 %

As the golden years came to an end, the participants had to pay more for their education. In the beginning of the 1980s state subsidies constituted approximately 15 – 30 % of total educational costs (Innst. S, no. 280, 1984 – 85). State subsidies per person in Norway continued to be significantly lower then in Sweden, Denmark and Finland (NOU, 1986:23). The Minister of Education had to admit in the beginning of the 1990s that adult education compared to the school system was lagging behind (St. forh. 1991-92, 8, p. 11).

Adult education appeared however as a public expense on other budgets. Due to increasing unemployment in the 1980s qualification measures and subsidies to vocational training schemes for adults rapidly surpassed the grants to general adult education. Already in the middle of the 1980s the expenditure to labour market courses was twice as high as to study work. In the first part of the 1990s, at the top of the unemployment rate, labour market courses received ten times the subsidies to the educational activities of voluntary organizations - or approximately four times the public subsidies to all other adult education put together.

In terms of resources it seems reasonable to conclude that in the beginning of the 1990s adult education largely had become a tool of labour policy, as also was the case in Finland (see Rinne and Vanttaja). This statement will furthermore be confirmed if we look at the quantity of education. Bearing in mind that the labour market courses averaged 400 study hours compared to 29 hours in general adult education the labour market courses amounted to 40 % of all lessons spent (Folk High Schools included) to adult education (Ministry of Education, 1995). At the end of the 1990s even though the numbers of labour market courses (and public spending) were cut by a half, a large share of adult education is vocational training under the auspices of labour market authorities.

However, this is not the whole story: The in-service training which is mainly paid for by the employer, is missing in these statistics (and there are no other statistics on this expenditure available). According to a survey in 1962 among a large number of enterprises, NOK 7.3 million was spent on vocational training (four times the public subsidy to adult education) – or 0.3 % of wage payments. There is good reason to believe that the private and public expenditure on vocational in-service training has increased relatively. An estimate is that Norwegian enterprises in the mid 1990s invested NOK 12 – 18 billion in competence development (NOU 1997:25) which far exceeds the public subsidies (less than NOK 4 billion).

Participation

According to a survey in 1953 approximately 4 % of the adult population participated in study work, i.e. evening schools, study circles, lectures and correspondence school education. In 1960s and 1970s, participation rose remarkably and in the beginning of 1980s it is estimated that 1 million people in Norway – a third of the adult population – participated in adult education. Since 1980s participation in the study work arranged by the voluntary organizations has decreased by 25 %. Enrolment in distance education is reduced from 200.000 in 1976 to 100.000 in 1998, according to Rekkedal "mainly …a result of continuously decreased financial support from the state". New surveys indicate however that the total participation is increasing. In 1996, 40 % of the sample of adults (16 – 79 years) had participated in adult education courses during the last two years. Compared with a survey in 1977 – 78 participation had increased by approximately 50 %, and adults in 1996 also participated significantly more often than before in several courses (Skaalvik and Engesbak, 1996). A recent survey indicated a continuing increase: 70 % of adults (18 – 79 years) said in 1999 that they had participated in adult education during the last three years (Skaalvik, Ljosland and Finbak, 2000). What we are witnessing is probably changes in preferences and new patterns of participation among men and women and the socio-economic groups.

Table 2. Participation in adult education according to three different surveys

Year	Age	Sample (N)	Period of participation	Total participation
1978 [5]	15 – 75	4 066	1 ½ year	24 %
1996 [6]	16 – 79	1 393	2 years	40 %
1999 [7]	18 – 79	1 837	3 years	70 %

Participation of men and women

A number of studies have revealed distinctly different patterns of participation between men and women. Men generally participate more in work-related education while women are the majority in general education. In working life the gap between men and women seems to have been largely reduced, while there still exist sexual differences among the total population. Table 3 shows the results from different surveys. (They are not comparable due to different design and differing periods of participation.)

---

[5] Skaalvik and Knudsen, 1979
[6] Skaalvik and Engesbak, 1996
[7] Skaalvik, Ljosland and Finbak, 2000

Table 3. Participation in vocational or work-related adult education (%)

	Participation among employees				Part. of total adult pop.	
	1972 [8] (1 year)	1986 [9] (1 year)	1993 [10] (1 year)	1996 [11] (5 years)	1978 [12] (1 ½ year)	1996 [13] (2 years)
Men	15	35	35	78	16	36
Women	9	28	33	73	7	26

If we look at the participation in general adult education we will find a majority of women. In voluntary study work the share of female participants have in recent years been stable at around 56 %. The reason is that women take more hobby and leisure-time courses than men. In general education (except hobby and leisure-time courses) the participation of men and women is however more equal. A suggestion is that men are oriented towards work and their career while women emphasize personal development more (Skaalvik and Engesbak, 1996). The 1999 survey shows this result (Skaalvik, Ljosland and Finbak, 2000):

Table 4. Participation the last three years in different types of courses (N = 1 837). (%)

	Work-related courses	General courses	Hobby- and leisure-time courses
Men	63	12	15
Women	58	13	22
Total	60	12	18

Participation in various socio-economic groups

A number of studies have documented that the more educated and skilled receive (and take) more adult education and training than the lower educated and unskilled. Although these differences in participation are slowly decreasing, they are still large. In addition, employees in higher positions participate more

---

[8] SSB Statistiske analyser no. 26; Voksenopplæring 1969 - 74
[9] NOS: Levekårsundersøkelsen 1987
[10] NOS: Arbeidsmiljø 1993
[11] Larsen, Longva, Pape and Reichborn, 1997, p. 104
[12] Skaalvik and Engesbak, 1996
[13] Skaalvik and Engesbak, 1996

often than unskilled workers in several courses and in a variety of different kinds of courses (Larsen et al., 1997).

Table 5. Participation in various socio-economic groups (%)

	Period	Unskilled workers	Skilled workers	Salaried employees with managerial functions
1979 [14]	1 year	12	27	45
1986 [15]	1 year	20	30	56
1991 [16]	1 year	23	32	56
1996 [17]	5 years	52	75	93

General and vocational education

A report in 1952 on participation in the Students' Free Education (later the People's University) stated that the main motives for studies were "special interest in the topic" or "good leisure-time occupation". Only a third considered studies to be useful for their vocation (SFU 100 år, 1964). A sample survey in 1977 – 78 (4 000 adults aged 15 – 75) indicated that motives for the majority of participants still could be found in the world of culture and education: 15 % participated in general education, hobby- or leisure-time courses compared with 11 % in work-related education (Skaalvik and Knudsen, 1979).

However, it is not always possible to distinguish between general, work-related or other types of education. Moreover the amount of participation will vary according to definitions of participation and what is included in adult education. On basis of several surveys between 1971 and 1983 a conclusion has been drawn that almost 80 % of all participation was work-related (Gooderham and Lund, 1991).

The unknown participation – due to the lack of statistics – is within in-service training. A cautious conclusion in Norwegian statistics (1993) is that half the adult education – in terms of participants – takes place in working life (Sosialt utsyn, 1993:140). A sample survey in 1996 by Skaalvik and Engesbak, corresponded to the 1978 study, confirmed the trend. Participation in work-

---

[14] NOS Levekårsundersøkelsen 1980
[15] NOS Levekårsundersøkelsen 1987
[16] NOS Levvekårsundersøkelsen 1991
[17] Larsen, Longva, Pape and Reichborn, 1997

related education had increased from 11 % in 1978 to 30 % in 1996. The main reasons for participation among employees are to "increase one's qualifications for the job" or "obtain more job security", i.e. the motives are to be found in the pressure for more qualifications and competence in working life (Larsen et al., 1997).

Table 6. Participation in work-related and general adult education (%)

		Work-related courses	General, hobby and leisure courses	Total participation
1978 [18]	1 ½ year	11	15	24
1996 [19]	2 years	30	21	40
1999 [20]	3 years	60	30	70

For 55 % of the person interviewed in 1996, the work-related coursed were organized by the employer or trade organization, these even arranged 30 % of the general education courses, a strong indication that the bulk of adult education in fact is in-service training. A study among employees in 1996 also showed that 63 % received in-service training in order to improve their work qualifications (Larsen et. al., 1997). An additional result from the studies is that adult education now is more equally distributed in according to age than before, especially for the well educated (Skaalvik and Engesbak, 1996).

Conclusions

In this lengthy historical perspective, adult education has passed through distinctive phases which reflect broader societal developments. In the shorter period, i.e. after the Second World War, adult education has been transformed from the sphere of culture to the world of work. The trend towards vocationalism is internationally observed and is pronounced in the new competence reform with a strong emphasis on workplace learning, documentation of the non-formal learning and incitements to further and continuing education for employees. Moreover there has been a trend from conceptualizing adult education as a cultural activity towards general or proper education.

---

[18] Skaalvik and Knudsen, 1979
[19] Skaalvik end Engesbak, 1996
[20] Skaalvik, Ljosland and Finbak, 2000

The development is here analysed as the combined effects of state policy, resources and personal demand (participation). In a previous article it is suggested that the institutionalization phase is succeeded by deinstitutionalization signifying a divestment of acceptance by the state of the responsibility for areas of adult education activities. A consequece has been greater exposure to the effects of market forces (Gooderham and Tøsse, 1996). Although the hallmarks of this trend are many, the state policy is ambiguous. On the one hand the new competence reform placed the main responsibility for adult education on the associations for employers and employees and fits well into the arguments of marketization, managerialism and economic adjustment to a global competition. On the other hand, the competence reform, as well as the other education reforms, is largely a state initiative followed by state investments. The left and right have in fact agreed upon a strong state involvement in the field of education alongside a more market-oriented economy – which is said to accord very well with neo-liberalism and neo-conservatism (Telhaug, 1997).

The move of focus from education to learning is fundamentally important for the ongoing transformation of adult education. This new learning paradigm in fact transcends the division of adult education into culture, education and vocational education. The boarders between culture, education and work are increasingly blurred as the current interest is the interplay of non-formal and formal education (see Wahlgren) as well as the combined effects of personal, general and vocational education.

The extended use of the concept of qualifications reflects this convergence of culture, education and work. As remarked by others this concept is no longer restricted to the area of labour-oriented training and education, but has become a universal paradigm for cultural development as well (Wildemeersch, Finger and Jansen, 2000:19). Furthermore, the concept of experience learning has served as a mediator between the personal growth philosophy and the vocational education, and between culture and work, since experience is considered basic for educational outcomes both from participation in cultural activities and workplace activities. A conclusion from the discussions of the dominant, emergent and residual is that culture seems to be a residual element while work and education converge into consideration of what is useful and will lead to better qualifications for working life.

A more radical conclusion to the hypothesis of convergence as the new emerging trend is that adult education is rapidly ceasing to be a separate educational entity. It has been increasingly transformed into further and continuing education "and from this, occupationally, into continuing professional development which takes it beyond the realms of education itself" (Jarvis, 2000). Adult education has no doubt lost its foundation in social movements. The movements themselves have lost membership and are crumbling away into newer associations with a looser structure and more demarcated aims. Accordingly "it is not possible", says Jarvis, "to regard adult education as a social movement any longer" - except for that it may survive as an action-oriented educational social movement for the elderly (Jarvis, 2000).

The increasingly use of the term further and continuing education (*etter- og videreutdanning*) instead of adult education (*voksenopplæring*) may be a growing sign that this new trend is emergent. However, this will imply a transformation of lifelong learning concept towards continuous competence development - or what some may view as a realization of lifelong learning – indicated in our statistics that participation is increasingly more widespread across the age-span of participants.

References

Bowles, S. and Gintis, H. (1976). *Schooling in Capitalist America*. New York: Basic Books.

Gooderham, Paul N & Lund, Jørgen (1991). *Voksenopplæring uten styring (?)*. Trondheim: NVI.

Gooderham Paul N. & Tøsse, Sigvart (1996). From philanthropy to deinstitutionalization: The historical development of the Norwegian adult education system. In *Social Change and Adult Education Research. Adult Education Research in Nordic Countries 1966*. Jyväskylä.

Jarvis, Peter (2000). The education of adults as a social movement: a question for late modern society. In Wildemeersch, D. Finger, M. & Jansen, T. (eds) (2000). *Adult Education and Social Responsibility*. Frankfurt am Main: Peter Lang.

Hake, Barry J, (1994). Formative Periods in the History of Adult Education: The role of social and cultural movements in cross-cultural communication. In (Stuart Marriot & Barry J. Hake (ed.). *Cultural and Intercultural Experiences in European Adult Education*. Leeds Studies in Continuing Education.

Innstilling om Organisering av og støtte til det frivillige opplysnings- og kulturarbeid (1960). Avgitt av Komitéen for utredning av det frivillige opplysnings- og kulturarbeid, oppnevnt av KUF, 1958.
Innstilling S. 280, 1984 – 85 *Om voksenopplæring. En del prinsippielle spørsmål og prioriteringer.*

KUF (1995). Voksenopplæring i Norge – omfang og ressursbruk.

Larsen, Knut Arild, Longva, Frode, Pape, Arne & Reichborn Anders N. (1997). *Bedriften som lærested*. Fafo rapport 212.

Nilsen, Egil (1958). *Interesser hos voksne*. Oslo: Universitetsforlaget.

NOS. *Voksenopplæring 1969 – 74.*
NOS. *Levekårsundersøkelsen* 1980, 1987, 1991.
NOS. *Arbeidsmiljø, 1993.*

NOU 1972:41. *Vaksenopplæring for alle.*
NOU 1997:25. *Ny kompetanse. Grunnlaget for en helhetlig etter- og videreutdanningspolitikk.*
NOU 1986:23 Livslang læring.

Skaalvik, Einar & Knudsen, Knud (1979). *Deltakelse i voksenopplæring.* Trondheim: NVI.

Skaalvik, Einar M. og Engesbak, Heidi (1996). Selvrealisering og kompetanseutvikling. Rekruttering til voksenopplæring i et tjueårsperspektiv. I S. Tøsse (red.). *Fra Lov – til reform.* Trondheim: NVI.

Skaalvik, Einar, Ljosland Ole Halvard and Finbak, Liv (2000). Voksenopplæring: Et landskap i forandring. In *CV* no. 3, 2000.

Statens folkeopplysningsråd 1934 – 1959. (1959).

Stortingsforhandlingene.
St. melding no. 43, (1988 – 89). *Mer kunnskap til flere.*
St. melding no. 42 (1997 – 98). *Kompetansereformen.*
St. prp. no. 1 (Budget)
St. prp. no. 92 (1964 – 65). *Om voksenopplæring.*
St. prp. no. 7 (1975 – 76). *Om lov om voksenopplæring*

Studentersamfundets Fri Undervisning (SFU) 100 år (1964). Oslo: Studentersamfundet Fri Undervisnings Forlag.

Studienytt.

Telhaug, Alfred Oftedal (1997). *Utdanningsreformene. Oversikt og analyse.* Oslo: Didakta Norsk Forlag AS.

Tøsse, Sigvart (1996). Det statlege engasjementet i vaksenopplæring 1934 – 1980. I S. Tøsse (red.) *Fra lov – til reform.* Trondheim: NVI.

Wildemeersch, D. Finger, M. & Jansen, T. (eds) (2000). *Adult Education and Social Responsibility.* Frankfurt am Main: Peter Lang.

Williams, Raymond (1977). *Marx and Literature.* Oxford University Press.

NEW DIRECTIONS OF ADULT EDUCATION POLICY IN FINLAND

Risto Rinne and Markku Vanttaja

Abstract

Equality of educational opportunities was one of the central themes of adult education policy in Finland starting from the 1970s until the end of the 1980s. A special target group for adult education was defined as those citizens with the least general and vocational education. Nowadays adult educational policy in Finland is characterized by marketization, emphasizing the role of labour market oriented adult education and de-emphasizing the goals of equality. There is a desire to use adult education as a means of helping people adjust to the pressures caused by the change toward an internationally competitive society. Increasing the productivity of work and supporting the success of national economic life have become the overwhelming goal of Finnish adult education. The strong belief in education as a guarantee of competitive ability among the Finns is shown by the fact that the level of active participation in training arranged by the employer is one of the highest in all OECD countries.

In 1995, approximately 1.6 million Finnish adults were participating in adult education. This is about 600 000 more than in 1980. This pronounced increase over a period of 15 years was mainly due to the increase in vocational adult education. Although the level of active participation varies sharply according to age, gender, level of education, socio-economic status and a person's position in the labour market. Those sections of the population with the least education are also the least represented in adult education, although they have been the special focus of the rhetoric of adult education for a considerable time. The goals of educational policy and the facts of participation in adult education have been in sharp conflict in this respect.

The point of departure for the educational policy of the 1990s seems to have been the assumption that the world is changing as a result of the globalization of the economy and technological development, and the fate of the individual is to adapt to these changes through education. No alternatives are offered. These changes are presented as if they were phenomena which occur irrespective of the actions of people, and the only possibility is to humbly acquiesce to them. The Finnish adult education policy strongly emphasizes the significance of lifelong learning and continual renewal as an individual survival strategy. According to the modern way of thinking a person is a "cognitive machine", which can be remodelled again and again in response to the changing requirements of working life. People are forced into an exhausting race which has few winners.

If it is indeed necessary to make great sacrifices at the altar of working life, productivity and competitive ability in the name of a policy of lifelong learning, it should be remembered that even in the field of learning the hopes and needs of people are not satisfied by growth in the production volume of economic life or national competitive ability. The fact is that people are spending less and less time doing salaried work. Many Finns have expressed the wish to voluntarily step aside from working life even before their actual retirement age. Meaning in life is more and more often sought outside the work place. This fact cannot be ignored even in adult education policy.[1]

Hasty and profound national changes

In Finland the changes in educational policy have perhaps been among the fastest in Nordic countries in the 1990s. After the dissolution of the Soviet Union and the collapse of the Berlin Wall, Finland changed from being a highly centrally governed Nordic welfare state to membership of the European Union and at the same time completely changed the course of traditional Nordic "social democratic" welfare state politics. The culmination point was the period of widespread economic depression in the beginning of the 1990s, but the reforms had already begun earlier, in the late 1980s. The strong state with its policy of standardization had to step back and make room for local policy and the influence of the market. The costs to the taxpayers were too heavy, it was claimed; the old Keynesian policy of full employment was forgotten and many social security nets were lowered in the fields of social policy, health care and education. The unemployment rate, which until then had been kept as low as a few per cent of the labour force through various labour-market operations, including education, was now growing to an unbelievable level. Finland was now unfortunately among the top three European countries in terms of high unemployment rates - between Spain and Ireland - with almost 20 per cent unemployed. Decentralization, deregulation, marketization, funding by results, managerialism, top-unit policy and all the other neo-liberal slogans became the everyday of Finnish political practice. At first they were very practical managerial decisions. The changed "culture of governing" was mostly legislated only afterwards. That was how it occurred in the field of education, for example. The massive legislation reform in Finnish education was carried

---

[1] The article is based on research by R. Rinne & M. Vanttaja "Finnish Adult Education Policies: Changes and tensions in the 1980's and 1990's. Helsinki: Publication of The Ministry of Education 67.

out only in 1998, after many years of planning and implementing the new policy (Rinne & Vanttaja, 1998; 1999).

The radical changes in Finland were not only carried out as a result of international changes. The political climate and political power relations in Finland were also radically changing. In 1987, Finland got its first conservative prime minister for decades, from the "Moderate Coalition Party". From 1991 to 1999 the first Minister of Education was also from same conservative party, first Mrs Riitta Uosukainen (1991-1994) and then Mr Olli-Pekka Heinonen (1994-1999). Many of the top positions at ministry level were occupied by conservatives, which was a very significant change compared to the old days when educational policy was very strictly governed by representatives of the Social Democratic and Centre parties. It was not by chance, or even only because of economic and structural changes, but also because of the activities of political agents that the educational politics changed so rapidly in Finland. Mr Olli-Pekka Heinonen, in particular, was a very active minister who drove Finland into the front row of the European Union by cutting down old bureaucratic political traditions and bringing in new, dynamic, neo-liberal ones. It was also during his period of office that the political power of the Ministry of Education was strengthened by strategic decisions, and the power of National Board of Education was gradually reduced. The Council for the Evaluation of Higher Education was closed, and evaluation became the main task of the National Board of Education, in addition to the evaluations ordered by the Ministry of Education. An organizational change was also carried out in the Ministry of Education according to which a separate section for adult education was established. In this organizational change the old advisory board for educational planning (1976-1997) was closed down, which meant that the old tradition of centralized manpower planning in the field of adult education was also abandoned (Rinne and Vanttaja, 1999; Lehtisalo and Raivola, 1999).

It is astonishing that during these years of radical change political debate was so restrained in Finland. In reality, the old social democratic and centralistic powers in educational policy had very few things to say. They could only shrug their shoulders; the consensus among the political parties about the "global and inevitable change" in Finnish educational policy was astonishingly great. It will be interesting to see what changes, if any, take place in Finnish (adult) education policy as a result of Prime Minister Paavo Lipponen installing a Social Democratic minister of education in 1999 as part of his second government. Ms Maija Rask is a woman from a small northern city (Kemi), a teacher of health care in a newly-established Finnish Polytechnic in civilian life, and she is a veteran social democrat – all quite the complete opposite of the former minister.

New market-driven adult education policy

In the broad lines of educational policy, the expansion of education has continued its triumphal march, but every activity labelled as educational no longer received the blessing of politicians. Nowadays, clear proof of the outcome of education is required. This change in direction in educational policy can also be seen in the discussions of the 1990s, which contained terminology familiar to the business world. Education has become a product that is sold, bought and priced just as other products are. In the field of education we now have clients instead of students, producers of services instead of teachers. In the new rhetoric of educational policy the buzzwords are internationalization, efficiency, quality, impact, competitive ability, evaluation, flexibility, free choice and individualization. Clear proof of the outcomes and efficiency of education are now required. Modern adult educational policy in Finland is also characterized by marketization, emphasizing the role of labour market oriented adult education and de-emphasizing the goals of equality. There is a desire to use adult education as a means of helping people adjust to the pressures caused by the change toward an internationally competitive society. The advantages of a market-based educational policy have been brought out at least in the form of dismantling the overlapping administration and bureaucracy, an increased awareness of costs among schools, and increased willingness to listen to expressed needs. Institutions of learning have had to consider the content and methods of education more than previously, and make their activities more effective and renew them (e.g. Tuomisto, 1998; Mem.1993).

Adult education institutions, as well as adult educators, have to be more attractive than before. They must be attractive and show their effectiveness to funding organizations and bodies. And they also have to try to gather more and more students who are able to pay at least some of their study expenses themselves. They have to use managerialism and use it effectively. Especially in the field of so-called liberal adult education this has created the need to exclude certain kinds of customers and close down those courses which do not bring in money. This marketization has also meant that education has become study-packages which are to be sold on the market just like any other product. Adult educators have to become advertisers and salespeople. This has also meant that money must be sought from those sources that offer it. More and more, adult education is being steered by market mechanisms in the direction of vocational and work-related education. The imperative to evaluate the results of every institution and department means greater competition and also, in the long run, probably closing down some older functions of adult education, i.e. those which are not marketable (Rinne & Vanttaja 1999; Sihvonen 1996; 1999).

In reality adult education in Finland is not working in a totally free market, since every institution still gets some public money, and in many cases it is the public authorities and adult educators themselves who decide what to offer – not the customers who decide what to buy. For example in the field of "labour market policy adult education" the customers have very limited freedom of choice. Thus, it would be best to describe the Finnish situation, at least in its modern form, as quasi-market-based adult education (e.g. Varmola 1996).

The changing profile of adult education

The role of adult education in the lives of the Finnish people has changed fundamentally in the last two decades. In the 1960s and 1970s the term adult education often referred to popular education undertaken at the free will of ordinary citizens. Studying to achieve one's leisure-time goals is still quite popular, but the number of people involved in this type of adult education has remained more or less the same from the early 80s until the end of the millennium. Nowadays, more and more adults spend their time participating in vocational studies. More clearly than ever before, being trained as an adult means preparation for working life or for the labour market. Increasing the productivity of work and supporting the success of national economic life have become the overwhelming goal of Finnish adult education. The increase in the importance of vocational adult education witnessed since the early 1980s can be seen as the clear mainstream in the definition of the adult education policy of the government, in committee reports, in educational policy discussions, in funding decisions, as well as in the practical implementation of adult education. (Rinne & Vanttaja 1999.)

In 1995, almost one-half, in other words approximately 1.6 million Finnish adults (18-64-year-olds) were participating in adult education (see Figure 1). This is about 600 000 more than in 1980. This pronounced increase over a period of 15 years was mainly due to the increase in vocational adult education. Approximately two-thirds, or a little over one million, of those actively studying were involved in vocational adult education, and the remaining third in general studies (Blomqvist et al. 1997, 9, 87- 94; Simpanen & Blomqvist 1992, 10).

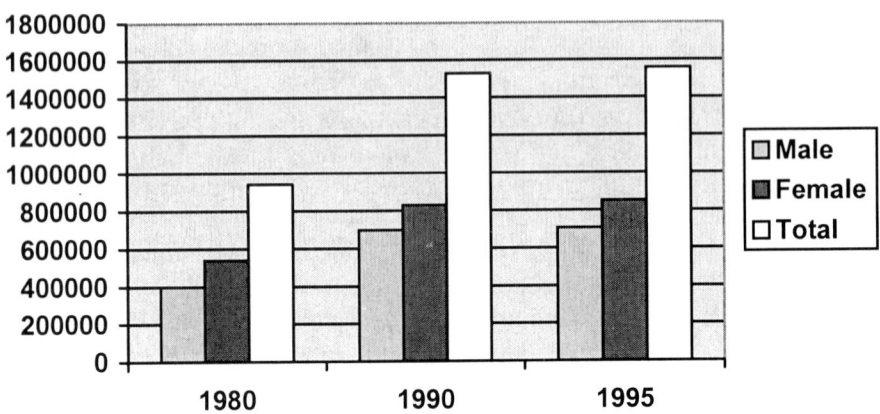

Figure 1. Participation in adult education in 1980, 1990 and 1995 (population aged 18-64)

The level of participation has increased particularly in the 1980s. The economic recession of the early 1990s seems to have slowed down the growth of adult education quite clearly, as the number of those involved has remained more or less the same between 1990 and 1995. However, the number of students does not tell the entire truth with regard to the intense expansion of adult education. Measured as the number of teaching hours, the volume of adult education has also increased vigorously in the 1990s. While the number of teaching hours used for adult education in Finland was 4.2 million in 1991, this sum had almost tripled to 12.4 million hours in 1997 (SVT 1999, 138).

Figures concerning the education of the adult population hide facts about educational inequality and significant differences between various groups. The level of active participation varies sharply according to age, sex, level of education, socio-economic status and a person's position on the labour market (e.g. Silvennoinen & Aaltonen 1999). Women are more active than men as adult students. In 1995, 53 % of those participating in organized education were women and 43 % men. This difference between the participation level of women and men has remained more or less the same from the beginning of the 1980s until the present day.

Those who most actively seek additional education are 30-54 year old Finns, of which as many as 54 % were involved in adult education in 1995. The probability of participating in adult education is clearly connected with one's level of education. Research concerning participation in adult education, both in

Finland and elsewhere, has regularly shown that the longer basic general education and vocational education people have, the more likely it is that they will be involved in adult education. This trend of accumulation has not changed in Finland during the 1990s. Those sections of the population with the least education are also the least represented in adult education, although they have been the special focus of the rhetoric of adult education for a considerable time. The goals of educational policy and the facts of participation in adult education are in sharp conflict in this respect (Havén and Syvänperä 1983; Rubenson 1991, 70; Rinne et al. 1992; Simpanen and Blomqvist 1992; Kivinen and Rinne 1993; Blomqvist et al. 1997).

Participation in adult education has increased in the 1980s among those with a comprehensive school and upper secondary school background on the one hand, and those with a tertiary education, on the other. The difference in level of participation between those with a short or a long basic education grew clearly in the 1980s, but has evened out a bit in the 1990s. Indeed, as can be seen from Figure 2, the differences between those who have completed a basic level education and those with a higher education background have been large throughout the entire 1980s and 1990s. For example, while three out of four persons with a tertiary education participated in adult education in 1995, less than one third of those with a basic general education did so (SVT 1999, 131; Blomqvist et al. 1997, 9).

The accumulation of participation can also be seen when examining socio-economic status. Upper managerial employees participated noticeably more actively in adult education. In 1990 as much as 83 % of this group had participated in adult education of some type. Lower managerial employees have also been more enthusiastic than average. Below average participation was found among the working class, entrepreneurs and agricultural entrepreneurs. Indeed, the participation level of agricultural entrepreneurs seems to have grown in the 1990s, reaching a level close to the average (48 % in 1995). The participation level of workers has also increased, which would also indicate that in the 1990s the differences between various socio-economic groups have been levelled to some extent. This levelling can be explained by the fact that unemployment has grown sharply among those from lower social groups, which has led to a quick growth in adult education for labour policy reasons. The increase in adult education among agricultural entrepreneurs, on the other hand, can be explained by the fact that Finland joined the European Union, which led to a structural transition and the training connected with it.

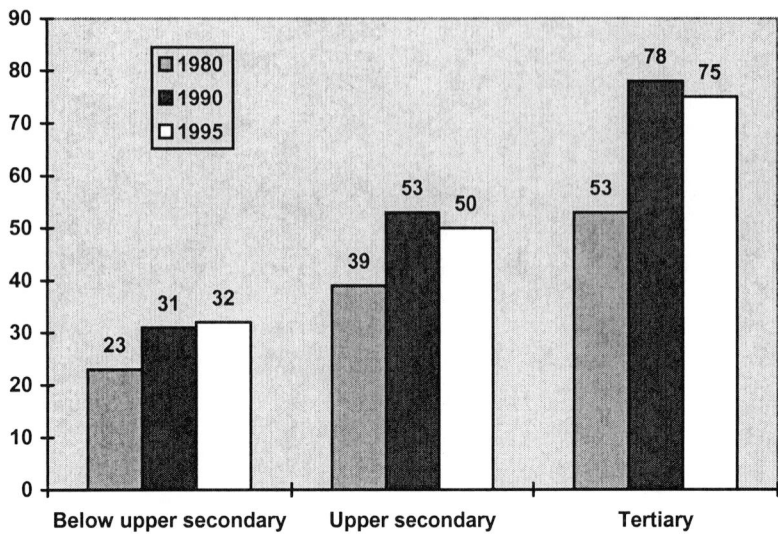

Figure 2. Participation in adult education in percentages in 1980, 1990 and 1995 by highest level of educational attainment (population aged 18-64)

The strong belief in education as a guarantee of competitive ability among the Finns is shown by the fact that the level of active participation in training arranged by the employer is one of the highest in all OECD countries. In Finland a little over one half of all wage earners had participated in personnel training courses in 1995. Of those countries included in the comparison Great Britain, where 42% of all employees had participated in personnel training courses, was closest to Finland in this respect.

Characteristic of personnel training in Finland compared to other countries is that although the participation rates are high, the number of hours per person is relatively low. In 1995 only 30.3 hours per employee was used for personnel training in Finland. In comparison to other countries Finland was placed fifth after New Zealand, Great Britain, the Netherlands and Northern Ireland. The highest figures were from New Zealand, with 39.3 hours per employee per year (SVT 1999, 134-135.)

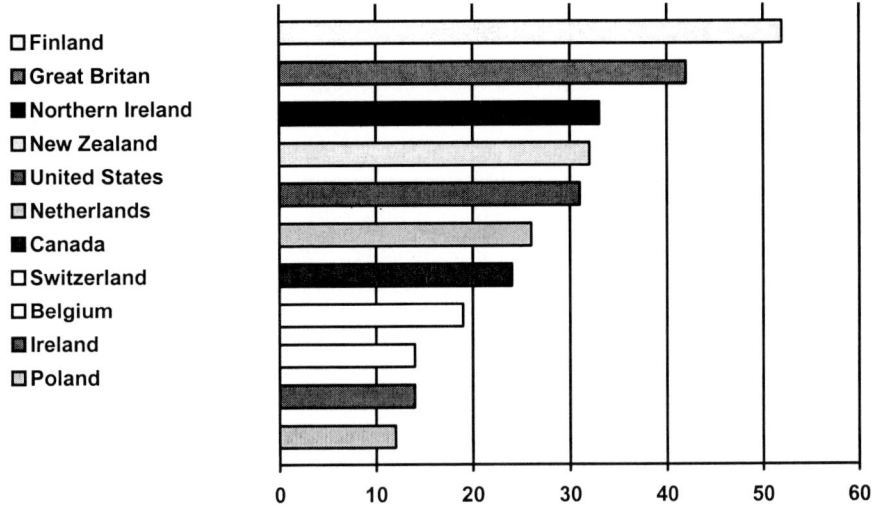

Figure 3. Participation in employer-sponsored training in certain OECD-countries in percentages in 1994-1995 (employees aged 18-64)
Source: SVT 1999, 134-135

Adult education as a tool of labour policy

A central goal of Finnish educational policy in the 1990s has been to increase the willingness to participate and the actual participation of unemployed people in training. The reason for this has been that the Finnish unemployment rate seems to have stabilized at a relatively high level for Europe. Marginalization from the labour market, in addition to short-term employment, is an everyday fact for hundreds of thousands of citizens. Activating the unemployed to participate in training programmes is justifiable, as we know that in addition to age, sex, educational level and socio-economic status, a person's status on the labour market is a central factor determining the level of participation. While approximately 60 % of the working population participated in adult education in 1995, the corresponding figure for the unemployed was 27 %. However, those unemployed who did participate logged in considerably more days on average (17.5) than among the working population (average 7 days per person) (SVT 1999, 132).

It is generally believed that education will allow those who end up unemployed to keep up in the ever-toughening competition. Without doubt, it has enabled many unemployed persons to find themselves a new career as adults, or at least to keep on the margins of the labour market. For many it has also created social contacts, structure and a meaning for life. Nonetheless, adult education as part of labour policy seems to function more commonly as a storehouse for those marginalized from working life and as a means of maintaining work motivation. An essential part of the mentality of the Finns, who value wage earning work highly, has been that it is not suitable for the unemployed to laze around out of the reach of official surveillance. Labour policy education has therefore become ever more clearly an activity that compensates for actual labour and allows control of the work force, through which the unemployed can earn their right to receive unemployment and social allowances (Rinne and Vanttaja 1999; Rinne et al. 1992).

It has long been a principle in Finland that the unemployed could not participate in full-time education without losing the right to unemployment benefits. A person was eligible for support on the same level as unemployment allowance only if he/she attended courses financed by the employment authorities. In many cases a person was sent to courses because the authorities demanded it, rather than of his/her own free will. This has given employment policy courses the flavour of compulsion. The policy of the first government of Prime Minister Lipponen that emphasized the activation and encouragement of the unemployed to participate in training gave a new shade to the country's adult education and labour force policy. In the same spirit there have been attempts to develop new forms of financial aid to students meant for those who are at the greatest risk of dropping out of working life completely. A special form of education insurance was tailor-made for the long-term unemployed, not without considerable political debate, but experience so far has shown that the willingness of the less educated sections of the population to participate in long-term training has not been noticeably increased, even though financial support equivalent to the unemployment allowance was used as an inducement. According to a statistical report of the Ministry of Labour, there have been a little over one thousand participants involved in this training during the one-year trial. The great majority of them (68 %) were 40-49-year-olds. Only about one-fifth (22 %) of the participants were over 50 years of age. The small proportion of those under 40 can be explained by the fact that in order to qualify for the financial support, the applicant had to have at least 12 years of work experience gained after the age of 23. The clear majority (62 %) of these students were women (Työministeriö 1998).

One of the most important goals of the reform was to provide basic vocational education to those long-term unemployed who lacked it. However, only a little over a quarter of the students (28 %) had completed only a primary, lower secondary or comprehensive school education. The majority (56 %) had either a lower or higher intermediate school education. Those with a lower or higher university-level degree accounted for 15%. The majority (60 %) who applied for the course were white-collar workers. There was a high proportion of applicants from the fields of nursing, social welfare, administration and clerical work. Thus, the typical person who benefited from the financial aid programme seems to have been a 40-49-year-old women with a vocational training who had been made redundant from a clerical job (Työministeriö 1998).

According to the study, financial reasons were the greatest barrier to applying to participate in adult education programmes. Without sufficient financial support, studying has proved to remain the hobby of the well-to-do (Nurmi 1995, 185; Blomqvist et al. 1997, 50). However, the experience gained from the education insurance system shows that applying for training and refusing to participate in training is not only a matter of money. Unwillingness to be trained would seem to have a much broader and deeper basis; it is a question of life-style and culture, as well as relating to the fact that education does not automatically create work or a job, even though it may improve a person's competitive status on the labour market.

In addition to unemployment, a problem that will become topical in both Finland and the entire European Union in the near future is the ageing of the population and its consequences. While the number of people of working age (15-64 year-olds) is clearly decreasing, the number of those over 65 is increasing significantly. In Finland the proportion of those of working age will be especially low compared to the number of children and the aged after the year 2010. An additional problem is the fact that many Finns take early retirement due to reduced working capacity well before the regular age of retirement. The willingness of Finns to retire early is attested to by the fact that the average retirement age is 58, and over one half of those aged 55-64 are presently retired. This change in the age structure and the willingness to take early retirement have increased discussion about the significance of adult education in maintaining working capacity. Adult education should also guarantee a qualified workforce to fill the vacancies left by early retirement and ensure that the members of this workforce have an up-to-date education. Otherwise Finland will find itself in a situation where there are simultaneously an abundance of unemployed persons and pensioners on the one hand, and few working taxpayers on the other. The consequences of this state would inevitably be a significant dismantling of public services and the crumbling of the foundations of the Nordic welfare state (Eva 1998; TM 1999).

A policy without alternatives leading to inequality?

Equality of educational opportunities was one of the central themes of adult education policy in Finland starting from the 1970s until the end of the 1980s. A special target group for adult education was defined as those citizens with the least general and vocational education. Activating this group to study and supporting them once they have undertaken to study has been considered especially important. On the basis of participation studies, the idea of educational equality and adult education as a "second chance" would seem to be an impossible dream. Those who participate most eagerly in adult education are those citizens who have already received a firm basic education, who are white-collar workers and who are at the prime of their working age and in the peak of health. The goals of adult education policy and the participation figures for various demographic groups have been in sharp conflict in this respect for decades (see Havén and Syvänperä 1983; Rubenson 1991, 70; Rinne et al. 1992; Simpanen and Blomqvist 1992; Blomqvist et al. 1997).

The declaration of educational equality has all but disappeared from the official educational planning texts of the 1990s. The educational needs of those who already have a degree have been emphasized to an ever-increasing extent during the present decade. Questions of equality have been referred to mainly in rhetoric criticizing market-based educational policy. The adult education policy of the 1990s has quietly accepted the situation described by the participation figures.

The point of departure for the educational policy of the 1990s seems to have been the assumption that the world is changing as a result of the globalization of the economy and technological development, and the fate of the individual is to adapt to these changes through education. No alternatives are offered. These changes are presented as if they were phenomena which occur irrespective of the actions of people, and the only possibility is to humbly acquiesce to them. According to the declarations of educational policy, however, people should have a positive attitude toward the problems that face them. These changes should be seen as opportunities, not threats, as the worn-out phrase goes. We must only believe in the ability of economic growth and fast technological development to produce well-being and try to keep up with the accelerating pace.

The Finnish adult education policy strongly emphasizes the significance of life-long learning and continual renewal as an individual survival strategy. According to the modern way of thinking a person is a "cognitive machine", which can be remodelled again and again in response to the changing requirements of working life. People are forced into an exhausting race which has few winners. The fact that the requirement for continuous re-education and renewal also has its reverse side. Seldom do we remember to ask if people really want to or if they really need to be continually preparing themselves for new tasks, to live under constant pressure to change and fear that their skills will become out-of-date and that their resources will be exhausted.

The newest launching of lifelong learning and continuous education can also be seen as one of the mainstreams of educational policy, in which people are subjugated to the station of a machine without a will of its own which exists for the benefit of faceless production. There is reason to ponder whether adult education is becoming the newest form of subjugation and manipulation in which the purpose of life, in the eyes of political decision makers, financial directors, employers and educators is to act as a workforce which can stretch in every direction, and the fate of which is to change at a pace determined by the "market powers" and the "invisible hand" of global development. If it is indeed necessary to make great sacrifices at the altar of working life, productivity and competitive ability in the name of a policy of lifelong learning, it should be remembered that even in the field of learning the hopes and needs of people are not satisfied by growth in the production volume of economic life or national competitive ability. The fact is that people are spending less and less time doing salaried work. Many Finns have expressed the wish to voluntarily step aside from working life even before their actual retirement age. Meaning in life is more and more often sought outside the work place. This fact cannot be ignored even in adult education policy.

References

Blomqvist, I. & Koskinen, R. & Niemi, H. & Simpanen, M. (1997). *Aikuiskoulutustutkimus 1995. Aikuisopiskelu Suomessa.* [Adult Education Study 1995. Adult Education in Finland]. Helsinki: Tilastokeskus 1997/4.

Eva (1998). *Harmaantuvat härmäläiset.* Raportti väestön ikääntymisestä ja yhteiskunnan muutoksesta. [Greying Finns. A Report on Aging Population and Change in Society].

Havén, H. & Syvänperä, R. (1983). *Aikuiskoulutukseen osallistuminen.* [Participation in Adult Education]. Tilastokeskuksen tutkimus 92. Helsinki: Tilastokeskus.

Kivinen, O. & Rinne, R. (1993). Adult Education, a Second Chance: Fact and Fiction. *Scandinavian Journal of Educational Research* 37 (2), 115-128.

KM (1993:31). *Humanismin paluu tulevaisuuteen.* [The Return of Humanism to the Future]. Helsinki.

Lehtisalo, L. & Raivola, R. (1999). *Koulutus ja koulutuspolitiikka 2000-luvulle.* [Education and Educational Policy Towards the 21st century]. Helsinki: WSOY.

Nurmi, K. (1995). *Miksi aikuinen opiskelee? Tutkintotavoitteisen opiskelun edut ja haitat aikuisen elämänkokonaisuudessa.* [Why Do Adults Study? Benefits and Costs of Degree Oriented Education in the Lives of Adults]. Annales Universitatis Turkuensis. Ser C. Osa 111. Turku: Turun yliopisto.

Rinne, R. & Vanttaja, M. (1998). *Aikuiskoulutustutkimuksen tila ja muutossuunnat Suomessa 1970-luvulta vuosituhannen loppuun.* [The State of Adult Education Research and Directions of Change in Finland from the 1970's to the End of the Millennium]. Helsinki: Aikuiskoulutusneuvosto.

Rinne, R. & Vanttaja, M. (1999*). Suomalaista aikuiskoulutuspolitiikkaa. Muutoksia ja jännitteitä 1980- ja 1990-luvuilla.* [Finnish Adult Education Policies. Changes and Tensions in the 1980's and 1990's]. Opetusministeriön koulutus- ja tiedepolitiikan osaston julkaisu 67. Helsinki: Opetusministeriö.

Rinne, R. & Kivinen, O. & Ahola, S. (1992) *Aikuisten kouluttautuminen Suomessa. Osallistuminen, kasautuminen ja preferenssit.* [Adult education in Finland. Participation, Accumulation and Preferences]. Koulutussosiologian tutkimuskeskuksen raportteja 10. Turku: Turun yliopisto.

Rubenson, K. (1991). *Aikuiskoulutuksen kehittäminen - markkinavoimien ohjattavaksi vai tavoitteiseen politiikkaan?* [Developing Adult Education – Steering of the Markets or Aim Oriented Policy?]. Aikuiskasvatus 11 (2), 66-75.

Sihvonen, J. (1996). *Sivistystä kaikille vai valituille. Kansalaisopistotoiminnan kehitys vapaasta kansanvalistustyöstä maksupalveluun.* [Education for All or a Chosen Few? The Development of Adult Education Centres from Liberal Adult Education to Tailored Training without State Subsidies]. Acta Universitatis Tamperensis ser A vol. 519. Tampere.

Sihvonen, J. (1999). *Kansalaisopistojen arviointi: Uhka opistojen itsemääräämisoikeudelle vai mahdollisuus toiminnan kehittämiseen?* [Evaluation of Adult Education Centres: Threat for Self-determination or an Opportunity for the Improvement of the Practice] Aikuiskasvatus 19 (2), 151-162.

Silvennoinen, H. & Aaltonen, S. (1999). *Työ ja koulutustarve. Aikuisväestön lisäkoulutustarpeet työelämässä.* [Work and Need for Educational. Need for further Education among Adult Population in Working Life]. Opetusministeriön koulutus- ja tiedepolitiikan osaston julkaisu 70. Helsinki: Opetusministeriö.

Simpanen, M. & Blomqvist, I. (1992). *Aikuiskoulutustutkimus 1990. Aikuiskoulutukseen osallistuminen.* [Adult Education Study 1990. Participation in Adult Education]. Tutkimuksia 192. Helsinki: Tilastokeskus.

SVT 1999. Education in Finland (1999) *Statistics and indicators.* Helsinki: Tilastokeskus.

Tuomisto, J. (1998). *Keskitetystä aikuiskoulutussuunnittelusta markkinoiden ohjaukseen – ja takaisin?* [From Centralized Adult Education Planning to Steering of the Markets – and Back Again?]. Aikuiskasvatus 18 (4), 268-280.

Työministeriö (1998). *Pitkäaikaistyöttömien omaehtoisen opiskelun tuki.* [Student Benefit of the Long Term Unemployed]. Tilastoyhteenveto 1.8. 1997-31.7.1998. Työministeriö 15.9. 1998.

TM (1999). *Työministeriö ja sosiaali- ja terveysministeriö1999. Ehdotus Kansallisen Ikäohjelman seurantajärjestelmäksi.* [Ministry of Labour and Ministry of Social Affairs and Health 1999. Proposal for Follow-up System for National Age Program]. Helsinki: Edita.

Varmola, T. (1996). *Markkinasuuntautuneen koulutuksen aikakauteen? Esimerkkejä ja tulkintoja ammatillisesta aikuiskoulutuksesta.* [Market Orientation: Entering a New Educational Era? Instances and Interpretations of Vocational Adult Education]. Acta Universitatis Tamperensis ser A vol. 524. Tampere: Tampereen yliopisto.

INTEREST AND MOTIVATION TO PARTICIPATE IN ADULT EDUCATION. A STUDY WITHIN THE ADULT EDUCATION INITIATIVE

Per-Olof Thång and Gun-Britt Wärwik

Introduction

Adult education policy reforms focus on economic growth and the limiting effects of unemployment. Another aspect of adult education is to help people strengthen their situation in life and reduce the educational gap between generations and social classes in society. So far, no Swedish educational reform for adults has been a success in this aspect. There are still many obstacles for people who want to participate in adult education, particularly among those with short formal education. This article is discusses some issues concerning interest and motivation among adults to participate in educational activities. Special focus is directed at a study of two Swedish municipalities. The aim of the study is to describe why participants have decided to enter education within the Adult Education Initiative (AEI) and if the education can be seen as part of their future plans.

Sweden has conducted several reforms in order to increase the possibilities for adults to participate in education. However, the reasons for the reforms have changed to some extent over time.

Adult education reforms

In 1967, the Municipal Adult Education (Komvux) was established to offer education at basic and upper secondary school levels. The aim was to remove institutional barriers for adults who wished to return to education after a period of work. Municipal Adult Education was originally meant to be a part-time education during leisure time in the evenings. The focus was to facilitate studies for the "reserve of ability". In the seventies, it was stated that the groups who were educationally most disadvantaged should be given priority. The focus was on equality and compensation for differences in school attendance between generations and social classes.

At the end of the 1960s the labour market training was expanding related to structural changes in the working life. The unemployment rate was very low (1.1 – 1.7 %). During this period a shortage of well-educated manpower was anticipated in some areas. Entrance requirements to higher education were also changed to make it easier for people with working experience and shorter formal education to get access. Recruitment to adult education has therefore been a question of major concern in Sweden since the beginning of the seventies. Resources were directed in order to recruit people who had had a shorter education and those with a weak motivation for studies (Government Bill 1970:35). According to Rubenson (1989), the reforms during the seventies could be seen as an attempt to broaden the earlier reform strategy that had focused on the renewal of childhood education.

"What the early seventies offered was an alternative strategy for social change based on a resocialization of adults rather than the socialization of children. There are parallels between this approach and that of literacy campaigns where initial efforts are directed toward adults in the knowledge that literate parents seldom have illiterate children" (Rubenson 1989:122).

The aim was to further increase the possibilities for the target group, people with short education, to make it possible to go from work to studies and then back to work again. In the middle of this decade some new laws for labour market were implemented. One of the most important was the legal right for time off (but not for financing) for general and vocational education. Another law was the right of the trade union representatives to recruit their members for participation in different kinds of adult education. The financial support for the adult students was also improved.

During the eighties, there was a growing awareness that despite the reforms, participation in adult education was still unequally distributed. People with short education were under-represented in adult education. The number of people with short education, especially women, had increased but it was largely those with a longer education who were recruited. It was particularly difficult to recruit older men. On the whole, Municipal Adult Education recruited even younger participants than before.

Studies by Lundquist (1989) showed that there is a clear connection between study financing and study intensity. In 1986, the rate of full-time students had increased in comparison with 1980. The most common means of study financing in 1986 was national study support. In 1980, most students financed their studies by working (Lundquist 1990). This change also mirrors contemporary developments in Swedish working-life on the whole. During this period, the unemployment rate still was very low in Sweden (1.5 – 2.5 %). Adult education, within both Municipal Adult Education and the Folk high school, were in many cases seen as an instrument for the rehabilitation of people with a difficult social situation and in need to strengthen their self-confidence, rather than as an instrument for high employability (Thång 1988).

During the first years in the 1990s, the unemployment rate rapidly increased in Sweden (10-12 %). Because of this, a major goal for the government is to halve the unemployment rate. The Adult Education Initiative (AEI), a five-year programme on adult education, is a part in this effort (SOU 1998:51).

The Adult Education Initiative (AEI) was started in 1997. The more humanistic aspects of adult education from the seventies were again replaced by a focus on economic growth and employment. Structural changes in the working life, due to the rapid technological and organizational development, have increased the need for a better skilled labour force (Sellin 1999; Tessaring 1999). A basic assumption is that access to a skilled labour force will lead to better conditions of economic growth.

The AEI reform followed an extended youth education. From 1994, all study programmes within the upper secondary school comprise three years. The AEI target group is primarily unemployed adults, who completely or partially lack three-year upper secondary school, another group is employees with short formal schooling. Those who have received the least of the public educational resources are now given a chance to catch up and with education they are expected to get a stronger position on the labour market.

A new form of study financing was introduced in 1997. This is a form of grant and is offered to adults aged 25 – 55 with short formal schooling. It is notable that the view of who is considered to have received a short education has gradually been modified during the years. In the middle of the 1970s the concept included people with six or seven years in school (Rubenson et al. 1977). During the 1980s the level was nine years in school which is the same as the compulsory education in Sweden (Fransson & Lundquist 1988). Today the concept refers to people with two years of upper secondary school or less (OECD 1995).

In short, there have been some reforms within the area of adult education in order to motivate people with short education to apply and attend.

The concept of motivation

Motivation is about why people think and behave as they do and also the intensity and strength in this. Motivation can create readiness for a change. Most people have an idea of what the concept implies. It is like an engagement or interest in something and a will to act and behave in a certain way or the power to achieve something, a goal-directed activity, but it is difficult to define the concept more precisely (Holmer & Thång 1996). A distinction can also be made between motive and motivation. Motive is about the reasons for doing something. Motivation can be said to be the energy which decides how much a person is ready or willing to invest in something or engage himself/herself in anything. The motivation can be explicit or not.

Motivation can also be an explanans, i.e. something which explains why anybody does anything, wants or wishes anything and is bound to the concept of intention and resolution. The latter was not accepted as a scientific concept towards the end of the 19th century as you could not operationalize and measure people's intention and resolution in a scientific way. In colloquial language the concept of intention and resolution has a high explanation value and is linked to the concept of motivation as explanans.

Motivation as an explanandum, i.e. motivation as an effect and result of people's experiences, is linked to motivation as knowledge, skill, understanding and self-confidence. A Swedish psychologist once said in a personal conversation that motivation is partly self-consciousness partly an experience of knowledge. He meant that motivation was the result of all this and that this assumption is part of a prior condition for continuing learning and knowledge development.

The concepts of motivation and experience are reciprocally dependent. Our experiences have a psychological quality, which belongs to the present. It is through the present our experiences are projected into the future. One could say that it is through the present and the actual situation of life that the past is bound with images and hopes of the future, i.e. motives and motivation.

Motivation can partly be viewed as a characteristic, partly as a relation. In this article we are chosen to regard motivation as a process and a relation rather than as a measurable characteristic.

Research in the field of motivation is characterized by a large number of theoretical approaches and has also been developed during the years. A criticism which is directed towards theories of motivation is the lack of "first"-person analyses of a person. It is often "third"-person analysis which is presented. A more and more accepted concept is the importance of a person's experience and feeling of being able to control, influence and steer his/her actions.

It is not unusual within (adult) education to dichotomize the concept of motivation. One distinction that can be made is between spontaneous and intentional motivation. Lyttkens (1994) argues that the stronger the individual's intention for competence development, the greater the scope of action and the less risk of experiencing a loss of meaning. Lyttkens also argues that a most important fundament in education and the development of competence is to get people to retain the purpose of their own learning and competence development.

Another distinction can be made between extrinsic and intrinsic motivation. Extrinsic motivation derives from outside the individual. Positive or negative reinforcements are important aspects in order to understand people's behaviour and actions. The subjectively expected utility is in focus (Greeno et al., 1996). Participation in adult education can be seen as a result of the individual's outcome expectations, that people make choices about what is of greatest benefit to them in the long run. Rubenson (1975) developed a theory about expectation in his thesis about interest in adult education among men with short formal education. Intrinsic motivation treats engagement as an internal property. One example is White's competence need, that an intrinsic need to feel competent is an innate characteristic of all human beings (Stipek 1996, p. 96.).

> "It is directed, selective and persistent, and it is continued, not because it serves primary drives, which indeed cannot be served until it is almost perfected, but because is satisfies an intrinsic need to deal with the environment" (White 1959).

Whether an individual is extrinsically or intrinsically motivated cannot be directly observed, it depends on how the individual experience the situation (Fransson 1978).

In a labour market education study, Thång (1984) presented a model of motivation: from thought to action. This focuses on the interaction between the individual and the context. This model illustrates the motivation of the individual as an experience, i.e. there is a dynamic relation between the individual and his/her context and surroundings. The idea of the model has been taken from Aristotle, who asks what makes a stone placed on a flat surface (want to) fall. Aristotle describes four co-working energies: impulse, resistance, position and will to fall. With this as a starting point Thång (1984) puts the question forward about which energies co-operate to make a thought change into action.

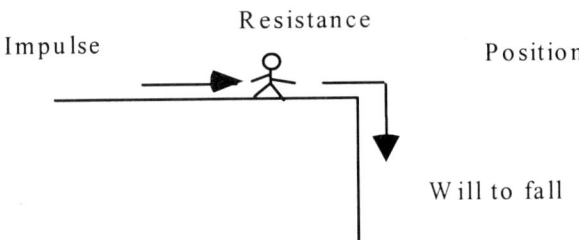

Figure 1. Motivation: From thought to action.

Participation in adult education can start with an *impulse*, a desire or a need to break an existing situation. For example, many people do not feel comfortable with their life and/or work situation and wish to get away from their current circumstances.

It is also common that people experience a *resistance* to change. People can bear within them a desire for education, but for some reason they do not allow these thoughts or desires to be fulfilled as actions. What a person considers possible or impossible can affect the resistance; his/her private economy, long distance to the education provider, and low self-confidence are other examples (May 1980; Fredén 1978).

Recent studies in Sweden show that many do not enjoy their job or type of work, but would like to change their employment or even occupation (Aronsson

& Göransson, 1977). To start education can be perceived by many adults as a social and psychological risk. A decision about adult studies can provoke feelings of insufficiency and even anxiety. Katzenelson (Fransson 1978) defines anxiety as a person's own instinct of self-preservation. How a person acts and behaves in situations which can provoke anxiety, threat or fear depends on his/her interpretation of partly the structure of the present situation, as well as the interpretation of his/her own capacity and power to cope with this situation. It is important to assert that it is a question of the individual's own experiences and interpretations. Fear and anxiety appear in situations which we partly meet with a lack of lucidity and structure and partly have low confidence in coping with the new and unknown. It is in those kinds of situations that we can experience lack of personal power. On the other hand, anxiety can be the motive and motivation which helps man to conquer impediments (Kierkegaard 1996, new edition May 1980).

The self image of people and the way in they are in relation to their surroundings has great importance for the decision to start adult education and how to realize and profit from education. The identity of a person can be another impediment to start adult education. People can strive to keep their identity even if it is dysfunctional and causes suffering.

The *will to fall* implies an orientation towards the future. There are some similarities with the *impulse*, but the orientation is towards something, not away from something. An obstacle for a person to change his/her life situation, can be the desire to get away from, or even flee, without knowing the aim or direction. In certain circumstances it could feel safer to cling to the known rather than confront the unknown. This illustrates how experiences cooperate with motives and motivations.

A release situation or event is often required in order for thoughts about something to change into actions. *Position*, i.e. circumstances, derives from the context, a situation and external conditions and relations and makes a person overcome internal resistance and external barriers. For example, unemployment or a divorce can act as a trigger to overcome a former resistance.

The concept of motivation is often used as an explanatory term. With the four concepts in Thång's model, an act can be described by motivation as an explicator; as explanans. But an act and the response it meets, effects in its turn the initial thought and motivation. Motivation in this instant is what is explained; as explanandum. A dialectic relation exists between motivation as an explanans and an explanandum.

Participation in adult education and training

It is well documented that participation in adult education is related to previous educational level. We also know that women dominate in adult education. During the autumn semester 1997, 65 % of the participants in municipal adult education had two years of upper secondary education or more. 10 % had some kind of post-secondary education. 33 % of the participants were men (National Board of Education 1999).

The situation within learning and training in working life is almost the same as within formal adult education. Younger people with longer education receive more education and training during working hours than older people with shorter education. The more educated the employee, the longer the course attended. The situation easily becomes a vicious circle; the shorter education tied to the more unqualified work with limited learning opportunities. The less possibilities to learn from the work tasks and to use one's competence at work, the less interest for learning and training. 46 % of the women and 43 % of the men participated in staff training during 1998 (SCB 1999a).

Borgström's (1988) study indicates that self-directed learning in Sweden is more frequent among people with longer education than among those with a shorter education. According to Borgström, self-directed learning may contribute to the reproduction of inequality.

Several Swedish studies have dealt with education and the work situation of employees with short education. Larsson et al. (1986) have shown that the shorter educational background one has, the less motivated he or she is for education and training in working life. In particular, older men with a low educational background experience difficulties in understanding the meaningfulness of formal schooling. At the same time, formal education is highly valued but it is not meant for them. One can say that they exclude themselves from education, formal education is meant for others and is of particular value for younger people (Alexandersson & Thång 1987).

Many employees with low levels of education within industry, and in many cases with less-qualified routine work, have an instrumental view of education and training. Education is regarded as useful if it is directly related to the work task. If the job does not demand any kind of education/training, they do not feel any educational need. In opposition to this, other studies (Larsson & Thång 1985) have shown that nurse's aids, working in hospitals, have a broader view of education, that education can have more effect than being directly related to the work task.

Another aspect is that education and training for the less educated within the industry very often focuses on the work force as a collective rather than the individual. In most cases, education does not become a real alternative until a person loses his/her job (Larsson & Thång 1994).

In his thesis, Holmer (1987) asked the question "What opportunities exist for enhancing education access among less-educated industrial workers and what is their potential for rectifying such an education?" (Holmer and Thång, 1996:5). He describes an effective distance towards education among many older workers. These attitudes and values influenced both their attempts to access, participate and make sense of the education offered.

"Adults cannot simplistically be seen as puppets acting according to expectations. Appreciation of education are influenced by views of labour as such, the actor's specific position within the labour process and of the actor's interaction with the environment, actually constructing it. Understanding of what is implied by education and what opportunities it can offer are conditioned by roles in the labour process, qualification demands and learning in working life" (p.5).

The studies presented make it clear that interest is related to what kind of activities a person takes part in. Holmer and Thång note that:

"Through becoming involved in activities which provide opportunities for learning, the motivation toward the development of new behaviour patterns evolves. Unqualified labour, on the other hand, leads to the development of passivity and acquiescence. Opportunities to learn and motivation for learning can be seen as two sides of the same coin" (p.19).

Dispositions towards education in the AEI

Aim of the study
One conclusion in relation to the studies presented is that the question of motives and motivation to participate in formal adult education is a complex matter. Motivation to participate can concern the entering process and the process that makes people stay in education. The specific study we want to discuss here concerns dispositions to act towards education within the AEI

(Wärvik & Thång, 1999a; Wärvik & Thång, 1999b; Wärvik & Thång, 1999c). A disposition to act is a broader concept than a motive. According to Thång (1984:232),

> *An attitude and a readiness to respond is a disposition to act towards a given phenomenon or object which includes a motive, an aspiration and intention to execute manual or mental actions or to bring about something found desirable.*

The study is focused on participants who entered the AEI during the first year of the programme in two municipalities in the western part of Sweden. The aim is to describe why the participants have entered formal education and if the education is a part of their plans for the future. Note that the focus is on participation in formal education, not on learning.

Method

Data was collected through interviews. Each interview lasted about one hour. The interviews were taped and transcribed.

Adults who enter an education can be expected to be very heterogeneous concerning motives, motivation, age, sex etc. We wanted a sample of people with different kinds of characteristics (age, sex, educational background and study focus). In total 50 people (25 from each municipality) were interviewed, 38 women and 12 men. The age range was from 21 – 54, the average age was around 34. Most of them participated in upper secondary education and only one in basic education. The majority of the interviewed were unemployed and nearly all of them (42) received the special grant connected to the AEI. Seven people received different kinds of combinations of state grants and state loans. One person financed the studies by work. The educational background was for most of them two years of upper secondary schooling (Table 1).

Table 1. Educational background.

Educational background	Number interviewed	%
Compulsory school (7 – 9 years)	14	28
Upper secondary school, interrupted	3	6
Upper secondary school, 1 year	2	4
Upper secondary school, 2 years	26	52
Upper secondary school, 3 years	4	8
Higher education	1	2
Total	50	100

There is also a variety educational content among the interviewed (table 2). In most cases they studied general subjects.

Table 2. Educational content and provider of education.

Educational content and provider of the education	Number interviewed	%
General subjects, municipal education	34	68
Vocational subjects, private and municipal education	4	8
General subjects, folk high school	10	20
Aesthetic subject [a], folk high school and municipal education	1	2
Other subject [a], folk high school and Municipal education	1	2
Total	50	100

[a] Combined with general subjects

The participants were interviewed after about one or two semesters of studies.

The municipalities

The study was conducted in two municipalities in the south-west of Sweden.

Municipality A is situated not far from a large Swedish town with a population of about 35 000. Of the inhabitants, 75 % work in the service sector, 24 % work in industry and 1 % in farming. For the country in total the same percentages are 70, 27 and 2 (SCB 1999b). The AEI classes are separated from the classes in the regular municipal adult education.

Municipality B is a rural district with around 9 000 inhabitants. 53 % work in the service sector, 38 % in industry and as many as 9 % work in farming. The AEI participants are integrated in classes in the ordinary municipal adult education as well as in folk high school.

The study was carried out in the spring during the first year with the AEI. During the actual semester 352 people participated in the AEI in municipality A and 162 in municipality B.

Result of the study

Many questions need an answer in order to shed some light over the motives. Why has education become an alternative? How well reflected is the decision to enter? According to the participants, is the AEI a voluntary activity? Many of the participants were unemployed when they entered this education. In both municipalities the local labour office and the AEI officers cooperated in the recruitment process. It is reasonable to believe that this situation can have some effect on the will to participate. What attitudes and readiness to respond, can be found about entering the AEI?

Among the interviewed, three dispositions to act can be described: a) an active b) a need to change the current situation in life and c) the decision to enter education is made by someone else.

Around half of the respondents (23) express an active disposition to act. They have entered the AEI because they wanted to take part in an education. Six participants within this group describe their future plans in a way that it seems reasonable to believe that they would have entered adult education even without the AEI. Other participants within this active group express a latent need to participate in adult education. Barriers to enter education before can have been work, childbirth and the financial situation. Long distance to the adult education provider has been a barrier for some participants from the rural district. Education seems to fit well into the current life situation and the financial aid connected to the AEI gave opportunities to participate without any financial obstacles.

"It's been a dream for several years to go back to school, to get the three years. I've been thinking about it for a long period but you do not deal with yourself when you have a job. But then I felt that this was quite a chance".

Another group (24) describe a more or less difficult situation in life and a need to change the current situation. The AEI offers an opportunity in a situation when they do not experience any other possibilities. They describe the decision to enter education as their own but the attention is not on the education, more on their own situation in life. The decision to enter education is not a part of a long-term plan, here and now is an important aspect in relation to the entering process.

" But I'm not that old, I'm 30. I've had the disease for several years now and when it also affected the wrists, I couldn't stand it any more. I wanted to do something, not just stay at home, being on sick leave. I just couldn't stand it. I wanted to do something useful and education is useful. (...) I just thought: now I'm leaving my job, I had no great plans".

Long-term unemployment can force an individual to enter education in order to keep the unemployment benefit. This was the situation for the third group (3) and they do not describe the decision to enter the AEI as their own. The current education is only another activity unemployed people have to take part in. They describe a distance towards the education. Education[1] has no value at all by itself.

"Interviewer: Why did you decide to enter the AEI?
The interviewed: Because I needed the unemployment money, I had only a few paid days left. I've had ALU and API and I thought I could take this now".

A question, which has arisen in recent years, is why so few men participate in adult education. Most of the men in our study express, in relation to the entering process, a need to change the current situation in life or that the decision to enter education was not their own, see Table 3. Education is an instrument to handle a more or less difficult situation in life. One cannot draw any general conclusions but it seems reasonable to ask if this mirrors the fact that men take part in adult education to a much less extent than women? That working class men are unwilling to take loans for education and that education becomes an

---

[1] Please note: education, not learning.

alternative for many men only when there are no other alternatives to handle a difficult life situation?

Table 3. Gender and the entering process.

	Men	Women	Total	%
Active	3	20	23	46
A need to change the situation in life/the decision to enter is made by someone else.	9	18	27	54
Total	12	38	50	100

A report from the U.K., "Excluded men", (McGivney 1999) discusses why so few working class men participate in adult education. The report speaks of a special male working class culture, which does not value education so highly but also that there are greater differences in participation between social groups than between genders. An important question related to this is if we have an adult education system that appeals to working class men as well as working class women?

Table 4 shows the relation between the length of the unemployment period and the entering process.

Table 4. Unemployment and entering process.

	Leave of absence	Unemployed part time or < 6 months	> 6 months	Total
Active	5	8	10	23
A need to change the situation in life/the decision to enter is made by someone else.	2	4	21	27
Total	7	12	31	50

A long period of unemployment is related to the b) category, a need to change the current situation in life and the c) category, the decision to enter is made by someone else. Note that among those with a period of unemployment of more than six months, i.e. long-term unemployment, 25 have been unemployed more than four years. However, many within this group have not been unoccupied, they have been employed hour by hour in the health care sector or have been on parental leave(s).

15 participants express long-term plans and the current education within the AEI can be seen as part of these plans. They know what they want to do in the future related to continued education and work. The education within the AEI is an instrument to reach the goal.

Seven out of ten do not express any clear plans for the future. Many of them want to be on the safe side when it comes to future plans, i.e. they want to be sure that a conceivable higher education will lead to a job. Only a few of the participants have a job. Many of them have experienced years of unemployment combined with activities for unemployed people and short periods of occupation. It is understandable if they want to be sure of getting a job this time. Many of them are middle aged with short education and they "know" that the labour market wants younger people with some kind of post-upper secondary education. Their self-confidence may not be the best. The participants within this group are more oriented towards work than towards education. It is interesting to note that during the period in education, several of them have realized that further education is a possible alternative. Usually motives are seen as an explaining factor, an explanans.

On the whole most of the participants are satisfied with the education and to be a student. Many of them have plans to continue their education within the AEI for another semester and yet there is no need to worry about the future. It is reasonable to think that future plans for many of them do not seem to be the most important thing just now. The education is in focus; not job seeking in an uncertain labour market which has given them such bad experience before.

During the interviews we asked some overall questions about the value of education for adults. Most of them seemed to relate the answers to their own life situation. All say that adults enter education to keep up with the competition in working life. The unemployed need more education so they can return to the labour market or the employed need a retraining course if they want to/have to get a new job. Education can also be a step on a way to a more qualified job. It is notable that all the interviewed say that education is a way to get a job but only one person says he is sure to get one after the education. He is taking a course in welding.

For most of those interviewed education is not just an instrument to get a job, personal growth is a very important aspect of education according to the participants. The later is very much related to participation in education for some time and a feeling of coping with the study situation.

Discussion

This study has focused on the decision process, when the individual decided whether or not to take part in the AEI.

The adult education reforms in Sweden have followed an extended youth education. The educational level among the population is still unequally distributed, among generations and social classes, despite the reforms. The motives for the reforms have shifted during the decades but several have been aimed at ensuring that people with short education take part in education.

The AEI is directed towards the unemployed and on a macro level can be seen as a reform, or an instrument to create an employable and a flexible workforce in order to promote financial growth. Participation in the AEI is voluntary so an important aspect of the AEI is to motivate the target group to enter.

The participants in our study describe the entering process in different ways. Some express an active disposition to act; they have entered because they wanted to take part in an education. Other participants have entered because they wanted to change their situation in life. In comparison with the motivation model described by Thång (1984) the former group has the focus *towards* something new. The later group has the focus *away from* something. They felt an *impulse*, a need to change. For many of them, long-term unemployment acted as a trigger to overcome the *resistance* to change (see also Larsson & Thång 1994). Another change in the context was that "everybody" talked about the AEI. It was on the news, the local labour office was involved in the recruitment etc. This meant that the AEI became a visible alternative. It was also for many people easier to enter when they knew that the decision did not affect their private economy, i.e. the unemployed received the same amount of money as if they had continued to stay at home.

Holmer (1987) describes an affective distance towards formal education among workers. According to his results, factors like position within the labour process and qualification demands affect the workers' understanding of what opportunities education can offer. Related to our result, it is important to notice that the interviews took part after about one or two semesters of study. It is reasonable to believe that more participants would have expressed that the decision to enter was not their own if we had made the interviews just after they had entered the education. After participating for a period, many people find the education interesting and worth the trouble, and that they were capable of handling the new situation. The decision to enter education can therefore be described in different words at the time of the interview than after a period in education.

The participants have different aims with their studies. Most of them become oriented towards work early in life. Some of them left school after compulsory education or shorter vocational courses. Many of the interviewed participants say that if they could choose between work and education the choice would have been work. One thing they all have in common is that they have stayed in education. Several say that they have started to think about further studies as an effect of the current education, despite the fact that they have no clear plans for the future. This indicates that a short period in education can change people's view of education and of their personal possibilities. This also mirrors the result by Larsson et al. (1986) that people with short education might have difficulties understanding the meaningfulness of education.

The interviewed group largely relate adult education to requirements on the labour market. The result also mirrors the public rhetoric about the need for a better educated work force. Many of the interviewed protest against the high qualification demands in the labour market, they say that even rather unqualified jobs require three years in upper secondary school. This can be compared with Hill's (1998) study of young men and women in vocational upper secondary programs. Her result shows that many of them do not think that the jobs they will get are so demanding as they are said to be in the public rhetoric. They had met a working life that did not need the increased competence level, that they cannot use their qualified education.

Another aspect of education is that it gives the participants general knowledge. Some of the interviewed describe for example that it is now easier to follow the public debate. Two subjects, Swedish and civics, are of special importance in this matter. This aspect of education is very much related to a more general experience of being good enough as a citizen and to get respect from other people. This is worth noting in relation to the emphasis on natural sciences and technology in the society.

References

Aronsson, G. & Göransson, s. (1997). Fasta anställningen men inte det önskade jobbet. En empirisk studie. *Arbetsmarknad & Arbetsliv.* 3, 3 s. 193 – 205.

Alexandersson, C. & Thång, P-O. *Förändras människan av utbildning?* Rapport nr 1987:06. Institutionen för pedagogik, Göteborgs universitet.

Borgström, L. (1988). *Vuxnas kunskapssökande. En studie av självstyrt lärande.* Stockholm: Brevskolan.

Fransson, A. (1978). *Att rädas prov och att vilja veta. Studier av samspelet mellan ängslighet, motivation och inlärning.* Göteborg: Acta Universitatis Gothoburgensis. No. 24.

Fransson A. & Lundquist, O. (1988). *Komvux rekryterar rätt! En jämförelse av rekryteringsmönstret till etapp 1 höstterminerna 1980 och 1987.* Göteborg: Institutionen för pedagogik och didaktik. Göteborgs universitet.

Fredén, L. (1978). *Att sakna möjligheter. En teoretisk och empirisk analys av depressioner utifrån Ernst Beckers socialpsykologiska teori.* Almqvist & Wiksell. Ak. Avh.

Government Bill 1970:35.

Greeno, J. & Collins. A. (1996). Cognition and Learning. In. D. Berliner and R. Calfee. *Handbook of educational psychology.* New York: MacMillan Library Reference.

Hill, M. (1998). *Kompetent för "det nya arbetslivet"?. Tre gymnasieklasser reflekterar över och diskuterar yrkesförberedande studier.* Göteborg: Acta Universitatis Gothoburgensis. Ak. avh. No. 126.

Holmer, J. (1987). *Högre utbildning för lågutbildade i industrin.* Göteborg: Acta Universitatis Gothoburgensis.

Holmer, J. & Thång, P.-O. (1996). *Motivation and Opportunities to Learn. Adult Education and Learning in Working Life.* Paper presented at the conference: Learning and Research in Working Life. Lund: Sweden.

Kierkegaard, S. (1996, nyutg.) *Begreppet ångest.* Guldsmedshyttan: Nimrod.

Larsson, S. & Thång, P-O. (1985). *Arbetets betydelse och utbildningens funktion. En empirisk studie av sjukvårdsbiträdens syn på arbete och utbildning.* Rapporter från institutionen för pedagogik, 1985:3. Göteborg: Göteborgs universitet.

Larsson, S., Alexandersson, C., Helmstad, G. & Thång, P-O. (1986). *Arbetsupplevelse och utbildningssyn hos icke-facklärda.* Göteborg: Acta Universitatis Gothoburgensis. No 57.

Larsson, S. & Thång, P-O. (1994). Principles behind the Generation of Adult Education in Local Arenas. In: Benn, R. & Fieldhouse, R. *Training and Professional Development in Adult Continuing Education.* University of Exeter.

Lundquist, O. (1989). *Studiesteg för vuxna, utveckling, utnyttjande, utfall.* Göteborg: Acta Universitatis Gothoburgensis. No. 72.

Lundquist, O. (1990). *Studiefinansieringens betydelse för nybörjare i komvux höstterminerna 1980 och 1986. En komparativ studie. Delrapport 1.* Göteborg: Institutionen för pedagogik, Göteborgs universitet.

Lyttkens, L. (1994). *Kompetens och individualisering.* Rapport nr 8, Agenda 2000, Ds 1994:18. Utbildningsdepartementet.

May, R. (1980). *Ångest, en utmaning: teorier, fallstudier.* Stockholm: Bonnier.

McGivney, V. (1999). *Excluded Men. Men who are missing from education and training.* Leicester: NIACE.

National Board of Education (1998). *Kunskapslyftet och den kommunala vuxenutbildningen.* Dnr 97:1646.

OECD. (1995). *Education at a Glance.* OECD indicators. Paris: OECD.

Rubenson, K. (1975). R*ekrytering till vuxenutbildning. En studie av kortutbildade män.* Göteborg: Acta Universitatis Gothoburgensis. No 13.

Rubenson, K., Bergsten, U., Bromsjö, B. (1977). *Kortutbildades inställning till vuxenutbildning.* Vällingby: Liber läromedel. Utbildningsförlaget.

Rubenson, K. (1989). Swedish Adult Education Policy. In S. Ball & S. Larsson. *The Struggle for Democratic Education. Equality and Participation in Sweden.* Sussex: The Palmer Press.

SCB (1999a). *Staff training: second half of 1998.* Örebro: Statistics Sweden.

SCB (1999b). Statistical yearbook of administrative districts of Sweden 1999. Örebro: Statistics Sweden.

Sellin, B. (1999). *European trends in the development of occupations and qualifications.* Thessaloniki: CEDEFOP.

Stipek, D. (1996). Motivation and Instruction. In. D. Berliner and R. Calfee. *Handbook of educational psychology.* New York: MacMillan Library Reference.

SOU (1998:51). *Vuxenutbildning och livslångt lärande.* Stockholm: Utbildningsdepartementet.

Tesssaring, M. (1999). *Human Resource Potential and the Role of Education and Training.* Thessaloniki: CEDEFOP.

Thång, P-O. (1984). *Vuxenlärarens förhållningssätt till deltagarerfarenheter. En studie inom AMU.* Göteborg: Acta Universitatis Gothoburgensis. Ak. avh. No. 47

Thång, P-O. (1988). *Vem går i grundvux och hur går det?* Göteborg: Rapport nr 1988:04. Institutionen för pedagogik. Göteborgs universitet.

White, R. W. (1959). Motivation reconsidered: The concept of competence. *Psychological Review*, 1959, 66, 297.

Wärvik, G-B. & Thång, P-O. (1999a). *Första året med Kunskapslyftet i Lerums kommun.* Institutionen för pedagogik, Göteborgs universitet.

Wärvik, G-B. & Thång, P-O. (1999b). *Första året med Kunskapslyftet i Hjo kommun.* Institutionen för pedagogik, Göteborgs universitet.

Wärvik, G-B. & Thång, P-O. (1999c). *Studier av Kunskapslyftet på lokal nivå.* Paper presented at the conference: Forskning i Norden, May 27 – 29, Tammerfors, Finland.

FACTORS BEHIND THE FINNISH HIGHER EDUCATION REFORM - THE ESTABLISHMENT OF AMK-INSTITUTIONS

Hannele Salminen

Abstract

A non-university sector of higher education has been gradually built up alongside the traditional university sector in Finland. It consists of the AMK-institutions, or polytechnics (institutions of vocational higher education). By August 2000, the system of higher education will be fully developed.[1]

This article discusses the planning process and the background of the reform, the factors that led to the renewal. On the one hand, there were shortcomings in the education system. On the other, there were powerful trends of change in society, as well as certain international, albeit largely coincidental, influences. The reform upgrading vocational higher education to AMK-institutions has been implemented as a gradual process of development and experimentation. This process differentiates the Finnish reform from the development of polytechnics in other countries. There was no direct international model for the Finnish AMK-institutions, but the reform was strongly connected with the general international discussion on education policy.

This article is based on the qualitative content analysis of data gathered through expert interviews and the official documents prepared during the period of reform by the educational administration.

Introduction

In many countries, a constantly growing part of each age cohort is participating in tertiary level education. In the OECD countries, the number of higher

---

[1] The term "AMK-institution" comes from the Finnish word *Ammattikorkeakoulu*, "AMK" for short. It is the term used by the OECD examiners of the non-university sector in their review report on Finnish higher education (1995,151-243), and also e.g. Teichler (1998: 477-478). Since the AMKs differ a lot from English polytechnics, it is also the term used here.

education students has quadrupled in a few decades. The rate of development has varied from one country to another, but the main line has been towards an increasing volume of higher education. In 1994, Papadupoulos compared education in Europe to education in the USA. According to him, the problem in Europe has been the relatively insignificant provision of higher education compared to the United States, where the trend has been towards expanding the university sector. The response in Europe has been to develop polytechnics. However, European countries had neither common practice, nor did they pursue similar educational policies: Each country developed its education system in its own way. The rationale and the problems behind the development differ, and thus the solutions may even have been converse. Many countries' response was to build a non-university sector alongside universities.

At the beginning of 1989 a public dialogue started in Finland concerning the restructuring of the education system. A large national pilot process was launched in the autumn 1991. It was in two parts: an experimental reform of upper secondary education and an experimental reform of higher vocational education. The latter instituted a non-university sector, the AMK-institutions. This article looks at the planning process and the reasons behind the AMK reform in Finland.

What were the reasons for setting up AMK-institutions, in the late 1980s and early 1990s?

In all education systems there are always several potential education policy themes which can be defined as problems that need to be solved and which demand educational measures. Only some of these themes are seriously taken up, and even fewer become targets for official measures. This is why it is interesting to examine why the polytechnics became the focus of interest in the beginning of the 1990s.

Many Central European countries including West Germany set up a system of polytechnics in the 1960s. Such foreign models were also discussed in Finland at the time. Before an educational reform was carried out in the 1970s, plans were being made in nearly every sector to develop vocational education. At that point, the idea of polytechnics also came up. There were aspirations within technical education to upgrade higher vocational education in engineering into polytechnics after the English model, and in the early 1970s a proposal was made to establish a polytechnic for engineering education. When the education reform was launched in the 1970s, these ideas were given up.

OECD experts evaluated Finnish education policy at the beginning of the 1980s. In their report they put forward the following questions: Would it be worthwhile to intensify cooperation between upper secondary education and vocational education, and would it be wise to develop a non-university higher education sector in Finland (OECD 1981)? At that time these proposals were not considered important, and the question of polytechnics did not come up in discussions in the 1980s. In Finland the idea of higher education institutions other than universities was alien and as yet unstructured. In the early 1990s the situation had changed and the upgrading of vocational education into higher education was debated again.

Shortcomings in the education system

In its report on education policy (1990) the Government suggested experiments of AMK-institutions and more flexible upper secondary education and training with a view to developing the Finnish education system. Before that there had been no need for polytechnics, because the higher education system worked quite well. The university sector was growing and was seen to offer enough openings. Similarly, vocational education had been undergoing a reform for over a decade and seemed to be improving. There was no special reason for seeking alternatives either in higher education or in vocational education.

Certain problems in the education system became apparent towards the end of the 1980s. The previous education system had been planned and created in the 1960s and 1970s (= the reform of upper secondary education and training). When that reform had finally been fully implemented towards the end of the 1980s, both society and working life had changed, as had the conception of education and learning. The education produced by the "new" vocational education was already out-of-date in many respects before it was fully implemented.

According to some researchers (e.g. Vuorinen 1991; Väärälä 1993), vocational education of that time was the product of an industrial society, which can be characterized as a society of science, applied technology and extensive exploitation of natural resources. Miettinen (1990) claimed that educational administration, curriculum planning and pedagogy were based on the principles of Taylorism and its views of human nature and learning: the aims of learning were defined as concrete actions, work and occupational tasks were seen as the result of isolated and simple acts, and vocations were scrutinized through task analyses which supported this point of view. The Government's education policy report (1990) also pointed out that vocational education constituted a system with several levels resembling the hierarchies of working life.

Some of the key reasons for the establishment of AMK-institutions were problems in the education system and education policy. The post-secondary education system seemed to be bursting with problems. In the late 1980s the Ministry of Education assessed the functioning of the system and found delayed graduation, increasing dropouts, widening demarcation between general and vocational education, large numbers of students with great expectations for study, and an inflexible education system which could not respond to the changing knowledge and skill needs (Ministry of Education 1989a). The education system was too rigid to meet the new demands of the labour market. Because young people's expectations and the needs of the working life did not match, there was double schooling and long study times. It was seen that educational resources were wasted in education which was not even planned to be used in the labour market. On top of this, vocational education in Finland, which had many levels and branches, was difficult to compare internationally. This was a specific additional argument for the AMKs. In 1993 there were three levels of vocational education leading to altogether 268 different diplomas. The diploma programmes, with few exceptions, were divided into separate lines: one for comprehensive school leavers, another for matriculated students. In 1995 Finland still had 170 vocational lines, Sweden had 16, Norway 10 and the UK 16 (Ministry of Education 1995, 65).

This analysis of the problems in the education system was generally accepted, although a number of widely different alternatives were suggested as a remedy (Ministry of Education 1989 b). Parliament also discussed the issue in dealing with the education policy report (Ministry of Education 1989 a; 1990). On the basis of the assessment, the Ministry of Education set the following goals for the development of education. One was to continue fostering equal opportunity in education for different population groups and meet the increasingly diverse educational demands of citizens. Education should motivate students better and meet occupational requirements more flexibly. Thus the objectives set from the outset for the pilot AMK-institutions clearly related to the education system: the main aim was to put right the problems in the education system, and there were objectives concerning the quality of education on top of this.

Changes in society and in the occupational structure are reflected in education policy discussion

Piloting the AMKs was justified in view of the known and foreseeable changes in working life at the beginning of the 1990s. These were rapid modifications in production and in the occupational structure and tasks, the use of new technologies, as well as environmental problems, which all had an effect on skill requirements and internationalization (Numminen & Lampinen 1990).

Towards the end of the 1980s people became aware of growing differentiation as a general trend in society. The linear career was said to be in crisis and the traditional demarcation between occupations was more changeable than before. Individual careers were more flexible than before: more and more people were working part-time and changing their place of residence, occupation or tasks. Instability had increased and the structures of the industrial society were breaking up. It was no longer practical to educate people for narrow tasks or permanent vocations. According to Väärälä (1993;1995), the Finnish reform of upper secondary and AMK-institutions was connected with an upheaval of the economy, which led to increased demands on educational outcome. Investment in education was also scrutinized more closely than before, the concept of accountability in education began to be discussed. Other reasons necessitating an evaluation of the socio-economic dimensions of the education system were the development of working life and the labour market and technological progress.

The first years of the 1990s are known in Finnish economic history as a time of exceptionally deep economic recession. Total production fell by 13 %, which resulted in the loss of almost 500 000 jobs. These are unusually high figures in the peacetime history of industrialized countries. Economic depression, low demand for labour, together with high unemployment rates, had an effect on education, raising questions of efficiency and quality. It was obvious that occupational structures were changing. A hierarchical system of education which emulated the structure of working life was no longer feasible, because occupational tasks were changing more rapidly than education. It became the aim of education to respond to the new qualification requirements.

Consequently, the planning of vocational education in the 1990s was based on the creation of broad basic occupational skills. It became evident that these skills, a high quality of education and changes in society demanded the creation of a non-university sector, AMK-institutions. Especially multi-field networks in upper secondary education and training and the new AMK-institutions were expected to enable students to plan and pursue their studies in a new way, combine studies in a new way, and construct new kinds of degrees.

Foreign influences in the planning of the Finnish non-university sector

There were polytechnics in many western industrialized countries, but their educational structures could differ greatly. Although the Finnish non-university sector is similar to both the Dutch HBO-institutions (*Hoger Beroepsonderwijs*) and the German *Fachhochschule* system, there are fundamental differences compared to both of them.

Research on the process of planning relating to the Finnish AMK-institutions has shown that the decision to create a non-university higher education sector derived from the personal interests and knowledge of those who were in charge of the planning. Especially the HBO-institutions (*Hoger Beroepsonderwijs*) in Holland and *Fachhochschulen* in Germany were well-known to the planners (Salminen 1997).

When the Finnish non-university sector was being outlined, the existing designs for the structure of polytechnics were studied, although the planners were not consciously looking for a model to imitate. Immediately when the issue was raised in Finland, Mr Taxell, the then Minister of Education, visited Germany to learn about the *Fachhochschule* system. During 1989 many German-Finnish seminars were arranged, as well as seminars where experts from the OECD and foreign research units talked about polytechnics and similar institutions.

Dorothy Firth's report for the OECD "Alternatives to universities" (published in 1991, but available in a draft version in 1989) set off a lively discussion in Finland. US community colleges and British polytechnics were well known in Finland, as well as the German *Fachhochschulen*, but the latter had not been visited by Finns very often. The Finnish planners visited Holland, but the Dutch model was just starting at the time when the discussion on the non-university sector began in Finland. A great deal of information was available concerning different types of institutions, and a large number of visits were made to investigate the systems in different countries. But the crucial influence of Firth's report was that it influenced thinking at the conceptual level. As the title reveals, the report made readers in Finland aware of polytechnics as alternatives to universities (Lampinen 1995).

Elovainio (1974: 252) points out that the earlier restructuring of Finnish higher education had not coincided with structural changes in the rest of Europe. The AMK reform was no different. There is one country which was carrying out a similar reform at the time: Austria launched polytechnics officially in autumn 1994, although they were based on a different model. Finland adopted the so-called systems model and Austria the opposite, a model based individual institutions each entitled to award its own degrees. Sweden, which has been the origin of so many of our reforms, was not the model this time. On the contrary: in 1995 it briefly looked as if Sweden were going to create a non-university sector similar to the Finnish one, but the proposal of the committee (Utbildningsdepartementet 1995) was not carried out in its original form.

This has described the new situation in society and how the demands for growing internationalization created pressure on the structure of the education system. It might be partly by chance that the interest in polytechnics coincided with the pressures deriving from problems in the education system. The planners' knowledge and relevant foreign influences can be regarded as the main reason why the choice fell on AMK-institutions when different options were being weighed up.

The planning process of the AMK reform

The Finnish public administration has a tradition of setting up committees to prepare reforms. In this respect, the AMK process was unique: there were no official committees for planning, nor did it start with a parliamentary communication. The discussion began with a proposal put forward by a group of senior officials at the Ministry of Education in early 1989. A large vision seminar was held in February the same year. The Ministry of Education emphasized that the vision was not a concrete proposal for development but an outline intended to activate education policy discussion and to give it structure. This was achieved: a lively discussion gained momentum on a national scale. Different kinds of models of higher education were put forward as a basis for the reform. Pilot AMK-institutions began to operate in autumn 1991.

In view of the tradition of appointing committees to prepare education policy measures and, if the committee institution is seen to mean that the formulation of education policy and educational arrangements are the state's responsibility, the AMK process can be taken as a conscious effort to use a new strategy in starting a reform. The fact that no committees were appointed may have been intended as a message of a whole new culture at all policy-making levels.

The previous education reforms had been centralized, with a planning and steering system in several steps. In the AMK experiment and reform the strategy was totally different. Both the time and the AMK reform were characterized by an effort towards decentralized administration. Lampinen (1995) said in an interview that the planning ideology somewhat coincidentally changed at the same time as the creation of AMK-institutions. Still one can believe that the decentralization of decision making was primarily meant to support the autonomy of the institutions being upgraded to higher education institutions, thus helping them to become parallel and equal to the universities.

The planning of AMK-institutions started first of all as a reform at the systems level in the vocational education. It was primarily intended to put right the problems in the education system. In my research on the establishment the Finnish AMK-institutions (Salminen 1997) I placed some essential features of the reform process into the hypothetical mission profile by Kaufman (1972, 1988) and Corrigan (1967), into the stages of the policy process by Harman (1984:15-17), and into the categories of public policy process by Lampinen (1992: 94-96). This analysis shows that the planning and development of the Finnish AMK experiment correspond well to the model put forward by Kaufman and Corrigan in their mission analysis, as well as to Harman's stages and Lampinen's categories. I have also compared the Finnish process with the systematic six-step change strategy devised by Bushnell (1971). Bushnell examines a change process on the level of schools and institutions, but in my research I applied the model to an examination of change in the whole education system. As a process, the planning and establishment of AMK-institutions followed many of the steps towards a systematic strategy of change presented by Bushnell.

Although there was a fresh, exceptional start to the AMK reform, and although there was no given planning strategy for the establishment of the AMK sector, an analysis of the reform and its planning with the above-mentioned theoretical models and frames shows that the planning and implementation of the reform seem to follow the general phases of a political process and reform.

Objectives of the MK reform, the polytechnics experiment

The main objectives of the reform were defined when the experiments began in 1991. The general objectives and the experiments in progress can be summed up as follows:

1. To raise the standard of education. Polytechnic diplomas will be made part of the higher education degree system. In contrast to university degrees, polytechnic qualifications will have a vocational and practical emphasis.
2. To react to changing needs for expertise and skills. The reform must find new study programmes to fill gaps in competence left by the old vocational education system and universities. Students should be given greater choice to fashion individual study programmes.
3. To make vocational education more attractive. The reform should provide a competitive alternative for young people with a good general education and an interest in higher education.
4. To improve the international compatibility of vocational education. The reform should lift higher vocational education into a sphere that comprises a non-university sector that is on a par with the university sector.
5. To make the vocational education system more functional. The reform should provide the occasion to set up larger, more efficient units with stronger material and intellectual resources. In fact, most of the new polytechnics will be multidisciplinary consortia formed by combining several institutions. Polytechnics should be set up to rationalize the educational network, while utilizing the synergy benefits of mergers and safeguarding the regional availability and impact of education.
6. To decentralize the administration of vocational education. The reform should transfer authority to the operational units, reducing normative administration and other central control.
7. To reinforce the regional impact of vocational education. The polytechnics should assume their proper role in developing the regional infrastructure by providing educational services as well as services and development supporting business and industry.

(Ministry of Education 1999)

The AMK reform was to be completed first by 1999, then by 2000 (Ministry of Education 1996). The first nine AMK-institutions obtained permanent licences on the 1 August 1996, the last ones will be issued in August 2000. After this the pilot phase will be over and the AMK reform will be completed.

Educational optimism and other values

Education policy is always based on certain values, pressures and limits and provides for certain structures as an answer or a reaction to specific problems, needs and challenges. Different and even opposing views are aired when decisions are made on education policy. Although the stated justification for the reform of AMK-institutions was the need for development owing to shortcomings in the education system and changes in society, there are naturally certain value choices behind an educational reform as well. In this reform, a choice was made to develop the level and status of vocational education as a whole. Other kinds of solutions would have been equally possible, for example to incorporate only some branches of vocational education into higher education. This alternative was also discussed during the experiment before the final solution took form.

Strong educational optimism can be seen to have had an effect on the establishment of non-university higher education, the AMK sector, in Finland. This optimism is typical of Finns. We have always believed in general education as a positive social resource and as a means of rising in the social hierarchy. Compared to many countries, such as the other Nordic countries, participation in general education has been high in Finland. The level of education has also risen steadily, counted in the number of people with diplomas and degrees from different levels of education. According to Elovainio (1992), faith in education as a means of social advancement was still in evidence in the early 1990s, for example in Finns' proportionately more active participation in general education compared with the other Nordic countries.

In spite of the cultivating mission of education, some of its central terms are defined by social economy. Educational optimism and belief in a fairly steady economic growth were still prevailing at the end of the 1980s. The approaching economic depression was not foreseen. From these starting points, an even more comprehensive education system with higher quality was planned. In Finnish society the different levels of education are hierarchical in terms of value and estimation. The higher education level is literally considered to be qualitatively and quantitatively better than other levels of education, and thus was also taken to lead to better knowledge and skills in any given field. According to Johnstone (1993), higher education is believed to be the prerequisite for gaining technology, productivity and other international privileges and for supporting economic growth. Higher education also forms and preserves values which define culture and its content in each community. Higher education is believed to be an important factor for social justice, equality and democracy.

Educational reforms usually concern either the whole education system or a large part of it. They typically aim at addressing several problems and shortcomings at the same time, and the objectives set for reforms extend far into the future. For example the objectives of the reform in Sweden in the 1950s and in Finland in the 1960s were to make the dualistic structure of education more coherent as well as build a more democratic education system.

Isling (1980) claims the main forces in reforms are changes in the economic force-field, caused by changes in production and in methods of production. Changes take place in the social structure and in consequential new interests and conflicts of interests (which lead to new and changing interests and conflicts of interests). Changes in society, such as educational reforms, derive from these conflicts. Underlying the Finnish AMK reform we can see interaction between Isling's ideological-cultural force-field B (problems and aims of the reform, opposition, values, ideas, beliefs) and the political-juridical force-field C (laws, regulations as a result of reforms; public discussion, opposition). The economic force-field A was favourable at the beginning of the reform.

Hernesniemi et al. (1995) mention three resultant features in the Finnish education system which essentially influence future economic growth:

1) The length of study in Finland is the longest in the world and the average age of university students is the highest of all the OECD countries.
2) Technical and natural sciences are emphasized in higher education; one third of degrees are awarded in these areas, which is one of the highest figures in the industrialized countries.
3) The number of people with postgraduate degrees has increased rapidly during the past few decades.

The two last facts seem to be positive in view of potential growth, but this inference is not totally unproblematic. Häyrynen (1992) claims that the most lasting effect of education seems to relate more to general mental skills than to job-specific skills.

Educational planning has been governed by the concept of macro-economic human capital (Raivola 1996). Belief in slow but certain return on investments in education is central to that concept. But the immediate needs of the learners are not taken into account. Formal education, regarded separately from the rest of society, provides partial, portioned, retrospective and prevailing knowledge which is bound to time and place, ready-made structures and routines. This is necessary, but not enough. Another viewpoint emphasizes more extensive learning possibilities in which the outside world is brought into the school and learning is extended outside the school. This was the rationale behind the effort to find new ways of interconnecting AMK-institutions and working life and to develop new ways of learning, project work and participation in "real working life" during studies.

Discussion on lifelong learning, which started in the 1960s, was rekindled before the 1990s. Lifelong learning was another argument for more extensive higher education and created pressures on raising the standard of education. This point of view gained great weight in education policy. The capability of the education system to react quickly to changes was emphasized. Belief in education changed into belief in learning. The definitions of lifelong learning highlighted the student's own responsibility for his or her own learning career. These themes are also addressed in the objectives set for AMK-institutions: individual, flexible studies, the student's own responsibility for combining them into a sensible degree, and opportunities for continuing studies within higher education.

Discussions

The first initiatives for polytechnics were put forward in 1960s, but it was not until the end of 1980s that this discussion took off and gained more weight in the education policy debate. In the first phase, several temporary AMK-institutions started operating in 1991 as pilot projects. The first nine permanent AMK-institutions began operating in August 1996, but the gradual process of experimentation and development went on for four years. This pilot phase sets the establishment of the Finnish AMK-institutions apart from the development of polytechnics in other countries.

The AMK-institutions evolved from former vocational institutions, which used to provide the highest-level vocational education. The AMK- institutions came about when specialized institutions were upgraded and merged into new, multi-field higher education institutions. The provision of vocational education was developed and incorporated into the higher education system. In a way, the reform divided the Finnish vocational education and training system into two: vocational institutions, which provide secondary vocational education and training, and AMK-institutions, which provide higher education.

Academic drift seems to be a virtually universal phenomenon in non-university higher education (Neave 1996). Polytechnics in both Holland and Germany kept their vocational nature and constituted a highly valued sector of higher education for years. Recently the degree system in German *Fachhochschulen* has been evolving towards the university degree system. It can nowadays be taken as an example of a mixed model. In the mid-1990s, the Fachhochschulen successfully seized the opportunity for claiming the right to award both a Bachelor's and Master's degree. Various experiments of implementing such a degree structure were underway on an experimental basis (Teichler 1998: 479). And in the late 1990s changes of legislation were made. On this basis, there seems to be a powerful drift towards assimilation into the university system. Because the non-university sector is quite new in Finland, this phenomenon is not yet in evidence, but some of the Finnish AMK-institutions have organized studies in cooperation with foreign universities which have the right to award Master's degrees.

The future of the Finnish non-university sector is closely connected with its ability to orient towards working life (Tulkki 1993). According to most assessments, the Finnish AMK-institution model is taking its own unique shape, and is going to be different from its international counterparts (Vehviläinen 1998). In my research (Salminen 1997) I came to the conclusion that it is not actually correct to discuss international models in this connection, as there were no direct models that would have been copied. The basic model of Finnish AMK-institution is a multi-field cluster of institutions providing education in different fields.

It is interesting that the severe economic depression which hit Finland in the early 1990s and the subsequent cuts in the education sector did not halt the AMK reform. As a matter of fact, many of the measures taken for economic reasons fit surprisingly well together with some of the pedagogical development aims. There were some aims which were both economic and pedagogical, such as cooperation between institutions; the merger of small institutions into larger, multi-field units; premises and other resources in common use; and more emphasis on independent work and study. Multi-field units enable students to combine studies of different fields flexibly into their degrees. It has to be said, however, that later when more cuts were needed, the pedagogical solutions were of minor importance in many situations.

At first the justifications and aims of the AMK pilot were mainly domestic. Development needs due to problems in the education system and changes in society were given as reasons for the AMK reform. Behind the reform there was also strong belief in a fairly steady economic growth, strong educational optimism and the idea of valuing education according to educational levels. Similarly, the discussion on lifelong learning argued for a non-university sector. In the beginning of the new millennium, growing importance is being given to the aim of adjusting the Finnish education system to the European environment and ensuring that it is comparable and comprehensible there.

One current topic discussed in the AMK context is vocational postgraduate degrees. They have been developed and prepared for a few years at the administrative level. Some international developments have slowed down the planning process.

On the 25 May 1998, the Ministers of Higher Education from France, Great Britain, Germany and Italy signed the Sorbonne Declaration with a view to harmonizing the structure of European higher education. It emphasized the creation of an European area of higher education as a key means of promoting mobility and employability and the Continent's overall development. To many the wording came as a surprise, since the Maastricht Treaty leaves decisions concerning education systems to the discretion of each member country.

After Sorbonne, political actions gained momentum, because already in June 1999 the European Ministers of Education convening in Bologna gave a joint declaration in order to establish the European Higher Education Area and to promote the European system of higher education world-wide.

The objective is a system essentially based on two cycles, undergraduate and graduate. Access to the second cycle would require successful completion of the first cycle, which takes a minimum of three years. The second cycle would lead to the Master's or doctorate degrees in many European countries. The present Finnish higher education system does not fit into this model without problems.

Germany and Holland, which both have a non-university sector resembling the Finnish one, have opened a route from polytechnics to the Master's degree. The Finnish AMK-degree is a Bachelor's degree. This means that the Finnish AMK-degree would not be comparable with the German and Dutch polytechnic degrees.

After the Sorbonne and Bologna Declarations it seemed evident that it would be necessary to solve the questions of the level/status of the AMK-degrees, the projected vocational postgraduate degrees and the Finnish licentiate degree in terms of international comparability.

The status of vocational postgraduate degrees in the degree system was what brought the planning process to a halt. The task forces preparing the reform could not find a solution. So the Ministry of Education postponed matters until the Government's policy line was known, which was forthcoming in the

Development Plan for Education and Research 1999-2004. The Government adopted the Plan in December 1999.

According to the Development Plan, vocational postgraduate degree studies of 40-60 credits will be gradually introduced in fields where there is demand for such qualifications on the part of employers. On the basis of piloting, the system of vocational postgraduate degrees will be eventually extended (Ministry of Education 2000: 38). The new degrees will also have a strong vocational orientation. At the planning phase, it has been envisioned that one criterion for admission would be some years of work experience after graduation. This would also prevent an AMK education from evolving into an automatic two-step degree-system. This would also support the idea that the new postgraduate AMK-degree would largely relate to the development of working life.

The new Development Plan for Education and Research is the first to mention research and development in connection with the AMK-institutions (Ministry of Education 2000: 38). According to Pratt (1997: 326), the question of research in non-university institutions gives rise to strong views in most countries. Finland is no exception. It has been debated for some years whether the AMK-institutions have the capacity and capability of carrying out research (read: are allowed), or is this the prerogative of universities alone. With reference again to Pratt (1997:326), most non-university institutions have an important task in offering advisory and consultancy services to firms. This activity is inherently investigative and generates a great deal of research. Research cannot be separated from the basic mission of the AMK-institutions, provided that research in AMK-institutions is more practically oriented than university research. Even less can it be separated from the new postgraduate AMK-degrees which will hopefully be developed in the near future. There are, however, opposed voices coming from the university sector now, as there were in the early 1990s, when the new AMK sector was being piloted.

References

Bushnell, D. S. (1971). A systematic strategy for school renewal. In D.S. Bushnell and D. Rappaport (ed.) *Planned Change in Education: a systems approach*. New York, Chicago, San Francisco, Atlanta: Harcourt Brace Jovanovich Inc., 3 -16.

Corrigan, B.O. & Kaufman, R. A. (1967). The Steps and Tools of the System Synthesis Process in Education. Operation PEP. San Mateo Country, Calif. Department of Education, December 1967. In R. A. Kaufman 1972. *Educational System Planning*. Prentice-Hall Educational Administration Series, INC. New Jersey: Englewood Cliffs, 63.

Elovainio, P. (1974). Korkeakoululaitoksen rakenne ja yhteiskunnan muutos. Helsingin yliopiston valtiotieteellinen tiedekunta. *Sosiologia* XI, 1974: 4. [The structure of higher education and change of society. University of Helsinki, Faculty of Political Science. *Sociology XI*]

Elovainio, P. (1992). Muuttuva koulutus. In O. Riihinen (ed.) *Sosiaalipolitiikka 2017; Näkökulmia suomalaisen yritystoiminnan kehitykseen ja tulevaisuuteen*. Juva: WSOY, 413-432. [Education in change. In O. Riihinen (ed) *Social Policy 2017; Views to development and future of the Finnish entrepreneurship*, 413-432]

Hallituksen koulutuspoliittinen selonteko Eduskunnalle (1990). *Suomen koulutusjärjestelmä, koulutuksen taso ja kehittämislinjat*. Helsinki: Valtion painatuskeskus. [*Government report on education policy to the Parliament 1990. The Finnish educational system, level of education and further development.*]

Harman, G. (1984). Conceptual and Theoretical Issues. In J. R. Hough (ed.) *Educational Policy. An International Survey*. London & Sydney, Croom Helm, New York: St. Martin's Press,13 -27.

Hernesniemi, H. & Lammi, M.& Ylä-Anttila, P. (1995*). Kansallinen kilpailukyky ja teollinen tulevaisuus*. Elinkeinoelämän tutkimuslaitos ETLA, Suomen itsenäisyyden juhlarahasto SITRA. Sarja B105. SITRA 145. Helsinki: Taloustieto Oy. [*National competitiveness and industrial future*. The research centre of commercial life, ETLA, The Finnish fund of independence SITRA.]

Häyrynen,Y.- P. (1992). Henkisten kykyjen tuottavuus ja 1990 -luku. In L. Lehtisalo (ed.) *Vaikuttaako koulutus.* Opetusministeriö: VAPK-kustannus, 51 -123. [Productivity of mental capacities and the 1990's. In L. Lehtisalo (ed*.) Does education have effects.* Ministry of Education.]

Isling, A. (1980). *Kampen för och mot en demokratisk skola. 1. Samhällsstruktur och skolorganisation.* A Dissertation for the Doctor's Degree in social sciences. University of Stockholm. Sober Förlag AB. *[Battle for a democratic school. 1. The structure of society and school organisation.]*

Johnstone, D. B. (1993). The Cost of Higher Education: Worldwide Issues and Trends for the 1990s. In P. G. Altbach. & D. B. Johnstone (ed*.) The Funding of Higher Education: International Perspectives.* New York: Garland Publishing, 3 -24.

Kaufman, R. (1972). *Educational System Planning.* Prentice-Hall Educational Administration series, INC. New jersey: Englewood Cliffs.

Kaufman, R. (1988). *Planning Educational Systems. A Results-Based Approach.* Lancaster. Pennsylvania. USA: Techonomic Publishing Co. Inc.

Lampinen, O. (1992). *The Utilization of Social Science Research in Public Policy.* Publications of The Academy of Finland 4/92. Vapk-Publishing. Helsinki: Government Printing Centre.

Lampinen, O. (1995). Opetusministeriön koulutuskokeilujen projektipäällikön haastattelu (H. Salminen) 31.10.1995. Helsinki. An interview of the project manager of the educational experiments in the Ministry of Education. 31.10.1995 by H. Salminen.

Miettinen, R. (1990). *Koulun muuttamisen mahdollisuudesta. Analyysi opetustyön kehityksestä ja ristiriidoista.* Helsinki: Gaudeamus. [*About the possibility of changing school. An analysis of development and conflicts in teaching.*]

Ministry of Education (1989 a*). Koulutuksen kehittäminen. Harjoitetun koulutuspolitiikan tarkastelua ja hahmotelmia peruskoulun jälkeisen koulutuksen kehittämisestä.* 16.1.1989.[*Development of Education. Paper on educational policy and future plans for the development of postcompulsory education.*]

Ministry of Education (1989 b). *Opetusministeriön valmistelemasta peruskoulun jälkeisen koulutuksen kehittämistä käsittelevästä muistiosta saadut kirjalliset lausunnot.* 16.6.1989. *[Discussion on the Ministry of Education's memorandum "The Development of Education"]*

Ministry of Education (1990). *Suomen koulutusjärjestelmä, koulutuksen taso ja kehittämislinjat.* Helsinki: VAPK. *[The Finnish Educational System, Level of Education and Further Development.]*

Ministry of Education (1993). *A background report for OECD's country research.* Helsinki.

Ministry of Education (1995). *Open School for the Youth. Three European Views on Developing Youth Education in Finland.* Report 5. Experimental Reform of Upper Secondary Education of Finland.

Ministry of Education (1996). *Education and research 2000. Development plan for education and university research for the period 1995-2000.* Government resolution 21st December 1995. Helsinki: Oy Edita Ab.

Ministry of Education (1999). The Finnish Education System. http://www.minedu.fi/minedu/education/polytechnic.html.

Ministry of Education (2000). *Koulutus ja tutkimus vuosina 1999-2004. Kehittämissuunnitelma 29.12.1999.* Opetusministeriö. Helsinki: Oy Edita Ab. [*Education and research years 1999-2004. A development plan 29.12.1999.*]

Neave, G. (1996). Homogenization, integration and convergence: the Chesire Cats of higher education analysis. In V. L. Meek et al. (ed.) *The Mockers and Mocked.* Oxford: Pergamon / IAU Press, 26 - 41.

Numminen, U. & Lampinen. O. (1990). Koulutuskokeilujen johtoryhmä 5.4.1990. *Peruskoulun jälkeisen koulutuksen kehittäminen.* Muistio. [The administrative group of the educational experiments 5 April 1990. *Development of post-compulsory education.* Memorandum.]

OECD (1981). *Review of National Policies for Education. Finland.* Paris.

OECD (1985). *Reviews of National Policies for Education. Finland. Higher Education.* Paris.

Palonen, T.& Rinne, R. & Kivinen, O. (1992). *Korkeakoulujärjestelmä ja reformipolitiikka. Seitsemän maan vertailu.* Koulutussosiologian tutkimuskeskus, raportteja 12. Turun yliopisto. [*Higher education system and reform policy. A comparison of seven countries.* Research of Unit for the Sociology of Education, report 12.]

Papadopoulos, G. S. (1994). *Education 1960 -1990. The OECD Perspective.* OECD. Historical Series. Paris.

Pratt, J. (1997). *The Polytechnic Experiment 1965 -1992.* The Society for Research into Higher Education & Open University Press. St Edmundsbury Press Ltd, Bury St Edmunds, Suffolk.

Raivola, R. (1996). *Elinikäinen oppiminen. Miksi tarvitaan uusi asenne ja uusi käsite?* Artikkeli Elinikäisen oppimisen Suomen komitean internet-sivuilla. http://www.freenet.hut.fi/EOK.[*Lifelong learning. Why a new attitude and a new concept is needed?* An article in the Finnish committee of life long learning, internet pages. http://www.freenet.hut.fi/EOK]

Salminen, H. (1997) *Miksi ja miten suomalainen ammattikorkeakoulu perustettiin. Tarkastelu suunnitteluprosessin käynnistymisestä ensimmäisten ammattikorkeakoulujen vakinaistamiseen 1.8.1996.* Kasvastustieteiden lisensiaatintutkimus. Jyväskylän yliopisto. [*Why and how the Finnish non-university sector was established. A study from the start of planning process till the first AMK-institutions were made permanent on the 1 August 1996.* A licentiate research in science of education. University of Jyväskylä.]

Teichler, U. (1998). The changing roles of the university and non-university sectors of higher education in Europe. *European Review*, Vol. 6, No 4, 475-487.

Tulkki P. (1993). Työelämän ja ammattikorkeakoulujen yhteys; Koulutussosiologian tutkimuskeskus, raportteja 18; 1993. *[Connection between working life and polytechnics.* Research of Unit for the Sociology of Education, reports 18;1993]

Utbildningsdepartementet (1995). *Yrkeshögskolan. Kvalificerad eftergymnasial yrkesutbildning.* SOU 1995:38. Stockholm: Regeringskansliets offsetcentral. [*Polytechnics*]

Vehviläinen, M.(1998). *Ammattikorkeakoulun opiskelijavalinnan seurantatutkimus. (Case Lahden ammattikorkeakoulu, diakonian instituutti).* Kasvastustieteiden lisensiaatintutkimus. Tampereen yliopisto, Hämeenlinnan toimipaikka. *[A follow -up study of choosing students to a polytechnic. Case Lahti polytechnic, institute of diakonia.* A licentiate research in science of education. University of Tampere.]

Vuorinen, P. (1991). Keskiasteen uudistus ja muuttuva työelämä. In J. Ekola & P.

Vuorinen & P. Kämäräinen (ed.) *Ammatillisen koulutuksen uudistaminen 1980 - luvulla. Selvitys uudistuksen toteutumisesta ja toteutusympäristöstä, osa II.* Ammattikasvatushallitus: Tutkimuksia ja selosteita n:o 30/1991, 1 -107. [The reform of upper secondary education and changing working life. In Ekola & Vuorinen & Kämäräinen (ed.) *Reform of vocational education in the 1980's. A report of implementation and environment of the reform, part II.* National Board of Vocational Education. Research and Reports no. 30/1991.]

Väärälä, R. (1993). Ammatin opettamisen murros. In H. Salminen (ed*.) Haasteita sosiaali- ja terveydenhuollon koulutukselle.* Helsinki: Opetushallitus, 13 - 23. [[Upheaval of teaching professions. In H. Salminen (ed*.) Challenges to the education of social and health care.* Helsinki: National Board of Education.]

Väärälä, R. (1995). *Ammattikoulutus ja kvalifikaatiot.* Lapin yliopisto. Acta Universitatis Lapponiensis. [*Vocational education and qualifications.* University of Lapland.]

REFORM 94 – CONSEQUENCES FOR ADULTS

Heidi Engesbak

Abstract

Reform 94 in Norway involves the latest changes in upper secondary education. The reform gives all students aged 16 to 19 years a statutory right to 3 years of full-time education leading to either vocational qualifications or university entrance qualifications. No such right was formulated for adults. The main focus in this paper is to discuss how Reform 94 has influenced adults' possibilities to participate in public upper secondary education. The period covered in this paper is the four years following the introduction of the reform, namely 1994-1997. The approach is twofold; (i) the need for qualifications for adults and how they meet the labour market demands of formal qualifications, and (ii) the accessibility of public upper secondary education for adults.

Introduction - New educational requests

Our post-industrial society has an impact on the individual's claim and need for more and higher formal education. Rapid changes in society and working life, including the changing role of the family, the separation of work, domestic and educational spheres, globalization and demographic changes all have effects on the request from the labour market for a more qualified workforce, and on the individual's request for more formal education.

With the rapid changes in production methods, practical skills must be related to general knowledge, which needs continuously updating. This situation puts new demands on competence and qualifications. For adults with low or non-formal education it has become more and more necessary to update their knowledge in order to increase the value of their work, to maintain their position or to get a (new) position. The value of formal education is decreasing at the same time, as adults in exposed positions understand that formal education is a means to improve and secure their own position.

The educational sector

In the period 1970 to 1990 we have experienced an increase in capacity within the educational sector. More people are enrolled in education. Compulsory 9-year primary and lower secondary education has been developed, and an increasing number of young people received an upper secondary education. The number of upper secondary pupils doubled in the period from 1977 to 1991.[1] Upper secondary education experienced a major change in 1976, and vocational training at the workplace was reorganized in 1980.

In 1980 and early 1990, Norway experienced a rather static situation in business and industry and the labour market became tight. Both the high unemployment and the increasing demand for well-qualified workers increased the demand for formal education. The rapid changes in society were combined with the demand from the labour market for updating the educational system. Since then, considerable developments have taken place in Norway. During the 1990s education became a political priority area, resulting in educational reforms, involving all levels of education. The guiding principle for the 1990s was the improvement of educational standards for the whole population by consolidating and improving the educational system.

One main political argument for the necessity of an educational reform was, for instance, that the link between school and industrial training was weak. There was little progress from one level to the next and many upper secondary courses did not give a 3-year education. Consequently there were too few positions for apprentices and insufficient opportunities to complete vocational training. In addition the arguments were that the specialization, particularly at foundation course level, was too extensive, with too many and too confusing options. The ideological goal was that all types of upper secondary education should provide pupils with university entrance qualifications, vocational competence, or documented partial competence.

Politically, Reform 94 was a response to changes in society in general and within the educational sector in particular. Reform 94 involved higher secondary education, both general education and vocational training. The most drastic changes have nevertheless been made within vocational and technical training. The labour market demand for broad competence and flexibility has therefore become central for vocational and technical training. Emphasis has been placed on developing broad competence, flexibility and a good foundation

---

[1] In 1977-78 the number of upper secondary pupils was slightly more than 135 000. This figure rose to approximately 255 000 in the school year 1991-92.

for advanced training. Moreover, the structure is to help to maintain a decentralized educational and training system. And all upper secondary education is to lead to full qualifications, either vocational qualifications or university entrance qualifications.

Educational policy 1994 to 1997

Education is decisive for employment, for the development of creative ability, for better exploitation of resources and for sustainable growth. Knowledge is often considered as a value, which will help individuals to raise their life quality. Education and the acquisition of knowledge are also acknowledged to be the main driving forces for change, innovation and growth in society and consequently a key to economic, social and cultural development. The possibilities to attain knowledge and education are therefore important both for individuals and society as a whole.

The principle of equality in terms of educational provision has long traditions in Norway, and the overall aim of the government, as stated in its Long-Term Programme 1994-97, has been to ensure equal access to education and training for all, independent of gender, social, geographical and cultural backgrounds. Raising the standard of knowledge and competence at all levels of education and stages of life was also a major objective. Moreover education is supposed to motivate people to acquire knowledge in a life-long perspective. According to the Long-Term Programme, the aim of education and training should be to prepare the population for changes in society and for jobs that have not yet been created. It also states that, general knowledge and continuously up-dating are important to meet rapid changes in production methods and society. Education is seen as a continuous process. Emphasis is put on knowledge and skills, which will provide a broad scope for renewal and continued learning in a lifelong perspective.

Reform 94 is composed to meet new demands of more formal education and knowledge. Therefore all youth aged 16 to 19 years were given a statutory right to three years' upper secondary education, with a corresponding obligation on the part of the regional authorities to provide an adequate number of places. No such rights were formulated for adults.

Approach

In this article I will focus on motivation and labour market theories and try to explain the desired participation by adults in upper secondary education. The main approach is in which ways Reform 94 has influenced the adults' accessibility and their possibilities to participate in higher secondary education in the 1994 –1997 period. Do we find equality in adult and youth access to upper secondary education in spite of the statutory rights given to youth? Is it still possible for adults to access upper secondary education? What is the relationship between the supply for and the demand after upper secondary education? Which alternatives do adults have in public education? The focus is therefore twofold: (i) Labour market changes and the need for formal qualifications, and (ii) Equality between youth and adults in participation opportunities in public upper secondary education.

Why adults participate in adult education

Most Norwegians have traditionally followed a path through life in which education is synonymous with youth, work with adulthood and retirement with old-age. Traditionally work is regarded as the only fully legitimate activity of maturity. There is "something wrong" with someone who is not working. Adult non-workers are considered to represent a social problem. According to O'Toole all adults who are not working have a second-class status in society.

> *"Women who take care of their children, the unemployed, the underemployed, the dropout, the elderly and even full-time students - all lack full working identities. They suffer both economically and psychologically from their second-class status..."* (O'Toole 1974:13).

Even so, education is no longer a process connected only with youth. Today it has been more and more common that adults take part in adult education, and the labour market now expects a higher degree of documented qualifications than ever before. An interesting question is what motivates adults to participate in adult education despite getting a second-class status while participating? Several researchers have tried to explain why adults participate in adult education, what motivates and stimulates them and what reduces their participation.

According to Havinghurst (1970) there are two basic aspects of education; (i) instrumental education and (ii) expressive education. Both aspects are important regarding life-long learning and adult education. Instrumental education means education for a goal that lies outside and beyond the act of education, i.e. the education is an instrument to change the participant's life-situation. *"Instrumental education is thus a kind of investment of time and energy in the expectation of future gain"* (Havinghurst 1970:17). Expressive education means education for the education's own sake. The goal lies in the act of learning and in the knowledge it self. *"Expressive education is a kind of consumption of time and energy for present gain"* (Havinghurst 1970:18). According to Havinghurst (1970) a competent person has to combine the two types of education at every stage of his/her life.

Houle (1961) studied participants by extensive holistic interviews, seeking common threads in adult learners' activity and motivation. Three subgroups were emerged: (i) Goal-oriented learners (ii) activity-oriented learners and (iii) learning-oriented learners.

Goal-oriented learners use learning to gain specific objectives, such as learning to speak before an audience, learning better business practice, and similar concrete objectives. According to the goal-oriented learner, learning is a series of episodes, which begin with a need, a curiosity or an interest. These learners seek the information and the knowledge where the knowledge actually is. Any institution or method will not limit the learning activities. The learner will select the optimal method, i.e. the method that best will achieve/realize the purpose, taking a course, joining a group, reading a book etc. *Activity-oriented* learners participate primary for the sake of participation or the activity in itself, rather than to develop a skill or to learn in general. They may take a course or a class to escape loneliness or boredom or an unhappy work situation, to collect credits or degrees. *Learning-oriented* learners seek learning for its own sake. The have a fundamental desire to know and grow through learning and their activity seems to be life long. These learners are enthusiastic. They take classes and courses, join groups and even change jobs for the learning potential offered.

Motivation towards participation in adult education varies during the life cycle.[2] Different stages or different ages have their own needs and motives that have to be fulfilled. In accordance with Cross (1981) adult education which increases ones chances of success is more attractive for the individual than other forms of adult education. *"Learning that will improve one's position in life is a major motivation"* (Cross 1981:96). This is one of two conclusions after a summary of research on motivation to participate in adult education. But at the same time she says *".. Just what will 'improve life varies with age, sex, occupation, and*

---

[2] The life cycle as an unit of social time has been employed extensively dating back to Margaret Mead (1928). As Honingman (1959:559) notes practically an entire culture can be described from the individual view, from the moment of impregnation or birth to death. There are various formulations of dominant developmental task of the adult life cycle. But almost all societies make a distinction between infancy, childhood, adolescence, adulthood and old age as divisions in the life cycle (Friedman 1970).

life stages". According to Cross (1981:96ff) teenagers and young adults are interested in upward career mobility. Adults with a good job want a better one, while adults without a job seek new career opportunities. Older people and those reaching career levels where additional education promises few extrinsic rewards, are often interested in learning that will enhance the quality of life and leisure.

Work-related motives are important in order to explain participation in adult education. Surveys have shown that labour market possibilities and improvements in ones own occupation career is an important motivation factor in adult education, and has become more and more important. Engesbak (1994) found that 75 % of adult participants in upper secondary education, participated in order to improve their position in the labour market. Engesbak and Rolfsen (2000) found that more than 80 % of the adult participants in study circles at university level were work motivated. Skaalvik and Engesbak (1996) found that adult participation in labour market-oriented education/courses tripled in the period 1978 to 1996. This indicates that labour-market needs and requests have become more and more important.

Labour market and qualifications

The focus on labour market and work-motivated learning might be explained by the changes in the labour market and the increasing request for formal skills and qualifications. Norway's industrial structure has undergone considerable change in the last 30 years. A significantly smaller percentage of employees work in industry and other manufacturing activities, while more people are employed in public and private services (Ellingsæter and Wiers-Jenssen 1997:9). Most OECD countries have experienced a similar trend, but the reduction in industrial employment and the increase in the number of public sector employees have been more pronounced in Norway.

Rapidly changing knowledge and technology are important factors in our society. Changes in scientific information and industrial techniques influence adult life by increasing the requirements for personal competence and extend the problem of human obsolescence.

New technology demands new strategies and new competence. Workers have to justify and update their qualifications and their skills for maintaining their positions in the labour market. This: *"... gives rise to short-term work perspectives and induces a relatively high degree of occupational insecurity, and accordingly, a relatively low degree of calculability and predictability."*

(Buchmann 1989:50). Buchmann (1989) draws attention to the structural changes in technology. According to her, these changes have altered the role of workers. *"Male occupation careers are beginning to take on 'chaotic' forms of professional trajectories previously found exclusively in female professional tracks"* (Buchmann 1989:48). Men's lifelong position in working life, with one (standardized) career is no longer the standard. Structural changes have affected the traditional positions of workers. Today it is natural to have more than one career (Acer 1992; Myles 1990; Halvorsen 1980). The probability of unemployment due to structural or economic factors is highly dependent on the individual's position in the labour market, age and sex (Buchmann 1989:49). Men with high occupational status are more likely to have stable and standardized careers endowed with high calculability and predictability (Eichorn et al. 1981). For workers, upgrading courses and further education therefore become more and more necessary as the main means to maintain their position in working life. Life-long learning, as a strategy to maintain a high occupational position is consequently necessary for most workers today.

Vocational workers who have an increasing chance to lose jobs through automation are forced to invest in further professional qualifications in order to preserve the marketability of their labour. This updating occurs in a time characterized by a high degree of flexibility among the work force. Workers have to renew their qualifications and overcome the constraints of specialization. That means that they have to acquire qualifications that can open as many employment opportunities as possible. This supports the tendency towards the individualization of professional updating, such as upgrading courses and further education (Buchmann 1989). An important manifestation of this process is a transfer of workers' further educational investments into leisure time (Negt 1984).

Even if the workers invest in education and formal qualifications, they are not secured a position in the labour market. The convertibility of professional investment into occupational positions and into a financial situation is not automatic or routine. It is rather uncertain and variable.

The increasing dependence of occupational status on educational certificates causes individuals to make educational investments in order to improve their chances for acquiring occupational status. A generalized increase in education stimulates what Bourdieu (1979) and Collins (1979) have called "The inflation of educational certificates". A structural concomitant of the overproduction of educational degrees is its continuity, this produces even higher educational demands as individuals struggle to achieve as high an educational degree as possible (Amos 1985). Competitions for educational certificates and the accompanying inflation and devaluation of education towards the labour market have become a structural constant in advanced industrial societies (Collins 1979). The processes are self-perpetuating causing shifts in the relationships between educational demands and occupations. For workers, this process causes a constant challenge for updating knowledge and new and better qualifications.

Figure 1. The relationship between labour market and individual's needs for education.

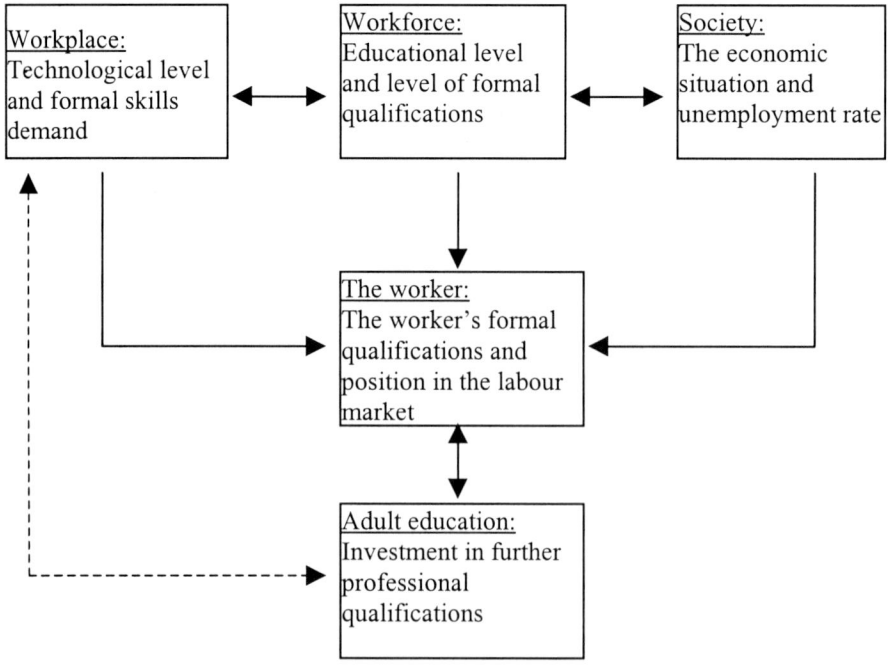

The structure and organization of the Norwegian system of education

The Norwegian government exercises its authority in matters of education through the Ministry of Education, Research and Church Affairs. The ministry is responsible for all levels of education, from primary and secondary to higher education, including adult education.

Figure 2. The education system.[3]

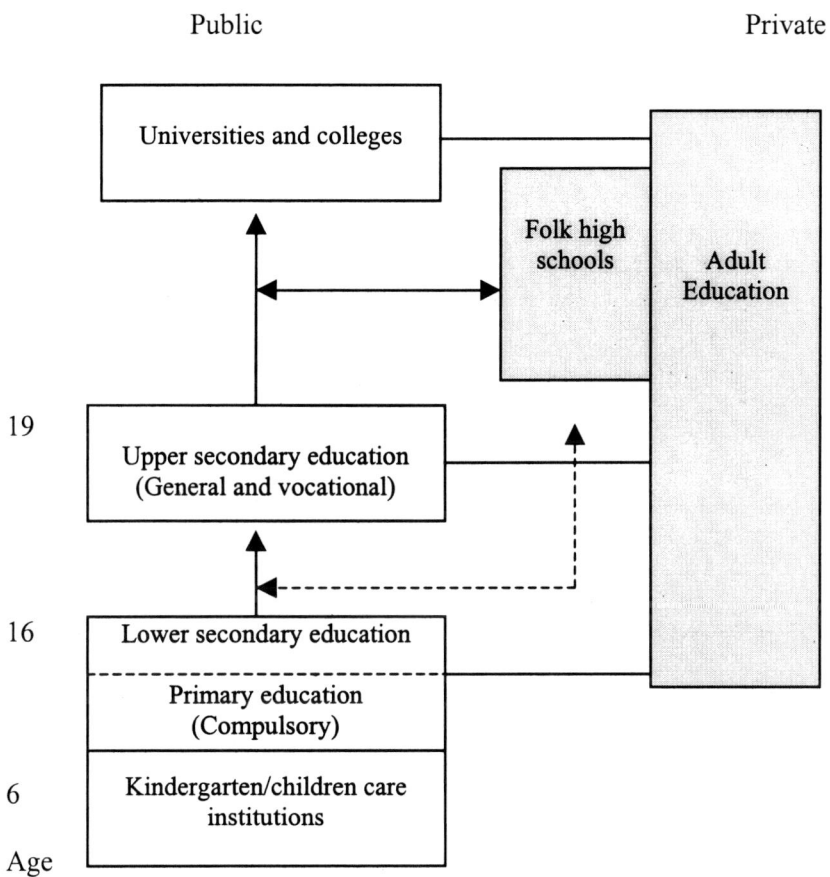

In 1997, the Norwegian government lowered the school starting age from seven to six, at the same time compulsory education was extended from nine to ten years.

Pupils normally start upper secondary education at the age of 16. All upper secondary courses lead to higher education or a recognized vocational qualification after 3 years (or, in the case of vocational courses, normally 4 years).

---

[3] KUF 1996.

Upper secondary education

Before 1994, adults had extra scores for age, work- and life experience. The consequence was that adults had intake priority when applying for public upper secondary education, when there was grade equality. Reform 94 gave a statutory right to a 3-year,[4] full-time upper secondary education for all teenagers between 16 and 19. Adults were not given a corresponding right.

It is the county municipalities who ensure that this right is implemented by arranging enough places in the various schools. In addition to providing places for young people with a statutory right to education, the county municipality must also ensure that adults aged 20 or more have an opportunity to obtain upper secondary education.

To take care of the adults' possibilities the government has set the minimum dimension equal to 375 % of an average birth-rate bulge. This means that each year-class in upper secondary education is corresponding to 125 % of the birth-rate bulge. 100 % per annum is used for teenagers' education. The spare 25 % is meant to cover adults' needs and applications for upper secondary education. But this 25 % is spread between (i) youth with psycho-social problems who need more than three years, (ii) youth who change their mind, and re-select courses, (iii) technical college, and at finally (iv) adults. In addition most county municipalities had a dimension higher than 375 % before 1994. This indicates that adults' possibilities regarding public upper secondary education has been worsened following the introduction of Reform 94.

The structure

After 1994 there were 13 different Foundation Courses.[5] This is a reduction from more than one hundred such courses. Specialization takes place in Advanced Courses I and II. Foundation courses, advanced courses I are school-based. Before 1994 the specialization started in Foundation courses. After

---

[4] When basic education in the school is combined with the completion of vocational training at a place of work, the training may last up to 4 years by combining the in-company training with productive work over 2 years.

[5] General courses: (1) General and Business Studies, (2) Music, Dance and Drama, (3) Sports and Physical Education.
Vocational courses: (1) Health and Social Studies, (2) Arts, Crafts and Design Studies, (3) Agriculture, Fishing and Forestry, (4) Hotel and Food-Processing Trades, (5) Building and Construction Trades, (6) Technical Building Trades, (7) Electrical Trades, (8) Engineering and Mechanical Trades, (9) Chemical and Processing Trades, (10) Woodworking Trades.

Reform '94 the specialization within the various subject areas takes place in Advanced Courses I and II.

Figure 3. Upper secondary education.[6]

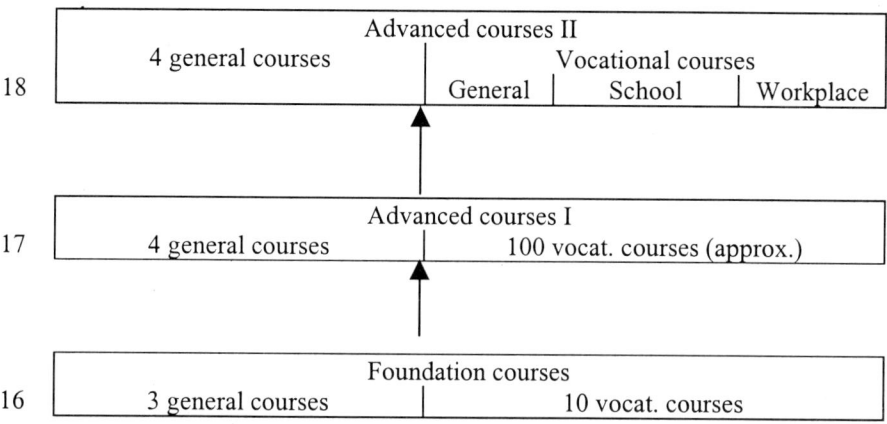

Age

After the first two years, alternative programmes for training in business and industry can be followed: (i) one year of training, or (ii) two years of training combined with productive work. The main model is a "2+2" one. This means, two years of vocational training in school and 2 years of final training (Advanced Course II) in a workplace. If a sufficient number of apprenticeship places cannot be secured, the county municipality must offer the trainees the opportunity of completing the training at school.[7]

---

[6] KUF 1996.

[7] Both those who take their final training at a training establishment and those who complete their vocational training at school take the same craft or journeyman's test and shall receive the same craft certificate or journeyman's certificate when they have passed the test.

Adults' access to public upper secondary education[8]

The demand

Table 1 The application for public upper secondary education. Foundation courses. 1994-1997. Number of applicants and variation in per cent.

School year	Adults		Youth		Total	
	Apply	% Variation	Apply	% Variation	Apply	% Variation
1994/95	16 720	-	63 496	-	80 216	-
1995/96	13 328	-20.3	61 689	-2.8	75 017	-6.5
1996/97	11 763	-29.6	60 722	-4.4	72 485	-9.6
1997/98	10 295	-38.4	60 417	-4.9	70 712	-11.9

In the autumn 1994, there were approximately 80 000 applicants to upper secondary education provided by the public sector. 21 % were adults. These adults applied for ordinary upper secondary education, equivalent to the teenagers. This means that the adults applied for 3 years of full time education, as ordinary pupils in ordinary classes.

In the period towards 1997 the percentage of applicants sank by 12 %. Even though we find a decrease in applications in the youth group, the largest decrease was among the adults. In the autumn 1997, there were nearly 40 % less adult applicants than 3 years earlier. The female applicants have decreased from 10 407 applicants in 1994 to 6 509 applicants in 1997, equivalent to a 63 % decrease. Also male applicants have decreased in the period, from 6 313 applicants in 1994 down to 3 786 applicants in 1997, a 60 % decrease. The amount of both female and male adult applicants for upper secondary education has decreased during the period.

In spite of the decrease in the demand, there is still a larger amount of female than male adult applicants. Table 2 below shows the sex differences in the application for public upper secondary education.

---

[8] The tables below are based upon Linda data, which covers all applicants to public upper secondary education. The Linda Data are made available by Norwegian Institute for Studies in Research and Higher Education (NIFU). Only those who apply for ordinary secondary education are included in the analysis. Those who apply for alternative education and those who apply for special reasons/disabilities are excluded from the analysis.

Table 2 Age and sex differences in the application for public upper secondary education. Vocational foundation courses. 1994-1997. Per cent.

School year	Adults Female	Adults Male	Youts Female	Youts Male	Total Female	Total Male	N
1994/95	62.2	37.8	48.9	51.1	51.7	48.3	80 216
1995/96	59.9	40.1	48.4	51.6	50.4	49.6	75 017
1996/97	60.6	39.4	47.9	52.1	50.0	50.0	72 485
1997/98	63.2	36.8	48.6	51.4	50.7	49.3	70 712

As we can see from Table 2, there is nearly a fifty-fifty distribution between the sexes. Also among youth there is no difference in applications between the sexes. Considering adults, there is a predominance of female applicants compared with males. The female dominance also increases in the period.

Preferences

Table 3 Applications for public upper secondary education. General and vocational foundation courses. 1994-1997. Per cent.

School year	Adults General	Adults Vocational	Youths General	Youths Vocational	Total General	Total Vocational	N
1994/95	13.9	86.1	51.7	48.3	43.8	56.2	80 216
1995/96	14.0	86.0	48.9	51.1	42.7	57.3	75 017
1996/97	17.0	83.0	48.8	51.2	43.7	56.3	72 485
1997/98	27.1	72.9	48.8	51.2	45.6	54.4	70 712

As we can see from Table 3, adults to a great extent want to participate in vocational education i.e. education leading to vocational competence like craft and/or journeyman's certificate. In the three first years after the introduction of Reform 94, over 80 % of the adults wanted to participate in vocational courses. In 1997 this decreased to 73 %. Compared with youth, there is a relatively high amount of the adults who want vocational education. Adults and youth then have different preferences and educational goals.

In 1994, 90 % of the adult female applicants and 80 % of the males applied for vocational courses. The corresponding amounts for youth were respectively 44 % and 52 %.

In addition to the differences between youth and adults in applying for general and vocational courses, there is also a difference in preferences in-between vocational courses. Female adults have relatively limited preferences. Most female applicants apply for Health and Social Studies or Arts, Crafts and Design Studies. Nearly 80 % of the adult females who apply for vocational courses apply for one of these two courses. The corresponding amount for youth is about 40 %. Male adult applicants have a more flexible application pattern. But also here, we find differences between the age groups.

The supply

Table 4 The supply and the level contribution[9] of public upper secondary education. Foundation courses. 1994-1997. Count.

School year	Adults Supply	Adults Contribution	Youths Supply	Youths Contribution	Total Supply	Total Contribution
1994/95	7 554	.45	57 200	.90	64 754	.81
1995/96	5 119	.38	55 794	.90	60 913	.81
1996/97	7 512	.64	56 193	.93	63 705	.88
1997/98	7 654	.74	56 147	.93	63 801	.90

In the autumn 1994, about 80 % of the applicants were offered a school place, this number improved to 90 % in the school year 1997/98. In 1994, less than half of the adult applicants were offered a school place, and in 1995 fewer than 40 % were offered a place. This amount increased radically between 1995 and 1996. In 1996 over 60 % and in 1997 nearly 75 % of the adult applicants were offered a place. This increase in contribution is not a result of an increasing number of school places, but a decrease in applications to public upper secondary education. As we can observe from the Table 4, the number of school places offered to adults is relatively stable (from 7.554 to 7.654, i.e. 1 % increase in the period).

---

[9] Level of Contribution = number of adults who were offered a school-place /number of applicants.

Table 5 Level of contribution of public upper secondary education. General and vocational foundation courses. 1994-1997. Per cent.

School year	Adults		Youths		Total		N
	General	Vocational	General	Vocational	General	Vocational	
1994/95	67.5	41.6	93.6	86.4	91.8	72.1	64 754
1995/96	72.2	32.9	94.7	86.4	93.4	72.2	60 913
1996/97	85.0	59.5	94.1	91.0	93.6	83.5	63 705
1997/98	91.9	67.8	95.0	90.9	94.8	86.4	63 801

As we can observe from Table 5, the level of contribution is relatively high among youth and among general courses. In the case of vocational courses, the level of contribution is rather low regarding adults, even if the level of contribution has increased in the period. In 1994, 42 % of the adults who applied for vocational courses, were offered a school place. This rose to 68 % in 1997. This implies that one of three adults who applied for vocational courses were not offered a school place.

Even if adults prefer vocational courses and apply to vocational courses to a greater degree than general courses, the number of vocational school places offered to adults has not increased in the period. In fact, in general courses we have had an increase of 1002 school places, while vocational courses experienced a decrease of 902 places. This indicates that the increasing level of contribution is not owing to an increase in supply of school places, rather a decrease in applications.

Discussion

After 1994, more or less all 16 year-olds carried on through upper secondary education. This has increased the educational gap between the generations. Young people have a higher education level on average than those who are older. Offering improved educational opportunities to the younger generations and increasing the educational level is a government response to the changes in society in general and the changes in the labour market in particular.

By giving the teenagers a statutory right to 3 years of upper secondary education without giving adults a similar right decreases the adults' possibilities in public upper secondary education and decreases the adults' possibilities in the labour market. By decreasing the possibility for adult attainment in upper secondary education, the groups at risk will be the ones that are hardest affected. Even if a relatively high amount of the Norwegians have more than 9 years of schooling, there are still 40 % of the adult population who have not (SSB 1996).

Adults lacking upper secondary education, dropouts and adults with vocational education which is no longer attractive on the labour market, need access to education to enable them to maintain or change their position or to (re-)enter the labour market. By reducing the adults' possibilities in upper secondary education, adults have fewer alternatives to improve their position in working life by their own means.

Education during adulthood is practically essential for competent performance of all development tasks. To keep up with the changing demands at the workplace and to be able to meet the changing competence demands, a renewal of skills and knowledge is required. Unskilled workers in an unsecured position in the labour market often want to secure their position and raise their level of skills. For many women (re-)entering the labour force after raising children this requires new qualifications and skills. All these require participation in instrumental education for successful achievement and realization. Most adults, who want more education and competence, are work motivated. They have specific job-related goals, and understand participation as means to goal-attainment, therefore most adults want to participate in vocational education, which is directly connected to the labour market.

Work has traditionally been regarded as the only fully legitimate activity of maturity. In many parts of the population this belief still exists. Excluding adults from public upper secondary education confirms the idea that adult non-worker represents a social problem. The focus on labour market education, and education at the work place can increase the impression that there is "something wrong" with non-working adults. Since we traditionally have followed a path through life where education has been associated with youth, work with adulthood and retirement with old age, it is difficult to understand that this has changed – that adulthood has to include both work and education – either simultaneous or at different stages.

Politically, Reform 94 was a response to changes in society and education. The educational opportunities for youth have been improved. In Reform 94, the government seems to have failed to meet the competence needs that adults have in order to meet the changing demands in working life. The competence reform is expected to be an educational reform for adults. Still, it remains to see how the competence reform will meet these needs and demands in the adult population.

References

Acker, J. (1992). "The Future of Women and Work: Ending the Twentieth Century" *Sociological Perspectives*, 35:53-68.

Bourdieu, Pierre (1979). *La distinction: critique sociale du jugement*. Paris: Editions de Minuit.

Buchmann, Marlis (1989). *The script of life in modern society: entry into adulthood in a changing world*. Chicago: University of Chicago Press.

Collins, Randall (1979). *The credential society: An historical sociology of education and stratification*. New York: Academic Press

Cross, K. Patricia (1981). *Adults as learners: Increasing participation and facilitating learning.* San Francisco: Jossey-Bass.

Eichorn, Dorothy H.,. Mussen, Paul H, Clausen, John, Haan, Norma and Honzik, Marjorie P (1981). *Present and past in Middle life*. New York: Academic Press.

Ellingsæter, Anne Lise og Wiers-Jenssen, Jannecke (1997*). Kvinner i et arbeidsmarked i endring. Integrering, marginalisering og eksludering.* ISF-Rapport 97:13. Oslo. Institutt for samfunnsforskning.

Engesbak, Heidi (1995). *Voksne i videregående*. Delrapport 95:1. Trondheim: Norsk voksenpedagogisk forskningsinstitutt.

Engesbak, Heidi (1996). *Reform 94 – også for voksne? Situasjonen for voksne 1 år etter reformen.* Trondheim: Norsk voksenpedagogisk forskningsinstitutt.

Erikson, Erik H. (1950). *Childhood and society* New. York : W. W. Norton. (Også utgitt: London: Imago, 1950.)

Friedman, E.A (1971). "Changing value orientations in adult life" In Hobert W. Burns (ed.). *Sociological backgrounds of adult education. Notes and essays on education for adults*. Chicago: Centre for the study of liberal education.

Halvorsen, Helge (1980)."Myten om den livslange arbeidskontrakten – kontrakt og kontraktsformer i arbeidslivet". In Ted Hanisch, Helge Halvorsen og Gunvor Strømsheim (ed.). *Marked for arbeid. Lønnsarbeider i velferdssamfunnet*. Oslo: Universitetsforlaget

Hanisch, Theodor Harald (1998). "The labour market in Norway". *Nytt fra Norge*. The Ministry of Foreign Affairs. November.

Havinghurst, Robert J. (1970). "Changing status and roles during the adult life cycle: Significance for adult education". In Hobert W. Burns (ed.). *Social backgrounds of adult education*. New York: Syracuse university.

Heath, Anthony (1981). *Social mobility*. London: Fontana Paperbacks.

Honigmann, John J. (1959). *The world of man*. New York: Harper & Brothers.

KUF (Royal Ministry of Education, Research and Church Affairs) (1996). The development of education 1994-96. Norway - National report. International conference on education, forty-fourth session, Geneva. F-2973 E

Mead, Margaret (1928*). Coming of age in Samoa: a psychological study of primitive youth for western civilization*. New York: Blue Ribbon Books.

Mertens, Dieter (1984). "Das Qualifikationsparadox: Bildung und Besschäftigung bei kritischer Arbeitsmarktperspektive". *Zeitschrift für pädagogik* 1984, vol. 30:439-455.

Myles, Gareth D (1990). Measurement and modelling in economics. *Contributions to economic analysis*; 195. Amsterdam : North-Holland

Negt, Oskar (1984). *Lebendige Arbeit, enteignete Zeit: Politische und kulturelle Dimensionen des Kampfes um die Arbeitszeit*. Frankfurt : Reihe Campus.

O'Toole, James (1974). "Education, Work and Quality of Life". In Dyckman W. Vermilye (ed.). *Lifelong learners: a new clientele for higher education. Current issues in higher education*. San Francisco: Jossey-Bass.

Ringdal, Kristen (1990). *Labour market structures and social mobility in Norway: a study in homogeneity and segmentation*. Trondheim: Department of Sociology, University of Trondheim.

Skaalvik, Einar M. og Knudsen, Knud (1979). *Deltakelse i voksenopplæring.* Trondheim: Norsk voksenpedagogisk institutt.

Skaalvik, Einar og Engesbak, Heidi (1996). "Selvrealisering og kompetanseutvikling: Rekruttering til voksenopplæring i et tjueårsperspektiv". I S. Tøsse (red.). *Fra lov til reform.* Trondheim, Norsk voksenpedagogisk forskningsinstitutt.

Thurow, Lester C. (1975). *Generating inequality: mechanisms of distribution in the U.S. economy.* New York: Basic Books.

DISTANCE EDUCATION AT THE TURN OF THE CENTURY – HISTORICAL BACKGROUND AND NEW DEVELOPMENTS ILLUSTRATED BY A CASE STUDY OF AN INSTITUTION IN CHANGE

Torstein Rekkedal

Abstract

The article is divided into two parts. The first is a short historical overview of distance education in Norway as it has developed from the establishment of the first correspondence school in 1914 till the situation today, where distance education courses and programmes in a wide variety of subjects are offered by different types of private and public organizations, institutions and cooperative networks applying a multitude of technologies. The second part describes the strategic transition of one specific institution from organising distance education with a firm basis in the traditions of correspondence education to distance teaching and learning on the Internet. This is mainly based upon my own institution as a case and the project research and evaluation studies connected to the development of the NKI Electronic College from 1987 till today.

Distance Education in Norway

To some extent Norway can be described as a showcase for successful distance education. For example, a 1977 German doctoral thesis, comparing private distance education in 16 countries, showed that Norway had the highest number of distance students per 100 000 inhabitants; 2.5 times more than second ranked Japan (Karow 1977). However, at that time, public distance education in Norway was virtually non-existent. This was mainly because the organizational structure of the higher educational system in many ways counteracted the development of an efficient distance education system. This situation of Norwegian higher institutions lagging behind many other countries in developing distance education changed from 1990 when the government initiated the establishment of The Executive Board for Distance Education at University and College Level (SOFF).

The first Norwegian correspondence school was established in 1914. Because of incidents during the Second World War when public schools were being closed and teachers arrested, enrolment in existing correspondence schools multiplied and more than sixty additional correspondence study initiatives were registered (Østlyngen 1947). When the government planned the reconstruction of the post-war school system, the coordinating committee for schools and education proposed to establish a public correspondence school encompassing all levels of education. This proposed "State Correspondence School" was supposed to develop courses and apply appropriate media dependent on the development of technology in the future. This idea was never realized. The planning process, however, resulted in the 1948 Act on Correspondence Education. According to the author's knowledge, the Norwegian 1948 act was for about 25 years the only law in the world specifically on regulating distance education. According to the law, the Correspondence Schools Council was established as an executive office to support the Ministry of Education in the regulation and accreditation of distance education schools and courses.

This legislation resulted in close governmental supervision of distance education courses and institutions. The establishment of formal governmental bodies working with distance education led to a close cooperation and over the years to a mutual trust between the private institutions, their organization Norwegian Association for Distance Education (NADE) and the Ministry of Education. There is hardly no doubt that the state supervision and cooperative climate resulted in the development of distance education of high quality in Norway. The general high level of quality has also been a result of systematic evaluation and research work on distance teaching and learning over the last 30 years.

In 1975, Parliament decided to provide financial support to correspondence students. Later, the state funding scheme was changed, and the government now supports the approved institutions directly through direct financial grants. This scheme of state funding has resulted in lower tuition fees. In addition, distance students may apply for state grants and loans on similar conditions as ordinary students in public and private schools and colleges.

Today, there are approximately 15 so-called independent distance teaching institutions accredited by the Ministry of Education. The two largest ones, NKI Distance Education and NKS Distance Education, both non-profit foundations, account for more than 80 percent of the yearly course enrolments. However, the number of enrolments has decreased from a peak of 200 000 in 1976 to less than 100 000 in 1998. Most probably, this decrease in enrolments has mainly been a result of continuously decreased financial support from the state.

In 1993, the Act of 1948 was abandoned, and the regulation of the activities of independent distance education institutions was placed under the Adult Education Act. This reform secured better integration of distance education into the national adult education system. Through this reform responsibility for quality was placed with the institutions themselves on a scheme based on cooperation between the distance teaching institutions and the Ministry of Education through NADE. As part of the change in legislation a Standing Committee on quality was established to support the institutions and constitute a link between the Ministry and institutions on quality assurance.

The independent distance education institutions offer a wide variety of programmes at secondary level and tertiary level. The majority lead to recognized exams and certificates.

Many programmes are offered in cooperation between distance learning institutions and public colleges and universities. In these programmes the distance teaching institution organizes the development of study material, recruitment and teaching/student support activities, while the public tertiary institutions take responsibility for the academic content and quality. The two largest institutions also offer their own higher education diplomas by separate accreditation by the universities and/or the Ministry of Education.

The idea of public organized distance education from the post-war reform work was never abandoned. During the 1960s and 1970s, new initiatives were introduced to establish a strong public institution for distance education. But contrary to many other countries, Norway decided not to establish a national open university, maintaining that there was neither an economic basis to support it nor a large enough population to justify it. Instead, the efforts resulted in the establishment of the Norwegian State Institution for Distance Education (NFU). It applies a "networking model" to promote distance education by initiating and coordinating the development and distribution of distance education programmes in collaboration with the National Broadcasting Corporation, publishers, the National Film Board, private distance education institutions and the public school and university system.

Following government reports and white papers during the late 1980s, the government established SOFF in 1990. SOFF's main objectives are to stimulate developments and experiments on distance education at tertiary level, coordinate activities, give some financial support, evaluate activities and recommend future developments. The governmental stimulation through SOFF has led to most universities and colleges becoming interested in distance education, trying out distance education and establishing separate positions and/or departments for distance education.

To facilitate collaboration between the universities and colleges SOFF has established a national network with both public institutions and a number of private educational institutions as participants. Since its inception in 1990, SOFF has provided support for the development of about 200 distance education projects at Norwegian universities and colleges. The courses that have been developed vary greatly by subject and programme of study. Most of the courses combine face-to-face meetings and distance teaching. Statistics for distance learners at public universities and colleges in Norway have not been collected very systematically, but in 1999 the number of students was estimated to be approximately 12 000, i.e. 7 % of the total student population in higher education (Toska 1999).

It is also clear that the level of commitment to distance education has varied among the institutions. The efforts to develop and offer distance study programmes have until recently only received cursory attention from senior-level administration. To a large extent, it can be said that initiatives have been driven forward by enthusiasts and pioneers among some academic staff and some of the administrative and technical personnel at the educational institutions.

However, the situation has changed during last few years. Administrators at the majority of the Norwegian universities have become very occupied with using technology to deliver flexible educational offerings for adult students. There are a number of reasons for this change. The so-called "Competence Reform" which includes legalized rights for all employees to take leaves of absence for updating their competence or take further education has led to demands that on educational institutions develop flexible courses associated with the competence reform. The development of network-based information technology with its assumed potential for supporting high quality distance education has drawn the attention of previously traditional institutions to new ways of distributing education. Both the possibilities and danger of the emerging global education market through the Internet have of course, also influenced Norwegian institutions.

In this new situation many higher institutions have shown increased interest in distance education. This has led to many higher education institutions developing strategies for distance education, new courses and programmes and collaborating in different ways through various kinds of networks and joint ventures to demonstrate their capabilities in terms of change and contribute to meeting the challenges of the competence reform (Toska 1999).

The Norwegian State initiatives on distance education at tertiary level are often mentioned as an example of the application of systematic government policies to direct the development of higher distance education towards clear goals with efficient use of resources through coordination, cooperation and financial support.

NKI and the Electronic College

The remaining part of this article discusses the theoretical background and practical reasons behind the decision of one specific institution, NKI (Norsk Kunnskaps-Institutt), to research and develop distance education based on computer mediated communication. It also reports the experience from teaching through electronic communication for more than 10 years.

NKI is a multiform teaching institution offering full-time and part-time programmes at secondary and tertiary levels. NKI courses and programmes are offered on-campus, by distance education or as decentralized courses. Local face-to-face classes or seminars may supplement the distance education programmes. NKI Distance Education is a separate unit and is organized as a dedicated distance teaching institution. The majority of the NKI distance education programmes are secondary level studies preparing for public or internal exams. The programmes at university and college level are offered in cooperation with Norwegian universities and colleges or through our own "Polytechnic College".

As a leading distance teaching institution in Norway, NKI had carried out research on teaching and learning methods and new technologies in distance education for many years (Rekkedal 1993). Our decision to direct our efforts to develop a distance education system based on electronic communication was taken in 1986 as a result of our continuous theoretical and experimental research on developing the NKI distance education system. Computer mediated communication was in this connection considered to be a medium that was qualitatively different from all other technological developments of media for distance education because of its flexibility and its potential of integrating the presentation of learning material in different forms and capacity for individual, small group and large group communication.

Distance Education and New Media

During the last 30 years distance education both nationally and internationally has generally changed from organising individual learning based on printed material and two-way communication via the ordinary postal system to multimedia learning based integrating print based media and new media, and more recently also the new communication technologies. NKI has followed these developments closely and tried to develop and modernize the distance education system along different lines:

1 Student support and counselling

The individual adult learner has generally great need for support to be able to cope with the studies normally in competition with other demands from job and/or family responsibilities. Research has shown that distance education systems should develop administrative and teaching support systems to help the students adapt to the demands of part-time studies to be able to succeed and complete. In this connection we have researched follow-up systems, initial and continuous counselling, training in distance learning study techniques, turn-round time involved in two-way communication and specific training for distance tutors (see e.g. Rekkedal 1985).

2 Media research

The correspondence teaching system of the 1960s has gradually been changed into a multimedia distance teaching system by the introduction of videotapes (both video-taped lectures and complete learning programmes) audio-tapes, computer software and laboratory kits, as well as, in some cases, video-conferences, radio and TV-programmes. Some of our research projects in this area have been carried out in cooperation with other distance teaching institutions and the Norwegian Telecom Research. Supported by and in cooperation with the Telecom we have carried out experiments on telephone tutoring (Rekkedal 1989), fax as a medium for individual tutoring and guidance (Rekkedal 1992), audiographics (Rekkedal & Vigander 1990), video, local cable television, satellite distribution and video conferencing (Holden 1992, 1993).

3 Computer mediated communication

Computer mediated communication has been one specific priority branch of the media research since 1986. NKI launched the so-called "EKKO Project" in

1986. The acronym, EKKO, denoted "Electronic Combined Education" (in Norwegian the combination of distance education and local face-to-face classes) a name that signified that the computer software should constitute a virtual school or classroom substituting the need for physical presence in a local class. The aim was to develop what we called the "Electronic College", a teaching system offering study programmes independent of time and space and facilitating flexible communication for administrative, social and teaching/ learning purposes. Our understanding was that the developments within computer communication would give teaching and learning possibilities, which would really change distance education dramatically. This article summarizes this research, experience and achievements (see also Paulsen 1990, 1992, 1998, Paulsen & Rekkedal 1990, Rekkedal 1999, Rekkedal & Paulsen 1997, Rekkedal & Møystad 1999).

Technology and competitiveness of distance education institutions

The rapid developments concerning new media and communication technologies constitute both new possibilities and dangers for distance teaching institutions. The new media create, at least in theory, the possibilities for preparing better and more cost-effective learning. At the same time, these developments have resulted in new types of institutions entering the education market, and have incited traditional schools, colleges and universities to offer media based teaching. Thus, distance teaching institutions and universities have encountered, sometimes unexpected, competition on the educational market. This situation was stated in extreme way by Tony Bates' introductory article in an issue of 'Open Praxis' focusing on technology under the title: "Hello technology! Goodbye, distance teaching institutions?" (Bates 1994). The changes in distance education caused by the emerging technologies has made some writers describe the new initiatives as 'third generation' distance education (e.g. Nipper 1989), the first being correspondence education and the second multimedia distance teaching. Until recently, it seemed that distance education institutions had not changed dramatically concerning the organization of their teaching and their application of new media. For instance, Bates (1990, p. 20) stated:

> "There is more talk than action about the use of technology in distance education. Even in the most technologically advanced of our member (EADTU) institutions, print, correspondence and face-to-face teaching still predominate. For most European distance learners, these are still the only media currently that really matter."

According to Bates (Ibid.) there were good reasons why the technological development had been so slow in the distance education institutions. One is, obviously, that distance teaching institutions have long traditions and investments bound up in the 'old' technologies and the natural inertia of large institutions acts against rapid changes. However, there are also rational reasons for the slow technological developments. Print, correspondence and face-to-face are well tried methods. As Bates (Ibid. p. 21) put it:

> *"The use of more advanced technology can be justified only if it meets one or more of the following criteria: lower costs; greater teaching effectiveness; increased accessibility to students. These are proving hard criteria to meet, so it is not surprising that there is still major academic and management resistance to the use of new technologies in most of our member institutions."*

We shall briefly comment on two other writers who have discussed the options available for distance education providers to be able to compete in the new technological environments, one representing the distance teaching universities, the other representing secondary education. John S. Daniel (1995), vice-chancellor of the British Open University, concluded in his analysis of the competitive advantages of the 'mega-universities' that:

> *"...networking students from their home computers should reinforce the competitive advantage of the mega-universities. Distance education has already evolved through two generations, correspondence courses and multi-media packages. The knowledge media ('the coming together of telecommunications, television and computing is producing a media environment for distance education that is more than the sum of its component elements' (p. 11)) represent a third generation of supported open learning that enriches distance education by giving students rapid communication with the people and learning resources of the academic community."* (Daniel 1995)

Margaret Gamlin (1995) of the New Zealand Correspondence School discusses the transition of distance teaching institutions from print and postal-based delivery of traditional correspondence education to a more immediate interactive technology-based delivery. She points out that the drive in many countries today to a competitive education system encourage conventional providers to use technology for innovative delivery of courses. However, most current technologies (such as audio and video conferencing, including audio graphics) tend to support the replication of the conventional classroom - the extended classroom model. She stresses the 'openness' of the correspondence education model and stimulated among others by Bates' (1994) article, she foresees a development in her institution, which builds on this openness and flexibility and learner centred focus, and changes the school's teaching into a 'multimedia' model.

The above considerations were the reasons behind NKI's decision to go in for the development of computer-based communication and the development of 'the Electronic College'.

NKI Electronic College – more than 10 years experience of computer mediated communication in distance education

In one of our early papers on computer conferencing entitled *'Computer conferencing - A breakthrough in distance learning or just another technological gadget?'* (Paulsen & Rekkedal 1988) we discussed developments of media and technology and concluded that computer conferencing or computer-mediated communication with its exceptional possibilities for developing flexible and open distance teaching of high quality, constituted a development that was qualitatively different from all other media. After more than 10 years of experience we can conclude that computer mediated communication and the Internet are becoming important technologies in distance teaching and learning. The introduction of the World Wide Web in the mid 1990s and increased access to the Internet both from the workplace and from home, factors which we did not foresee in 1987 when we introduced our first electronic courses, are changing the world of distance education.

The virtual school

The basis of our ideas for establishing the 'Electronic College' was largely taken from Hilz (1986), introducing computer conferencing as a means to establish a 'virtual classroom' with computer-based communication structures similar to those normally taking place in the normal classroom. The 'virtual school' as, we conceived our aim, should not only emulate the classroom activities, but all other places and activities within the school system.

Morten F. Paulsen (1989), the Director of Development of the Electronic College, pointed out the following requirements for the virtual school:

1 It should emulate all the main tasks of a school: teaching, administrative and social.
2 It should be generally available concerning geography, technology, economy and student competence.
3 It should be independent of time, i.e. continuously available and accept asynchronous communication.
4 It should emulate the different needs of human communication, one-to-one, one-to-many and many-to-many.

Some important functions of computer conferencing in distance education

Based on NKI experience and information from other sources (e.g. McCreary and Van Duren 1987) some important functions for the computer conferencing system in distance education were identified:

Distribution of information: Distance teaching systems have a large need for increased efficiency in updating and distributing information to students, full-time and part-time teachers and administrators.

Examples: Information about courses, seminars, student associations, examinations and updating of learning material.

Two-way communication between tutor/counsellor/administration and student: In most distance teaching systems, the submission of assignments for correction and comments is an important element. It has been demonstrated that long turn-around times may have destructive effects on course completion (Rekkedal 1983). It also takes a long time for students to receive answers from their tutors when they really encounter problems in their studies. To some extent, the telephone has been applied as a means of communication. Electronic mail is independent of both time and space.

Examples: The student may ask questions at any time, without the time delay of mail services. In principle, draft solutions may be submitted and commented on, thus introducing a more flexible organization of tutoring and assessment. If desired, student answers may be made available to other students, before or after the submission of their work. On-line computer-scored tests, as a substitute for off-line testing which we have seen in some distance learning systems can also be included in the system. On a higher level, two-way communication may be used for the guidance of individual student projects.

A substitute for face-to-face teaching, introduction of group discussions and project work: A number of distance learning systems include the possibility of face-to-face meetings with tutors and/or fellow students. For many distance learners, the possibility of taking part in such activities are restricted. Some theorists have argued that direct teaching may have disruptive results on student autonomy and ability for self-study.

Examples: While face-to-face teaching in distance learning systems often seems to have developed into lecturing/presentation of subject matter, computer conferencing concerns information exchange and discussion. Discussions taking place in the classroom can develop into exciting experiences in group learning. The discussion is time and space independent, the medium seems to foster equality of status between students, and between students and tutor. Specifically designed group learning methods may be applied, such as group submission of assignments, group learning and presentations, group seminars and project work.

The public tutorial: Student questions of a general academic or administrative nature may be accessible to all students, as a question from one student normally will be of interest to others. Pre-produced comments on general aspects of a course can now be distributed on-line, and the tutor is given an opportunity to expand on the pre-produced learning material.

Peer counselling: As peer counselling and informal cooperation is a natural part of the on-campus activities of any teaching institution, the possibilities in computer conferencing are obvious. It has been demonstrated that computer conferencing in general may give peer help in solving problems - often from an 'unknown friend'. In large-scale systems, where hundreds of students are studying the same subject, peer help may be of particular importance.

Free-flow discussion: A number of educational conferencing systems has formally established informal meeting places for continuing discussions such as the "Cafeteria", or "Local Pub". Through the computer, informal discussions and student association activities may be included.

The Library: A collective database can be developed within the conferencing system, to facilitate the availability of relevant articles, short lectures etc. to the distance learner.

Registration, administration, teacher conferences etc.: Modern distance learning systems have developed complex administrative systems for student monitoring. These systems can and should be integrated with the conferencing facilities.

Development of teaching material: The system may efficiently be used for cooperative development of printed material - both within the institution and between institutions.

User directory: The system contains information on its users, e.g. where one may find fellow students with common interests. Phone numbers and addresses can be made available. The information actually increases possibilities for direct communication and via other media.

Initial stages of the EKKO Project

The aim of the project was to: Develop a computer-based conferencing system for distance learning and apply the system for experiments in different contexts to gain pedagogical and administrative/organizational experience in order to install conferencing as a standard option for NKI distance students.

The project followed these stages:
1. Introductory search in the field.
2. Development of a specific conferencing system on the NKI mini computer, HP 3000.
3. Pilot experiments with "on-campus students".
4. Study visits to institutions in Europe and North America.
5. Pilot projects in distance learning.
6. Introducing computer conferencing on a larger scale in distance learning.

The First Generation: 1986-1993

The first version of EKKO - the computer conferencing software emulating the 'Electronic College' - was designed and implemented during 1986. During autumn 1986 we carried out the first pilot experiments with on-campus students. In the autumn 1987 the first distance education course was delivered to a small group of 4 students. The next semester, spring 1987 two additional courses were offered. From the spring semester 1990 NKI Distance Education offered a complete college programme (equivalent to one year of full-time studies) based on computer mediated communication. This programme in 'Administrative computing' included a total of 10 different courses. In addition, from the same semester, NKI offered its distance training programme for distance tutors through the same system.

During its most intensive period EKKO served more that 3 000 users, including on-campus students, prospective students, active distance students, former students, tutors and administrative staff. The system included an e-mail system, closed and open conferences for administrative, teaching and social purposes, and bulletin boards. During the first generation period the 'Electronic College' delivered more than 1 000 courses with an average completion rate of above 80 %.

The following were some of the effects and experiences of the first generation of the 'Electronic College' at NKI:

From 1990, NKI was one of few institutions in the world that was delivering a complete study programme based on electronic communication. Prospective distance tutors could qualify for their work through distance education based on computer communication. The system was applied also for administrative communication and discussions. Full-time staff members had been qualified to teach through the conferencing system, and a part-time staff of competent computer conferencing tutors had been built up.

Computer conferencing had been applied in subjects with different didactic solutions; subjects emphasising individual study, subjects with emphasis on group discussion and project work. To be able to exploit the possibilities for discussion, group learning and peer support, most of the initial courses required the students to start at the same time and follow a fixed common progression during the semester towards the exams. This made the computer conferencing courses less 'open and flexible' than the 'correspondence type distance courses'. Many students expressed clearly that they preferred - or actually demanded - the freedom known from unpaced individual study. Thus, courses where the students could start whenever they wished and study at their own pace were introduced. The students who experienced this individual freedom in their studies were generally positive. Consequently, in 1997 NKI took the strategic decision that flexibility and individual freedom for students to organize their learning should be the basis for the future developments. There is no doubt that this decision was a sound one, and quickly resulted in large increases in enrolments. For the future we see a great challenge in developing didactic arrangements combining the flexibility of individual unpaced study with the possibilities for social interaction in the virtual school environment.

We also learned during the first generation experiments that teaching via computer conferencing often becomes 'labour intensive' on the part of the tutor. Originally we had a hypothesis that the supposed increase in learning quality in the 'virtual school' could be compensated by less emphasis on the development of learning material. So far, our experience has not at all supported this assumption. Thus, it seems that investments in pre-produced learning material will be approximately the same as in other large-scale systems if the total quality is to be satisfactory.

The tutors reported that teaching via EKKO had been very stimulating, however, highly demanding concerning the number of hours spent and the 'continuous' attention needed. We also saw a challenge in developing teaching/learning techniques and strategies that stimulate student-student communication without putting unrealistic demands on tutor resources.

Concerning student participation, NKI' experience and experience in other settings, such as the British OU (Mason 1990), proved that conferences may become too small or too large. The users fall into groups of 'active', 'less active' and 'passive users'. There must be a sufficient number, or 'a critical mass' of active users to make the conferences attractive.

It seems necessary to have an active conference moderator in the conference. The tutor (or another person) must take the role as organizer, active contributor, and/or social integrator. After we formally engaged one student as host of the 'on-line cafe', the social activity and student satisfaction and motivation seemed to increase considerably.

The teaching/learning and administrative functions which can be handled by the system, and the quality and quantity of contributions depend on whether participation in the system is voluntary or obligatory. Voluntary participation may result in low activity, which may become a self-fulfilling circle of diminishing interest.

In our first generation of computer conferencing courses we experienced a somewhat higher number of non-starters than in comparable correspondence courses, probably due to initial technical difficulties, and higher completion rates among the starters. Students having completed courses based on computer conferencing had higher examination achievements than both correspondence students and face-to-face students. We do not have data to make certain whether these differences are a result of characteristics of the media/methods or differences in recruitment.

In general, the students reported favourable attitudes to computer conferencing as a form of study. They seemed to be more active in the social conferences than in the academic conferences. This could be a result of the fact that most NKI courses depend a lot on individual work and assignments for submission rather than group discussions. Most students stated that the mail system was the most important subsystem of the first generation of EKKO. This may indicate that the optimal way of organising the studies had not been found. On the other hand, it seems that many part-time distance learners have to find time efficient study strategies to be able to cope with the demands of study beside work and family demands. This means that many would not give priority to social or academic interaction relative to individual study and exercizes in preparation for their exams. This seems to be in line with other findings indicating that part-time distance learners often adopt time saving techniques in their approach to learning to survive the demands of study as well as work, family and societal pressures (Lockwood 1992, Marland et al. 1990).

The Second Generation: From 1994-1996

NKI considered the first generation of the electronic college to be quite a success - both as a computer system, as such, and also concerning how we managed to organize the distance learning system. We continuously followed other developments in teaching/learning methods and software on the market and examined different products, such as CoSy, PortaCom and FirstClass, with the aim of developing an improved 'second generation' system. When we had to introduce new solutions because of replacement of the old host computer, the requirements were that the system should:

- be based on standard software
- provide access to the Internet
- be attractive to all NKI departments and available from any computer network within NKI
- be attractive to possible collaborators
- be as user friendly as possible

From 1 January 1994, the new 'open' Electronic College was introduced. This second-generation system was based on a philosophy of being as open as possible to other networks and services. Accordingly, it was based on Internet, e-mail and the Listserv conferencing system. From the beginning the user interface for modem users was text-based. The second generation stimulated the development of many new courses and study programmes.

All the courses and programmes developed after the introduction of the second-generation system were unpaced and put no limits on times for enrolment. This solution was chosen as a consequence of our conclusions from an interview survey among EKKO students on recruitment and study barriers:

«...it is a major challenge to develop methods and organizations in distance education based on computer conferencing systems which take care of the students' need for autonomy and flexibility.» (Rekkedal 1990, p 92)

The first semester with the new generation was marked by transitions and adjustments to the new system. In some ways, the old system was felt more to emulate an 'image' of a virtual school. The open system introduced new problems due to lack of standard interpretations among e-mail systems. However, students and staff seemed to adjust and became familiar with the new system. The general access to Internet resources outside NKI seemed to be an advantage that was appreciated by students. Access to the Internet was offered to all tertiary level students at NKI and consequently the application of Internet resources could be integrated in some of the study programmes.

The Third Generation 1996: From small-scale experiments to large-scale operation

The third generation was introduced with the first web-based courses in 1996. The web-service could be regarded as a two-level system. The top-level, the NKI Electronic College homepage provides general information about the college such as course descriptions, prices, contract form, contact information, support information, and an article library on online and distance education. The graphical and user-friendly web-interface introduced opportunities such as hyper linking and multimedia presentations. However, there were also new challenges such as access control and copyright issues.

The second level, the course homepages, is pass-worded and can only be accessed by NKI employees and fee-paying students. The course homepages are designed with a set of templates to secure some course conformity. A typical course homepage provides links to each of the study guide units, to the tutor's e-mail address, to the class discussion forum, to external Internet services and resources, to a course evaluation form, and possibly to multiple-choice assignments. The study units are also often designed so that the students can benefit from printing out the material.

There is no doubt that the decision taken in 1996 to base the Electronic College on standard Internet servers and client software used by the ordinary Internet user was a sound one. Today the Electronic College offers 20 complete study programmes at secondary and tertiary levels and 150 different courses. Course enrolments have increased rapidly. Course enrolments doubled every year between 1995 to 1998, and were well above 3 000 in 1999 (however, only 15 percent of the NKI distance students).

Most of the students live in Norway, but there are students logging into the college from 15 different countries. The Electronic College puts great emphasis on facilitating learning according to the students' needs, which could be described in the following way: A student may enrol at any time to any of the programmes and courses or personal choice of courses and follow his or her own progression schedule. The College is open 24 hours a day 365 days a year. The students may choose to study individually or take part in academic discussions or leisure and social communication with fellow students, teachers and alumni. Concerning the conferences, we have chosen a combination of 'push' (contributions sent as e-mail to all members of a conference) and 'pull' (contributions archived and accessible to all members) technology.

The organizational and didactical choices that emphasize flexibility and individual freedom have been firmly based on continuous research and evaluation studies. This choice of pedagogical approach leads to some great challenges in organising cooperative and collaborative learning activities. However, evaluations have given clear indications that the students will not give up their individual freedom for more group-related activities (Rekkedal & Paulsen 1997). It seems that the most important advantages of Internet study emphasized by the students, are the same that characterize distance study in general. In addition, many students point to the practical easiness of e-mail communication, rapid turn-around of assignments and questions and support from fellow students in the academic conferences.

Recently, we have also made some attitude measurements to see whether the students are satisfied with their learning experience in World Wide Web-based courses. In short, we may conclude that (Rekkedal 1999):
- 86 per cent of the students agreed that "it is possible to achieve excellence in courses that are taught on the WWW" (only 2 per cent disagreed)
- 94 per cent agreed that "My enrolment was facilitated because the course was on the WWW" (3 percent disagree)
- 90 per cent agreed that "I would enrol again in a WWW based course" (no one disagreed)
- 88 per cent agreed that "I would encourage a colleague or friend to enrol in a WWW-based course" (1 per cent disagreed)

Some conclusions

In a recent book, *Globalising Education*, the British Open University researcher, Robin Mason, states:

> "There is little doubt that the Web is the most phenomenally successful educational tool to have appeared in a long time. It combines all the media...: text, text-based interaction, audio and video as clips, and with somewhat less robustness, multi-way interactive audio and video." (Mason 1998)

We agree – and there is no doubt that distance teaching institutions have to adapt to the new technological reality. If they do not, we are afraid that the question mark in Tony Bates' 1994 article could be removed. We believe that both traditional educational institutions and dedicated distance teaching institutions face great challenges to change and adapt to the demands from a market of adult students who need continuous and recurrent development of their competencies and who require the individual freedom to learn how, when and where they prefer. We believe that the Internet is changing the whole concept of what distance teaching and learning is, and that distance learning will be seen as more attractive to a growing number of people. We believe that distance teaching institutions that do not change dramatically during the next few years to apply the Internet and Web for distribution and communication will not survive.

However, we also believe that the distance teaching institutions are in the best position to develop and organize the teaching and learning system for the distance student of the third millennium. We believe that Desmond Keegan is right when he argues:

> "... that web based education is best regarded as a subset of distance education and that the skills, literature and practical management decisions that have been developed in the form of educational provision known as 'distance education' will be applicable mutatis mutandis to web based education. It also follows that the literature of the field of educational research known as distance education, is of value for those embarking on training on the web." (Keegan 2000)

In this connection we would also like to refer to Professor Otto Peters, who in his address to the 19th World Conference in Vienna in June 1999 on "The University of the Future – Pedagogical Perspectives" concluded with the belief that *"the university of the future would look more like a distance teaching university than like an ordinary university"*.

An important question remains: How can this technology be applied to represent a more attractive and efficient learning environment for distance students, and how can we design the courses and tutoring and administrative systems to make distance education based on computer mediated communication really cost-effective?

Sometimes it seems that educators believe that presenting the students to the Internet as a resource of information and means of communication solves the problem of offering effective and efficient education at a distance. Our conclusion is that this is not at all the case. The challenge for distance teaching institutions is to find ways of planning, organising and facilitating learning for students with different preferences concerning learning strategies and needs for competence development independent of time and place restrictions. This means that the medium itself does not solve any problems (Clark 1994). We must learn how to design instructional programmes including student learning activities based on this new medium to achieve optimal outcomes for different kinds of learners in various subjects and having differing aims and objectives.

If we manage, the change that is taking place in distance education from correspondence teaching to teaching and learning on the Internet will also change the position of distance teaching and learning from being at the periphery to becoming the centre of activities in the world of education.

References

Bates, T. (1994). Hello, technology! Goodbye, distance teaching institutions? *Open Praxis, V. 2, 1994, pp. 5-7.*

Bates, T. (1990). The Challenge of Technology for European Distance Education. In: Bates, A. W. (ed.): *Media and Technology in European Distance Education*, pp. 17-26. Heerlen: EADTU.

Clark, R. E. (1994). Media Will Never Influence Learning. *Educational Technology, Research and Development, v. 42, No 2, pp. 21-29.*

Daniel, J. S. (1995). *The Mega-Universities and the Knowledge Media. Implications of new technologies for large distance teaching universities.* Master thesis. Quebec: Concordia University, Department of Education.

Gamlin, M. (1995). Distance Learning in Transition; The Impact of Technology: A New Zealand Perspective. Keynote address to *The EDEN Conference 'The Open Classroom' Distance Learning and New Technologies in School Level Education and Training, Oslo.*

Hilz, S. R. (1986). *The virtual classroom. Building the foundations.* New Jersey: New Jersey Institute of Technology.

Holden, G. (1992). *Videokonferanser som del av undervisningsopplegg i fjernundervisning.* Bekkestua: NKI/SEFU.

Holden, G. (1993). *Multipunkt videokonferanse. Evaluering av fjernundervisning via video.* Bekkestua: NKI/SEFU.

Karow, W. 1977. *Informationen. Privater Fernunterricht in 16 Landern. Ubersicht und Vergleich.* Berlin: BBF.

Keegan, D. (2000) Seamless interfaces: distance education and web-based training. *Istruzione a Distanza, 2000, 1.* Rome: University Roma Tre.

Lockwood, F. (1992). *Activities in Self-Instructional Texts.* London: Kogan Page.

Marland, P., Patching, W., Putt, I. & Putt, R. (1990): Distance learners' interaction with text while studying. *Dist. Ed., 11, 1, pp. 71-91.*

Mason, R. (1990). Refining the use of computer conferencing in distance education. In: Croft, M., Mugridge, I., Daniel, J. S. & Hershfield, A. (eds.). *Distance Education: Development and Access.* Caracas: ICDE.

Mason. R. (1998). *Globalising Education – Trends and Applications.* London: Routledge.

McCreary, E.K. & Van Duren, J. (1987). Educational Applications of Computer Conferencing. *Canadian Journal of Educational Communication,16, 2, pp. 107-115.*

Nipper, S. (1989). Third generation distance learning and computer conferencing. In: Mason, R. & Kaye, A. (eds.) (1989). *Mindweave. Communications, Computers and Distance Education.* London: Pergamon.

Paulsen, M. F. (1989). *En virtuell skole. Del I. Fundamentet i EKKO-prosjektet.* Bekkestua: NKI/SEFU.

Paulsen, M. F. (1990). EKKO: Experiences. In: Bates, A. W. (ed.). *Media and Technology in European Distance Education.* Pp. 235-239. Heerlen: EADTU.

Paulsen, M. F. (1992). The NKI Electronic College: Five years of computer conferencing in distance education. In: Paulsen, M. F. *From Bulletin Boards to Electronic Universities: Distance Education, Computer-Mediated Communication, and Online Education.* Pp. 2-17. University Park, Pennsylvania: The American Center for the Study of Distance Education.

Paulsen, M. F. (1998). *Teaching Techniques for Computer-Mediated Communication.* Doctoral Thesis. University Park, Pennsylvania: Pennsylvania State University.

Paulsen, M. F. & Rekkedal, T. (1988). Computer conferencing - A breakthrough in distance learning, or just another technological gadget? In: Sewart, D. & Daniel, J. S. (eds.). *Developing Distance Education.* Papers submitted to the 14th ICDE World Conference in Oslo. Pp. 362-365. Oslo: ICDE.

Paulsen, M. F. & Rekkedal, T. (1990). *The Electronic College. Selected Articles from the EKKO Project.* Bekkestua: NKI/SEFU.

Paulsen, M. F. & Rekkedal, T. (1996). *Technology for Adult Learning in Norway - Including a Case Study on the NKI Electronic College.* Report for the OECD Study B6 on 'New Delivery Systems and Changing Demand on Education'.

Rekkedal, T. (1983). The written assignments in correspondence education. Effects of reducing turnaround time. *Dist. Ed., 4, 2, 231-252.*

Rekkedal, T. (1985). *Introducing the Personal Tutor/Counsellor in the System of Distance Education.* Stabekk: NKI.

Rekkedal, T. (1989). *The Telephone as a Medium for Instruction and Guidance in Distance Education.* Bekkestua: NKI/SEFU.

Rekkedal, T. (1990). Recruitment and Study Barriers in the Electronic College. In: Paulsen, M. F. & Rekkedal, T. (1990). *The Electronic College. Selected Articles from the EKKO Project.* Pp. 79-105. Bekkestua: NKI/SEFU.

Rekkedal, T. (1992). *Telefax som medium for toveis kommunikasjon i individuell fjernundervisning.* Bekkestua: NKI/SEFU.

Rekkedal, T. (1993). Practice Related Research in Large Scale Distance Education, Experiences and Challenges. In: *Research in Distance Education – Present situation and forecasts.* Umeå: University of Umeå, Sweden.

Rekkedal, T. (1999). *Courses on the WWW – Student Experiences and Attitudes Towards WWW Courses – II.* Evaluation Report Written for the Leonardo On-line Training Project, MMWWWK.

Rekkedal, T. & Paulsen, M. F. (1997). *The Third Generation NKI Electronic College. A Survey of Student Experiences and Attitudes.* An evaluation report written for the Leonardo On-line Training Project, MMWWWK.

Rekkedal, T & Møystad, E. (1999). *Recruitment Barriers to Learning on the Internet. Survey among active correspondence students and prospektive students at NKI.* Bekkestua: NKI.

Rekkedal, T. & Vigander, K. (1990). *Forsøk med bruk av telewriter i matematikkundervisning.* Bekkestua: NKI/SEFU.

Toska, J. A. (1999). Norwegian University Collaboration in Open and Distance Learning. Presentation on *CREAD Conference in Vancouver, September 21-23*.

Østlyngen, E. (1947). Korrespondanseundervisning i Norge. *Norsk Pedagogisk Årbok 1946-47, 173-183*.

WORKING LIFE AND NON-FORMAL EDUCATION

Bjarne Wahlgren

Abstract

Using an analysis of Nordic adult education, *The Golden Riches in the Grass* advances the thesis of a Nordic think tank, where non-formal education - folkeoplysning - contributes to or would be able to contribute to the promotion of the qualifications in the labour force. The Nordic Council of Ministers consequently took the initiative to establish a Nordic research project. This was implemented as collaboration between four research institutions in Norway, Sweden, Finland and Denmark in 1996; and focus has been placed upon the relations between working life and non-formal education.

An analysis of 16 cooperative projects was made between non-formal educational institutions and companies – four in each country. These were selected according to "best practice" principles. The conclusion of the project was that in general it is difficult to find evidence that the collaboration between non-formal education and working life has been mutually supportive. No conditions can be pointed out that strengthen personal development in a democratic perspective, either concerning the content or form of the education or the learning environment. However, there are a few exceptions where the content of the education differs from other types of job retraining programmes, and where personal existential conditions, both at the workplace and outside, are emphasized. A distinctive feature of these examples is that there is common understanding between the company and the non-formal educational institutions which is important in developing comprehensive personal qualifications.

The experience of these few examples might form the basis of further studies. Not least because the workplace need for personal qualifications – which also include attitudinal, cultural, and ethical aspects – is likely to rise in the years to come.

Introduction

In 1995, the think tank for Nordic cooperation, appointed by the Nordic Council of Ministers, published the report *The Golden Riches in the Grass – Lifelong Learning for All*. One of the repeated themes of the report was the relations between the labour market, trade and industry and learning during working life on the one hand, and the personal, the general, and lifelong learning on the other. In the report this was described as being a dialectical relationship.

Consequently, the think tank called the attention to the need for research in order to procure systematic and practicable knowledge concerning learning during working life, the development of learning environments, and life competence.

The Nordic Council of Ministers accepted the request, and FOVU (the Steering Group for Nordic cooperation on non-formal education - folkeoplysning - and adult education) took the initiative to start a Nordic research project lasting three years in 1996, called *Working Life and Non-Formal Education*.[1]

The research project has been undertaken as a comparative study of conditions in Norway, Sweden, Finland, and Denmark. The most essential data are 16 case studies, four in each country, that have been described and analysed according to a common questionnaire. The 16 cases are chosen to describe "best practice" in the field.

There is little common Nordic research within the field of (adult) education. Most of the material is research, viz. accumulated national experience under a common theme[2], explanations[3], and comparative analyses[4]. So, the research project attempts to prepare the way for new knowledge by implementing a systematic comparison between four countries in the Nordic community.

---

[1] The research project is described in full in Wahlgren, Eidskrem, Sjösten (1999). The Danish part of the project is described in Wahlgren (1999).

[2] See e.g. *På ny – erfaringer fra et nordisk netværksprojekt om voksenundervisning* (1988) which consists of accumulated experience from various projects, focusing upon "vulnerable groups".

[3] See e.g. Johan Engelhardt (1982) and Kim Mørch Jacobsen (1982). It is characteristic of both publications that they describe what (at that time) went on and was topical within Nordic adult education.

[4] See e.g. *Nye veje i voksenundervisning og folkeoplysning. En kortlægning af forskning, forsøg og udviklingsarbejde i Norden 1978-83* 1983). The publication - which is a follow-up upon an earlier analysis – has a descriptive character. This also applies to the publications *Folkeoplysning og voksenundervisning – hvad koster det i de nordiske lande?* (1983) and *Folkbildning och vuxenundervisning i Norden. Struktur – omfång – ekonomi* (1997). They are both surveys of activities, legislation, and economy within the field.

The Project

In *The Golden Riches of the Grass* it is often pointed out that the labour market and trade and industry need labour with comprehensive qualifications. It is a fact that, besides professional qualifications, general and personal qualifications are demanded to be able to manage a job today. It also appears that the demand will be increasing in coming years, especially within the two last mentioned categories of qualifications.[5]

The difference arises when it has to be decided how the various demands for qualifications are weighed in relation to each other, how the contents are to be of the generally qualifying education, and which educational institutions are to contribute to qualifying the workers.

Traditionally in a Nordic context, non-formal education has played an important role in adult education – not least in connection with a broad general and democratically founded qualifying of the workers. Against this background it makes sense to clarify what non-formal adult education contributes in connection with the broad qualifying of the labour force.

Accordingly, the following complex of problems forms part of the project:

> *To what extent can non-formal education contribute in a fruitful way to qualifying the labour force? What is the content and what kind of education is part of this collaboration?*

The Concept of Non-Formal Education

In the project, non-formal education is limited institutionally to the adult educational associations (and in a Finnish context also adult education centres) and the folk high schools (and in a Danish context also the day folk high schools).

A delimitation has also been undertaken concerning the content. The starting point is the common features which historically have been characteristic of Nordic non-formal education.[6]

---

[5] In a Danish context these views are presented in *National Kompetenceudvikling: Erhvervsudvikling gennem kvalifikationsudvikling* (1997) and in *Uddannelse og erhvervsliv. Handlingsprogram for national kompetenceudvikling* (1998).

[6] See Wahlgren 1999), Ch. 2, pp. 5-11. See also Jacobsen (1989).

Traditionally non-formal education has been connected with a sense of community and democracy. Non-formal education has contributed to strengthening the people's sense of community. As non-formal education is intended to contribute to this sense in principle it must be aimed at everyone – at the people. It must be able to make people participate in such a community. Non-formal education must contribute to the individual acting democratically. Non-formal education must contribute to a strengthening of the will to democracy and the ability of acting democratically.[7]

The formation aspect in non-formal education is two-sided. Partly the relations to the existential situation of the individual, partly the relations to the community and the ability of functioning in such a community.

This doubleness in the Nordic concept of non-formal education must be maintained as an important feature – not least in relation to international concepts of adult education where emphasis is upon the individual and self-management.[8] Kjell Rubenson writes about this, "While the Andragogical position disappears and focus is upon the individual, the methodology of non-formal education also takes the collective into account. In study circles this is expressed in terms of common search, common work towards common objectives".[9]

This is to say, in the research project we delimit the concept of non-formal education both institutionally and concerning the content in which non-formal education is defined as an activity which considerably emphasizes personal formation and development, viz. the existential development of the individual in relation to a democratic community.

Data Collection

Three part studies form part of the research project. The first is an analysis of the policy-documents that are available in the four countries. The second is four national surveys of the collaboration between working life and non-formal education. The third is 16 analyses of courses where cooperation between working life and non-formal education is emphasized.

---

[7] Concerning the relation between personal development and democratic action, see Lindgren (1996), p. 183f.
[8] E.g. in the Andragogical tradition represented by Malcolm Knowles (1973).
[9] Rubenson (1995), p. 109

The Analysis of Policy-Documents

An analysis of documents forms part of the project. These documents formulate the official (state) adult educational policy. The documents in question are analysed with a view to stating the relation between working life/non-formal education. Delimitation has been undertaken concerning time (ten years), and the analysis is limited to ministerial concepts.

The Analyses

We have analysed the cooperative relations working life/non-formal education in the four Nordic countries in order to choose the sixteen cases in a qualified way, and in order to evaluate how the results of the case analyses can be generalized. Because of different registries the analyses have been done differently in the four countries.

In Finland the analysis has been implemented through interviews with key personalities. In Sweden the analysis consisted of applying to several of the national non-formal educational organizations. This applies to Norway, too. Applications have been sent to the University Extension Courses, to the Workers' Educational Association, and the study circles in the towns.

In Denmark the analysis was undertaken twice. The first time consisted of applications to the national non-formal educational organizations. Information from these organizations was followed-up through interviews by telephone with the local departments. The second time a registry was used where courses could be identified where non-formal educational institutions had implemented education of workers. These courses were contacted in writing and followed-up by telephone interviews.

Description of Cases

The main content of the collected data are four selected cases in each of the four countries.

The criteria of the selection have varied from country to country. In Finland, Sweden, and Norway the best have been selected among a small number of possibilities. Cases have been selected that meet the formal criterion, viz. that there is cooperation between a firm and a non-formal educational organization concerning courses over a certain period (at least one week). In the three countries cooperation between working life and non-formal education is not very common, consequently the choice of cases is limited. In the cases where it has been possible to choose between various cooperative courses, the courses with most "substance" have been chosen, in short, where cooperation between non-formal education and working life has been most extensive.

In Denmark the choice of the four cases took place in the analysis where 50 relevant courses were found. The four cases have been chosen according to "best practice" and according to the wish that various types of education were represented (evening classes and day folk high schools) and that there was to be a political diversity.

As mentioned above, the research project is a collective product in a difficult and not very widespread discipline: the cross-national cooperation within the field of educational research.

In principle there are two ways of doing research cross-nationally. One is to establish a division of labour so that each country solves part of the whole assignment, and subsequently the results are collected. The second method is to illustrate the complexity of problems of the project according to national differences. That is, to illustrate the differences and similarities in the demands for qualifications in the various countries, the differences and similarities in the organizational conditions, and the differences and similarities in the applied pedagogy. This method was chosen for this project. It is a precondition for this method that systematic comparisons can be made about central variables between the participating countries.

To satisfy this demand a common question framework for the collection of data was prepared for the research project. In all, 63 questions were prepared to collect information in each case from each of the four countries. The question framework deals with the following themes:

- The position of the firm during the course
- The non-formal educational organisation
- What do the firms demand?
- What do the workers demand?
- The role of the non-formal educational institution
- The content and form of the education
- The learning environment
- The teachers' qualifications

Within each theme between five or ten subquestions were asked – in all 63, as mentioned above. The questions were open and general, illustrated by the following questions concerning the role of the non-formal educational institution: *Has the educational institution particularly considered the consequences of the education in question being non-formal? How does the educational institution participate in the planning of the education? What is the impact on the non-formal educational institution regarding self-perception and future development, that such cooperation has been initiated? Is it a question of de-ideologizing or a strengthening of the educational and formative perspective?*

The questions were answered by interviews with representatives from the firms, representatives from the non-formal educational institution, and the participants in the courses. These interviews were supplemented by observing the participants during the courses and in the environment on the whole. Further, the written material was included that described the activity.

The extent of the data collection varies considerably from case to case, due to practical and resource conditions. From the very intensive case study, based upon extensive presence and interviews (often where the research institution worked with the case beforehand) to few interviews, some of them by telephone. The typical case description is based upon the participants observing the education, interviews with key figures (from the firm, from the educational institution, and among the participants), supplemented by available material in writing.

In each case the answers were written systematically, according to the question framework. The size of each case description varies from 6 to 20 pages.

Results

The main thesis of the project is that in principle there is a symbiosis between working life and non-formal education. While the training at the workplace mainly aims at qualifying the labour in relation to production and the market, non-formal education mainly aims at qualifying the individual in relation to society and in relation to living a meaningful life. However, the question is to what extent the data material supports the thesis that non-formal education in its content, form, or learning environment contributes with anything considerably new in connection with qualifying the workers in relation to working life.

The Content of the Education

Concerning the content, to what extent can we talk of improving the education, related to the workplace, just because the education was implemented by a non-formal educational institution? To what extent is it emphasized in the sixteen cases that the individual develops existentially in relation to a democratic feeling of community?

There are differences when we compare the content of the four cases. These differences can be systematized in two variables. One describes the degree of professionalism, from topic-centred professionalism to knowledge-centred professionalism. The second variable describes the degree of connection with the working procedure, from the job-specific to the general and everyday. Graphically, the national variations can be described as follows:

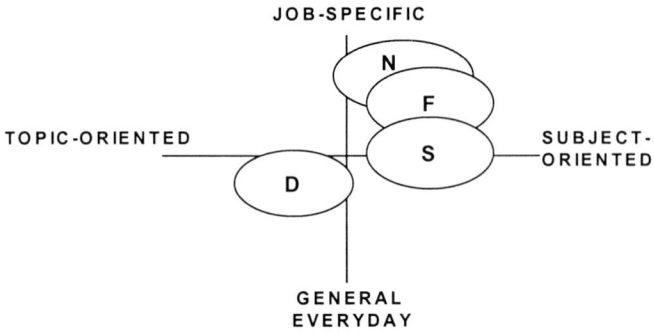

The Norwegian and the Finnish cases are very much alike, in general they are closely connected with qualifying the labour force. The content is traditional subjects, such as mathematics and science, and functional subjects, such as economics and management, however, all subjects are closely connected with the conditions of production. In the Swedish cases the education is less directly connected with job-specific demands and contains traditional subjects to a higher degree, especially foreign languages. In the Danish cases the education is correspondingly less directly connected with job-specific demands, however, contrary to the Swedish education, are centred on general everyday subjects.

It is necessary to be careful about attributing too much importance to the national differences. However, it seems to be a reasonable conclusion that there are differences, and that these differences can be related to the following conditions:

In the case of Norway, non-formal educational activities are connected with some kind of (formalized) professional training.

In the case of Finland, non-formal educational activities are connected with qualifying the workers in "small and medium-sized firms".

In Sweden, non-formal educational activities are connected partly with the job rotation projects, partly with the recent ideas of a "knowledge lift"[10], in short, a more formal qualification.

In Denmark, the relation between working life and non-formal education is deeply rooted in the Act on Adult education grants[11] emphasizing both the general personal qualifications and the more vocationally oriented.

Leaving the national differences aside and watching the general tendencies across the countries we can place the cases in the following three categories: the knowledge-oriented education, the job-related education, and the personal qualification education.

In the knowledge-oriented education the content is chosen and argued for according to traditional "school subjects", e.g. foreign languages, mother-tongue teaching, mathematics, science, and computer studies. The teaching is only indirectly related to the working situation, for instance in the shape of "staff benefits" or a general qualification – a knowledge lift – which the workplace is going to benefit from indirectly and in the long term.

This kind of education can be implemented with a greater or smaller connection with conditions that develop societal, cultural and personal aspects. However, the pivotal point is the "school subject" and the acquisition of it. In these courses the connection with non-formal education does not really supply anything to the content of the education beyond what can be found in all good education. Four of the 16 cases can be placed in this category.

In the job-related education the content is chosen and argued for according to the immediate needs of the workers in relation to carrying out their daily work.

---

[10] See Rubenson, Tuinmann, Wahlgren (1999). The knowledge lift is identical with the Adult Education Initiative described in the article of Thång and Wärwik.
[11] See Eklund and Wandal (1992).

The education is related to the working situation. The cases with emphasis upon job-related topics, such as instructions, management theory, organizational theory are placed here. Likewise the subject-oriented education which is related to the work, e.g. "psychology and psychiatry" within the social sector.

This education is also implemented with greater or smaller connection with conditions that develop societal, cultural and personal aspects. However, the pivotal point of the education is the qualification in relation to the job. Also in these courses it is difficult to find how the connection with non-formal education really supplies anything to the content of the education beyond what can be found in all good adult vocational training. Eight of the 16 cases are placed in this category.

In the personal qualification education the content is chosen and argued in accordance with the wish to strengthen the workers' personal development according to an idealistic and democratic perspective. The education is related to the workers' everyday life, both at the workplace and outside. Here the cases are placed that emphasize topics that are connected with the individual worker and his/her position in a social interplay at the workplace.

In this education the pivotal point is the individual worker and the development of the individual. The subject-oriented and job-specific aspect of the education is subordinate to this pivotal point. Only in these – relatively few courses – do we find examples that the connection with non-formal education really supplies innovative perspectives about the content of the education.

It is characteristic of the courses that the aim of the education is broad and closely connected with the development of the individual worker. For instance, in one of the courses it is stated that the aim is:

> *"To enhance the motivation, to make the individual want to understand and possibly change old habits and patterns of actions, to enhance the understanding of who you are and know yourself in the role as collaborator, and make the individual see him/herself and his/her working conditions in a new perspective."*

Further, it is characteristic of the courses that the firms want to and are able to formulate demands for comprehensive personal qualifications. Correspondingly the educational institutions are well aware of the enlightening background they represent, and they wish to maintain this background very consciously. The course is developed in collaboration between the firm and the non-formal educational institution according to a mutual understanding of the importance of personal development.

It is in the category *the personal qualification education* we find a symbiotic relation between working life and non-formal education. Three or four of the 16 cases belong to this category.

To summarize it can be stated about the contents of the education that there are few examples in the 16 cases that cooperation between the workplaces and the non-formal educational institutions has resulted in any barrier-breaking and new contents when qualifying the workers. Most of the courses can be characterized as knowledge oriented education where the contents of the education are chosen and argued according to traditional and beforehand existing "subjects", or as job-related education where the contents of the education are chosen and argued according to the workers immediate needs in relation to the carrying out of their work.

Only in few cases are there examples that the content of the education is innovative in relation to traditional adult vocational training. In these courses emphasis is upon a personal qualification education, and the content of the education is chosen according to the wish to enhance the personal development of the worker.

Three conditions are characteristic of these courses:

1. One is that there is a common understanding between the firm and the educational institution as regards the importance of developing comprehensive personal qualifications that are neither job-specifically job-rooted nor rooted in the subjects.

2. This agreement is expressed in a broad, personally oriented objects clause for the courses.

3. The courses are all run in large and medium-sized production firms.

The Form of Education

Does the very form of non-formal education contribute to qualifying for the qualifications of working life?

In the pilot report of the project it was discussed whether there is a particularly "enlightening" form of non-formal education. Is it a fact that being together in non-formal education differs from other kinds of being together where education takes place? In the pilot report it was pointed out that there are certain Nordic differences in the concept of these conditions. Especially the Swedish, and partly the Norwegian tradition, is more inclined to maintain that non-formal education has a special educational form, an "enlightening" pedagogy, than is the case in Finland and Denmark.[12]

Against the background of an analysis of Swedish conditions Kjell Rubenson concludes that *the distinctive mark of non-formal education to a high degree lies in the pedagogy and the methodology.*[13] Activity and conversation are considered to be key concepts of the work which is supposed to be built upon the experience of the participants and result in a wider insight, reaching beyond the particular topics. At the same time Rubenson points out that the methodology of non-formal education also includes the "collective". *Through common work towards common objectives* it becomes a practical training in democracy, he says (cf. above).

In a Norwegian connection Sturla Bjerkaker likewise points out that non-formal education can be *characterized by the equal dialogue, the free and voluntary process of learning, the development of knowledge based upon experience, and the meaningful participation.*[14]

In connection with the discussion of the concept of non-formal education it is pointed out above that a democratic aspect must be included. This aspect must be noticeable in the participants' involvement in the decision-making processes, in the fact that their experiences and qualifications become part of the education, and that the educational conversation is democratic, and that the participants are equal part in these activities.

The project studied the extent to which these conditions form part of the studied cases.

It is common to the four countries that the form of non-formal education, "the study circle pedagogy" is of central importance to the teachers, and especially in the planners' and the principals' minds. However, the form of non-formal

---

[12] Wahhlgren (1995), p. 14f.
[13] Rubenson (1995), p. 106f.
[14] Bjerkaker (1998).

education as a "pure" study circle pedagogy cannot be found in the cases. There are various modifications, and there are various reasons for these modifications in the Nordic countries.[15]

In the Norwegian cases there are examples that the external (and formal) demands for the extent and content of the education restrict the possibility of influence by the participants.

In the Swedish cases there are examples that the specific demands of the subject and the demands from the firms restrict the influence of the participants. This is in spite of the fact that the principals especially emphasize the use of the study circle pedagogy.

In the Finnish cases it seems as if both tradition and the demand for a measurable output restrict the influence from the participants and the involvement of their experiences.

In the Danish cases there are examples that the standardization of the courses restricts the influence of the participants. It also seems as if involving the experience and activating the participants are considered to be more important than the participants' influence - especially their influence upon the introductory presentation of the education.

In short, the national differences can first and foremost be found within the framework of the education - and to a lesser degree in the pedagogical tradition.

As mentioned earlier, the various characteristics of the form of non-formal education are emphasized when we only look at the purpose and intentions of the education. However, a "pure" non-formal education, the study circle pedagogy, is not used in practice. This does not imply that the education does not work, or that it is inferior - or experienced as being inferior. On the contrary, it is a fact that because the form of non-formal education is modified, it works. The form is adapted to the reality of the education, viz. the participants, the firms, the non-formal educational institutions, and to a certain degree also the teachers actual concept of good education. That is why it works. However, for the same reason there is nothing innovative in the form of education given in the studied courses.

---

[15] It has been described in various connections that "the study circle" is modified. For instance, Jan Byström describes that development into "class" is the most common, which our study also shows. Byström (1983), p. 53f.

What is left is the discussion to what extent the "enlightening" aspect - both in its "pure" and in its modified forms - contributes with anything important in relation to educating workers. Is it able to contribute something considerably (new) in connection with qualifying the workers for working life?

On the one hand it is important to maintain that the participants' activity is a precondition of learning, and that the participants actively taking part in the various decision-making processes is a precondition of more comprehensive and profound learning. Besides, it is important to state that the education is expected to implicitly mean democratic learning when it takes place in a democratic form. According to these basic views it must be considered of great importance that the "enlightening" form is part of, or forms the basis of part of the education of the workers.

On the other hand, there is not much radicalism left today in the "enlightening" form such as it has been put into practice here. By now it is accepted in general, both in the theory of adult pedagogy and in the practical adult education that the participants influence the education, that the participants' qualifications are involved, and that the participants actively take part in the educational conversation.

These principles are found again in many different adult pedagogical "movements". For instance in the andragogical principles, in problem oriented teaching, run by the participants, and in the experience teaching. Likewise, they have gained a foothold far into the institutionalized Nordic adult education, and this applies to both general adult education and the education which are more directly aimed at the labour market (the labour market training).

Accordingly, the conclusion is that the "enlightening" form does not radically contribute to renewing the education of the workers and their qualifying for the labour market, instead its place in adult education strengthens the development of an adult pedagogy where emphasis to a rising degree is upon influence from the participants, the involvement of experience and dialogue.

The Learning Environment

An important factor in adult learning is the environment or context in which the learning takes place. There is common agreement concerning this point.[16] In the

---

[16] See e.g. Wahlgren (1999a), *Guldtavlerne i græsset* (1995) page 70f, Jarvis (1987 and 1997), Darkenwald, (1989).

research project, the learning environment is defined as the social context in which the learning takes place. The learning environment includes the kind of interplay between the participants in the learning situation and the climate in which the learning takes place.

In the project there is a distinction between two aspects of the learning environment. One aspect is attached to the education, the other to the working situation. The following has been studied:

1. What conditions are emphasized about the learning environment in the education?
2. What considerations have been made concerning the learning environment at the workplace?

There is a surprisingly considerable accordance in the Nordic cases that the learning environment in education is of great importance to the learning. Similarly there is broad agreement concerning the conditions that form part of and are important in this connection, viz. the interplay among the participants, confidence, openness in the dialogue, and positive relations among the participants.

These conditions are given different priorities in the different data sources, and they are described in various concepts. Concepts are used such as: confidence, trust, openness, a good atmosphere, a warm atmosphere, a relaxed atmosphere, informal atmosphere, positive relations, and the participants feeling like good friends.

The conditions which are emphasized in the cases are important pedagogical issues, consequently it is important that they are emphasized. On the other hand, these are conditions which are commonly accepted in both adult pedagogy and in the practical adult education. Thus it is not innovative to maintain that the interpersonal relations in the education must be positive. Nor is it innovative that it can be demonstrated that the relations are positive. Satisfaction with the education and with the social relations is a logical result of good education - and occurs just as often as the opposite.[17]

---

[17] In a Danish study of cross-sectorial adult educational courses about half of the participants state that they "quite agree" that there is a "good atmosphere between the teacher and us", and that there is "a good atmosphere in the group". By and large this depends upon the form of the cross-sectorial work. Aarkrog a.o. (1995), p. 75-77.

It is remarkable that all education, on the whole, takes place at the educational institutions. That is, in the classrooms of the adult educational associations or the folk high schools. Only a small part of the activities takes place at the workplaces. Only part of this learning is directly connected with the work, viz. the Swedish job rotation projects and the Danish follow-up activities in one of the cases.

It was to be expected that in the projects there were reflections on and concrete work with the learning environment at the workplace and learning at the workplace. For instance, considerations concerning the workers' influence upon the work process and the connected learning. However, this cannot be found in the projects. There are no considerations how the learning environment of (non-formal) education might play together with the place of work as a learning environment.

Summary and Discussion

It is evident that the ideas of the Nordic think tank concerning the wish to promote and strengthen the relations between working life and non-formal education have not been implemented to any great extent since the think tank wrote the report *The Golden Riches in the Grass*. However, this does not imply that the considerations were erroneous. There are still very good reasons to establish and enhance such cooperation.

One of the reasons is that companies need to develop personal qualifications in connection with establishing new fields of production which imply active involvement of the workers. The research on qualifications points out this need, and it is emphasized that it is becoming greater. In this connection it is evidently a reasonable hypothesis that in the future the need for personal qualifications also comprises attitudinal conditions, and beyond this, cultural and ethical perspectives.

Another reason is the wish from the non-formal educational institutions to enter into a closer interplay with working life. Evidently there is a fruitful challenge to the Nordic non-formal education to re-establish the relations with working life. Thus this cooperation - with its historical roots - would be given new life in a new societal situation.

If the cooperation between working life and non-formal education is going to be strengthened in practice it must be given higher priority by the non-formal educational institutions. At the same time it must be re-evaluated what non-formal education is able to contribute.

The ideological profile of the non-formal educational institutions in relation to working life must be enhanced. The non-formal educational institutions must realize what is the strength of non-formal education in comparison with other suppliers of adult education. They must realize this to themselves and to working life.

References

Aarkrog, V., Ramsøe, A., Storgaard, A., Wahlgren, B. (1995). *VUP – Erfaringer og perspektiver.* København: Arbejdsmarkedsstyrelsen & Undervisningsministeriet.

Bjerkaker, S. (1998). Med folkopplysning som basis. In *Studienytt* No. 1-98.

Byström, J. (1983). *Studiecirkelns pedagogik.* Stockholm: Brevskolan.

Darkenwald, G. G. (1989). *Enhancing the Adult Classroom Environment.* In Hayes (ed.). *Effective Teaching Styles.* San Francisco: New Directions for Continuing Education, No. 43.

Eklund, S., Wandall, J. (1992). *VUS. Resultater og perspektiver.* København: Danmarks Lærerhøjskole & Udviklingscenteret for folkeoplysning og voksenundervisning.

Engelhardt, J. (ed.) (1982). *Voksenundervisning i Norden.* København: Nord.

Folkeoplysning og voksenundervisning – hvad koster det i de nordiske lande? (1993). København: Nord 1993:32.

Folkbildning och vuxenundervisning i Norden. Struktur – omfång – ekonomi. (1997). København: TemaNord 1997:584.

Guldtavlerne i græsset. Livslang læring for alle (1995). København: Nord, 1995:2.

Jacobsen, B. (1989). The Concept and Problem of Public Enlightenment. In *International Journal of Lifelong Education, Vol. 8*, No. 2, p. 127-137.

Jacobsen, K. M. (1982). *Voksenundervisning – for hvem til hvad?* København: Nord.

Jarvis, P. (1987). *Adult Learning in the Social Context.* London, New York, Sydney: Croom Helm.

Jarvis, P. (1997). Power and personhood in teaching. In *Studies in the Education of Adults Vol. 29, No. 1, April 1997.*

Knowles, M .(1973). *The Adult Learner: A Neglected Species.* Houston: Gulf Publishing Company.

Lindgren, L. (1996). *Kan en filthatt stärka demokratin? Om mål och ideal i folkbildning.* Stockholm: Carlssons.

National kompetenceudvikling: Erhvervsudvikling gennem kvalifikationsudvikling (1997). København: Undervisningsministeriet.

Nye veje i voksenundervisning og folkeoplysning. En kortlægning af forskning, forsøg og udviklingsarbejde i Norden 1978-83 (1983). København: Nord.

På ny – erfaringer fra et nordisk netværksprojekt om voksenundervisning (1988). København: Nord 1988:25.

Rubenson, K. (1995). Vad är folkbildning? Nogra jämförande funderingar om folkbildningsbegreppet. In B. Bergstedt & S. Larsson, (ed.) (1995). *Om folkbildningens innebörger.* Linköping: Mimer.

Rubenson, K., Tuijnman, A., Wahlgren, B. (1999). *Från Kunskapslyftet till en Strategi för Livslångt Lärande.* SOU 1999:141. Stockholm: Utbildningsdepartementet.

Wahlgren, B. (1995). *Arbejdsliv og folkeoplysning. Rapport fra pilotprojekt.* København: Forskningscenter for Voksenuddannelse.

Wahlgren, B., Eidskrem, I., Sjösten, N-Å. (1999). *Arbejdsliv og folkeoplysning.* København: Nord.

Wahlgren, B. (1999). *Arbejdsliv og folkeoplysning.* København: Dansk Folkeoplysnings Samråd.

Wahlgren, B. (1999). Læringsmiljø for voksne. In Jensen, C N (1999). *Om voksenundervisning.* Værløse: Billesø & Baltzer.

Uddannelse og erhvervsliv. Handlingsprogram for national kompetenceudvikling (1998). København: Undervisningsministeriet.

MANAGEMENT EDUCATION AND ORGANIZATION DEVELOPMENT

Juha Kettunen

Abstract

Management education in the Nordic countries reflects the historical development in the successful economies of the United States, Europe and Japan. Scientific-professional management education is a mixture of the German model which emphasizes the scientific values of universities and the American style general management education which stimulates practical values in addition to scientific values. The American style business education leads to highly valued degrees which are favoured in many types of companies. This has favoured, at least in part, active labour mobility in the United States. Management education is firm-specific in continental Europe and Japan, where employment histories are long. General management education encourages the participants to learn a wide range of possibilities and widen their scope beyond their specific jobs. It emphasizes practical training which fills the gap between university knowledge and the needs of the employers. The universities in continental Europe, especially in Germany, adopt a scientific approach. This has left the responsibility of management education primarily to non-academic institutions and consultants. Special competence is learnt at universities and practical knowledge is acquired mainly in companies and other organizations. Management education is also firm-specific in Japan, where practices adopted from other countries are applied to suit the economic and social background. On the other hand, many Japanese concepts have been adopted in Western countries.

Introduction

The integration of management education with the needs of employers is an important feature in the planning of executive education and the development of organizations. Often education provides theoretical knowledge, but the needs of companies and other organizations are tied to their everyday activities. Professional management must apply scientific, abstract and complex knowledge to practical situations in the real world. This article studies the development of management education is studied from historical and cultural perspectives and some ideas are presented about how management education has been used in organizational development in the successful economies of the United States, Europe and Japan.

Management education can be divided into undergraduate 'pre-experience' studies at business schools or universities and postgraduate training for experienced individuals. Germans make a distinction between 'job capable' (*berufsfähig*) and 'job ready' (*berufsfertig*), where graduates are considered 'job capable' and become 'job ready' through practical work (Locke, 1989).

It would be waste of resources to give a large number of people management training at undergraduate level or just after graduation. It usually takes years of on-the-job experience to test whether individuals are destined to be managers. Graduates usually work during their first years in specialist jobs. Companies choose their future executives after they have several years of work experience, evaluating personal character and aptitudes and then providing them management education to those deemed suitable.

Lifelong learning has become an important principle in modern educational policy. Thus everyone should have the opportunity to develop their skills and knowledge at any time in their lives. A key characteristic of lifelong learning is a constant interaction between one's career and further education. Often the time between learning a new idea and putting it into practice is short.

This article first describes the development of management education from a historical perspective. This serves as a background for the next section, which presents some aspects on how management education can be used as a tool for personnel management and organizational development. The last section summarizes the main results of the study.

Management education in a historical perspective

General management education

One important distinction between undergraduate and management education is that undergraduate education takes the students directly from school. The latter recruits participants with undergraduate degrees or, alternatively, students with non-university degrees but only those with practical experience in management positions. These studies usually lead, especially in the United States, to the prestigious title of Master of Business Administration (MBA).

American management education is general and practical rather than specialist compared to that in many other developed countries. If the practical application of learned knowledge is neglected, there is a gap between one's university education and what the companies and other employers expect. MBA programmes are general and practical rather than academic. The prestige of this degree is measured in the labour markets. The possession of an MBA could earn a significant salary premium, allegedly as much as 45 per cent in the mid-1980s in Britain, as pointed out by Tiratsoo (1998).

The excellence of American management is linked to business schools, where the MBA is a well-known product of management education. Graduate management education expanded rapidly in the last decades, with over 90 000 MBAs obtained in the United States in 1995 (Economist, 1996). The reputation of American management was good even before the Second World War, but American influence on international management education was distinct only in Britain. Clearly the MBA courses have not been a remarkable reason for the fame of the American management, because the number of participants in MBA programmes was very small during the 1940s. The MBA programmes at that time were not very demanding in the academic sense. A report on American business education even recommended a thorough upgrading of American business education (Gordon and Howell, 1959). It seems paradoxical then that the American business schools could use the high reputation of the American management practices and produce an outstanding educational product, the MBA, which had a great influence in many countries.

The teaching method is an interesting characteristic of US business schools. The case method originated at Harvard Business School, where the Law School of the university was its source of inspiration. It was thought that practical cases from actual companies would train the students in the skills needed on the job. This approach can be criticized on the ground that the practical reality, i.e. the cultural and institutional factors, is not usually the same as that in the cases. The approach of management techniques was another main teaching method. It was favoured during the 1960s and 1970s when operations research was popular. This method has especially been used at the graduate schools of Carnegie-Mellon University in Pittsburgh and Stanford University (Gemelli, 1996).

American business schools have usually close connections with companies, because their education and research has a practical orientation. Professors often have work outside the university as consultants and managers of companies. The aim of American business administration courses for career professionals is to make the participants more capable and ready to fulfil the management needs of employers.

The export of American management education to Western Europe

After the Second World War, the US and UK policy makers tried to recover and reform European business and industry under the auspices of the European Recovery Programme. The US Technical Assistance and Productivity (USTAP) programme sponsored business education and retraining for thousands of European managers (Carew, 1987 and Hogan, 1987). The management training spread American corporate and production practices throughout Western Europe.

USTAP organized National Productivity Centres in many European countries. These centres hosted seminars, workshops and distributed manuals, journals and articles about American style management. Visiting teams of European managers also attended courses at business schools and universities in the US.

The number of foreign students in business education programmes increased dramatically (McGlade, 1995). Often foreign scholars trained in US management programmes returned to their home countries to reform educational curricula or introduce new methods adjusted to their cultures. That satisfied the need for management education in these countries.

At the end of 1950s American business schools started to lose their prestige. Some British students had given unsatisfactory reports concerning courses. The pressure was intense, the size of the class groups was too big and the case method was considered invalid. Pressures increased gradually to create a destined European method for business education (Platt, 1960).

In the late 1970s and 1980s, the fierce Japanese competition forced American companies to send managers to Japan to learn about such Japanese management doctrines as JIT, TQM, Kaizen and process-manufacturing. American and also European business schools, consultants, business people and other practitioners tried to absorb the effective operation management practices from Japan (Locke, 1996).

Plenty of European management institutions have been founded, particularly since the 1980s. The number of MBA programmes has been increased dramatically in Great Britain and in many other European countries. European students have complained about the reliance of the case method practice used at

Harvard Business School. Thus European teachers have developed and presented alternate models to American style management education (Gallagher, 1993).

The Americanization of the management education decreased with the spread of alternate methods of management education with more culture specific methods of education. Because the American tradition of management education favours practical training over the study of pure science, it has been a notable barrier in exporting its management education to Europe. The competition from European and Japanese business schools has forced the American schools to present a more global view of management education.

There were recruitment difficulties at the end of the 1980s in Britain as the economic growth slowed down. Many business schools started therefore to focus on the client. This orientation led to an increasing number of part-time programmes. Also, many programmes were customized for particular groups of clients. One in five of the MBA graduates in 1995 had taken a traditional full-time programme (Tiratsoo, 1998).

Specialist competence in continental Europe

The formation of special competence of managers is an alternative strategy to general management. People initially study a speciality at universities in Germany, as in many other countries. After graduation they may take a job at a company, gradually rising through the ranks of their company to the top positions. A study carried out in 1990 showed that reaching the highest management level takes an average of 24 years in the largest German companies (Bauer and Bertin-Maurot, 1992). The managers thus have time to develop a loyalty to their companies. The long time span allows them to deepen their specialist competence as well as helping them easily identify the resources of the company.

Industry representatives criticized the business economics (*betriebswirtshaftls-lehre*) at German universities considering it too academic and lacking in practical skills (Brinkmann, 1967). The difficult transfer of academic knowledge into one's occupation has been emphasized. Social and communication skills have also been suggested for improvement (Konegen and Grenier, 1994).

The American example inspired a handful of people to change the German system during the post-war period. Vaupel (1952) pointed out the need for general management education, which would require specialists to learn a wider variety of subjects, thus widening their knowledge of fields beyond their own specialities, i.e. increasing their abilities to handle a variety of situations.

German academia has almost as long tradition as American business schools. German faculties teach specialities such as accounting, finance and marketing to pre-experience students. The essential difference between the post-war American and German systems has been that the Germans have been avoiding the teaching of general management to post-experience students. The German companies have used non-academic institutions and consultants in management education. Usually this is short-term training or consulting of career professionals.

The German emphasis on research clearly differs from the American approach. German business economists are trained in scientific methodologies and with the objective of extending scientific knowledge in particular areas of theoretical study. On the other hand, the purpose of the American system is usually to solve practical problems. The value of results depends on how practical they are in business (Locke, 1984).

Firm-specific training in Japan

The prewar Japanese universities got strong support from the government, and commercial education had reached a reasonably high level. The Japanese system is rather similar to those of continental Europe, though Japan was considered more advanced than Germany and the other Anglo-Saxon countries (Nishizava, 1994, Sugiyama and Nishizava, 1987).

Before the Second World War, studies at Japanese universities were considered rather theoretical, and the idea of 'scientific management' was therefore adopted. A key idea of 'scientific management' was efficiency, which had both theoretical and practical aspects. It has been pointed out that the secret of high productivity is not in the machine but in the unreserved and efficient collaboration of the worker and the boss (Hutton, 1953).

'Americanization' is the key-word for the development of the Japanese educational system after the Second World War. The Japanese system was considered as too specialist and vocational by the American experts, who believed that the way to prepare cultivated citizens was by focusing on the arts and more general studies.

Quality control was extensively diffuse in post-war industry. The improvement of quality was, therefore, an important factor in the recovery of the Japanese economy. Statistical quality control especially had an important role in education. Numerous organizations were created for quality education during the 1940s, such as Nikka Giren (Japanese Union of Scientists and Engineers), Nihon Kikaku Kyokai (Japanese Standards Association) and Nihon Noritsu Kyokai (Japanese Management Association). Two prominent external training organizations were also created during the 1950s: Nihon Sangyo Kunren Kyokai (Japan Society for Industrial Training) and the Nihon Seisansei Honbu (Japan Productivity Centre) (Okazaki-Ward, 1993 and Sakamoto, 1964).

At the end of the 1950s the Japanese system of business education started to transfer from teaching American management techniques to a more Japanese system. The importance of in-house training gradually increased. The Japanese Productivity Centre started a one-year full-time course of management consulting for professionals in 1958. The aim was to apply overseas management techniques in a way suited to Japan's economic and social background. The management education was carried out using firm-specific training methods (Okazaki-Ward, 1993 and Sakamoto, 1964).

Individual companies increasingly organized their own management programmes during the 1960s. In-firm management education extended rapidly at the same time as the economic growth was strong. Many companies incorporated their own educational policy. For example, Hitachi opened its own executive school in 1960. The educational programmes of Japanese companies assumed the participants had strong loyalty and commitment to the company; i.e. they expected lifetime employment in the same company. That system worked rather well during the period of rapid economic growth.

Organization-specific training assimilates knowledge and management techniques, but, on the other hand, it takes into account the cultural features of the organization. That strengthens the coherence of the organization. This increases job tenure and people may rise to the top positions through internal hierarchical ladders after many years of work in the same company. That limits the recruitment of managers from the other companies. The features of a company's operations and management may be so specific to that organization that it cannot be copied by competitors.

Many large companies have their own executive schools. On the other hand, consultants and external training centres like the Japanese Management Association and Japan Productivity Centre have had an important role in the firm-specific training of the small and medium-sized companies. They have filled the gap between the needs of companies and higher formal education. A vast majority of Japanese business leaders have degrees from business schools or graduate schools, but after their formal education and work experience the specialist in-house training has had an important role in management education.

Scientific-professional management education in the Nordic countries

Sweden established the first business school in the Nordic region in 1909. That soon attracted a number of followers in the other Nordic countries. The new business schools were viewed as competition by the faculties of law at the universities and the institutes of technology. Non-academic commercial institutes were undoubtedly also interested in protecting their interests (Engwall, 1992). Also the non-academic commercial institutes could have been interested in protecting their fields (Engwall, 1992). However, a number of business schools were established and business education became part of many universities starting in the 1950s.

German business schools (*handelshochschulen*) served as a model for the Nordic schools. German teaching staff was initially used and the first Nordic teachers had studied in Germany. By the 1920s the orientation turned gradually towards the US as a result of study trips made by Nordic professors and students (Engwall, 1992). After the Second World War the American orientation became very strong (e.g. Amdam and Norström, 1994).

Economics and business administration dominated the curricula in business education. Accounting and finance studies were the core in business administration, but later organizational and marketing problems became more and more important. The Nordic schools also put emphasis on language training and many other practical skills such as typing and shorthand (Sandström, 1977).

An important feature of Nordic management education is that the research orientation has German or continental European, rather than American, roots. In this way the business schools show that they belong to the academic family rather than among the existing commercial academies (Engwall, 1992). The education is thus not only a continuation and renewal of professional skills, but also furthering the teaching of a scientific approach and applying the results obtained by this method to practical situation.

There are three popular forms of management programmes in Finland. The longest and most well-known is the MBA. It is similar to the MBA programmes in other European countries. The other popular programme is Professional Development (PD). The European Euro Pro programme and international Professional Degree programme are the grounds on which the PD programmes in Finland have been built. Euro Pro education began at the initiative of companies and universities to meet the needs of industrial and economic development. The PD programmes were started at the end of the 1980s in Finland (Hujala-Huttunen and Varjo, 1994). The third popular form of management education is the 'long executive programme'. The JES (*Johtaminen eurooppalaisessa Suomessa*) programme of the Finnish Institute of Management (Lifim) is a good example of this kind of programme.

Helsinki School of Economics and Business Administration started the executive MBA programme in 1983, following the model of Stanford University's MBA programme. The JOKO Executive Education Ltd at the business school is responsible for the programme. At the Helsinki University of Technology, the Department of Industrial Management is responsible for the Euro MBA programme, but at the other universities the continuing education centres organize the executive management programmes.

There are MBA programmes at the University of Jyväskylä, Lappeenranta University of Technology, University of Oulu, Swedish School of Economics and Business Administration, University of Tampere, Turku School of Economics and Business Administration, University of Vaasa and University of Kuopio.

There were hundred PD programmes in 1997 in Finland. Nearly every university has PD programmes, except the three business schools with MBA programmes (Laiho, 1998). The PD and MBA are not official degrees in Finland, but in many cases these programmes have been included in postgraduate degrees at the decision of the professor who is responsible for postgraduate studies. There are also non-academic institutions and consulting companies with their own profile of training.

There were 99 000 students participating in continuing education at Finnish universities in 1995. The share of students was 6 per cent in labour-market training, 21 per cent in in-house training and 73 per cent in other training programmes. The share of hours of education was 29 per cent in labour-market training, 10 per cent in in-house training and 61 per cent in other training (Laiho, 1998).

Currently management education can be understood as a result of its historical and cultural background. The character of Nordic management education can be described as scientific and professional. It means learning which is based on scientific knowledge, which is in turn successfully applied using job experience. It combines theory and practice. According to a study by Laiho (1998), the Finnish participants in Professional Development programmes considered that both the professional and scientific aspects of the programmes are important. The professional importance was considered slightly more valuable than the scientific importance.

Organizational development using management education

General management education in organizational development

The offer of a general management education is an incentive for the managers of companies, and because it increases the rate and depth of the organization's development, the employer often pays the tuition. The development project of management education is an important tool to allocate human resources to a project that would otherwise be too burdensome to organize.

It is useful for both the company and the school to nominate a mentor at a company and a tutor at the university to supervise the development project. Often the reports of the projects are presented to the management board and are thereafter official documents in the organization. Education is an important instrument to develop the thinking of the participant.

There are also small development projects within the courses, which can be used by the participants in their own work experience. Since the courses offered cover a variety of academic fields, they expand the knowledge of the participants and their capabilities to deal with a variety of job situations.

The development projects can be seen as the employer's investment in human capital. It creates a return during the period of study, because the ideas are supposed to be applied to practice. It is also an investment from the participant's side considering the fact that the persons will probably spend part of their own leisure time to study.

In many practical situations it can be seen that if the persons do not participate in the development of the project and the solution of the problem, there will not be real changes and intellectual growth. The knowledge and ability to run the process may disappear with the visiting researcher or consultant. On the other hand the personal experience and everyday thinking may not be enough for the widespread understanding and discovering new solutions, but the person remains within the limits of the prevailing practices.

The literature within the programmes also increases the incentives to follow current professional knowledge. It is required that the participants write essays about the books read and also apply new knowledge in their own job or organization. Often they find it easy to make organizational innovations which can instantly be applied to practical situations.

It is difficult for an organization to grow only by providing some information to the persons to employees and waiting until they produce innovative solutions. Fricke (1994) emphasizes that these innovations are the results of a process in which the participant has an active role. Therefore, the strategies given outside the organization cannot be successfully used in development processes, where new innovative solutions are sought.

The ability to possess the necessary knowledge, to apply it in a practical situation and obtain successful results from the process is needed on the job. These are also requirements for research skills. A critical research orientation is needed to pick through the plethora of information and in order to use it to advantage in one's work. Engeström (1986) points out that the purpose is to approach the ideal of work with theoretical control.

A degree in general management education and work experience are the indicators of management capability and readiness. This status creates a positive image for the person and also the organization. Hence general management education possibly increases the probability that the person is seeking better job opportunities and the probability that a job search will be successful. In the US, where a degree in business administration is favoured, job mobility is large.

The prestigious MBA can be a bonus for managers who complete a satisfactory number of specific tasks and achieve their targets. The possibility of attending classes in a management programme can be used in advance to increase incentives for efficient work.

PD and MBA programmes are based on a personal study plan and they may take two to four years to complete. Often the programme strengthens the commitment of the person to the company. It is important for the employer to also have a written contract with the participant so that the person is committed to staying in a company for a minimum length of time. Undoubtedly the employer will think of other incentives for the manager at the end of this period. For example, bonus pay, partnership or a pay raise is often given.

Firm-specific training in organizational development

There may be different views between the employer and employee about whether management education should be general management education or specific in-house training. General management education is valuable, because diplomas or certificates from particular programmes can also be used to find better jobs at other companies. On the other hand, the in-house training is valuable for the company because it is often precisely tailored to meet the needs of the organization.

The knowledge from in-house training stays in the company, because the knowledge of participants in it is tied to the culture of the organization. A similar argument is also true for general management if the person has long-term employment in the company. An alternative may be that the knowledge disappears with the consultant, who learns most in the process.

There is a mixed type of management education which is targeted for the individual participants from a specific industry or occupation. For example, in Finland there is an MBA programme concentrating only on Soviet trade and entrepreneurship. These kinds of programmes are difficult to build for oligopolistic industries, for example, for banking and the forestry industry, where the markets are dominated by large competing companies.

There are also programmes which are tailored for companies with specific needs, for example, to provide a mix of general management education and in-house training. Thus there are PD and MBA programmes in Finland that are tailored for large organizations or business networks. These kinds of programmes combine the interests of the participants and the organization.

Client-centred planning has led to programmes that are customized to meet the specific needs of the employer or the individual needs of the participant. The personal study plan creates a framework for study and forges a link to the employer's needs. For example, some Finnish PD and MBA programmes have individual enrolment for courses and a flexible modular structure so that the person can start at any time.

Conclusions

American style general management education has had an important effect on management education in many countries. In this method the gap between university knowledge and the needs of the employers is filled by on-the-job training. General management education widens the scope of the participants beyond their specific jobs, encouraging them to use a wider variety of resources. These studies usually lead to prestigious titles, which are useful during people's whole career in one or more companies.

In continental Europe, and especially in Germany, people study specialist subjects at universities, where scientific methodology is pervasive. Practical knowledge is learned mainly on the job, while management education is taught primarily by non-academic institutions and consultants. Specialist competence has great value for allowing persons to rise to the top positions after long employment in the same company.

Japanese managers are even more loyal to their companies than Germans. The management education is usually firm-specific in Japan, where knowledge from other countries is adopted and applied to suit to the company's economic and social background. Thus they have created management techniques that cannot be easily copied. The coherence of the organization is strong and lifetime employment is usual.

In the Nordic countries, and especially in Finland, a scientific-professional management education is favoured. It is a mixture of the German model, which was prevalent before the Second World War, and the American model, which became important after the war. The academic features, and especially the research orientation, is important. However, the professional competence is even more important.

Management education is an important tool for employee and organizational development. A decision has to be made about whether general management education or in-house training is used. General management education can be a bonus for the managers, but in-house training is often more precisely tailored to meet the needs of the organization. The customer orientation has led to the availability of many specially tailored programmes, and flexible, modular programmes which are individually designed. There are thus industry or occupation specific arrangements that are open to individual participants; or general management training customized for companies.

The change of the business environment and the development of new technology needs foresight and adaptability on the part of management. General management education which can be transferred from an area to another is needed. On the other hand, new types of professions will appear and thus bring the need for new types of specific education.

References

Amdam, R.P. and Norström C. J. (1994). Business Administration in Norway 1936-1990. In L. Engwall and E. Gunnarsson (eds), *Management Studies in an Academic Context*, Acta Universtiatis Upsaliensis Studia Oeconomiae Negotiorum 35. Uppsala: Almqvist and Wiksell, 66-83.

Bauer, M. and Bertin-Mourot B. (1992). L'Etat, le capital et l'entreprise au sommet des grandes entreprises. «Les 200". Comparaison franco-allemande, *La Revue de l'IRES*, 10: Autumn, 31-70.

Brinkmann, G. (1969). *Die Ausbildung von Führungskräften für die Wirtschaft. Ein Forschungsbericht über Probleme der Hoch- und Fachhochschulausbildung von Kaufleuten und Ingenieuren.* Cologne: Universitätsverlag Michael Wienand.

Carew, A. B. (1989). *Labour Under the Marshall Plan, The Politics of Productivity and the Marketing of Management Science.* Manchester: Manchester University Press.

Economist, The (1996). Dons and dollar, 15 July.

Engeström, Y. (1986). *Learning by Expanding.* Helsinki: Orienta-Konsultit.

Engwall, L. (1992). *Mercury Meet Minerva.* Oxford: Pergamon Press.

Fricke, W. (1994). Scientific Knowledge, Social Change and Action Research. In T. Kauppinen and M. Lehtonen (eds.) *National Action Research Programmes in 1990s.* Ministry of Labour, Labour Policy Studies 86. Helsinki: Hakapaino.

Gallagher, K. (1993). *The Chronicle of Higher Education*, 40: 15, 1 December.

Gemelli, G. (1996). American Influence on European Management Education - the Role of Ford Foundation, in R. P. Amdam (ed.), *Management, Education and Competitiveness. Europe, Japan and the United States.* London, Routledge, 38-68.

Gordon, R. A. and Howell J. E. (1959). *Higher Education for Business.* New York: McGraw-Hill.

Hogan, M. (1987). *The Marshall Plan: America, Great Britain and the Reconstruction of Western Europe, 1947-1952*. Cambridge: Cambridge University Press.

Hujala-Huttunen, E. and Varjo, A. (1994). *Kasvatus- ja opetusalan PD-koulutus - akateeminen vastaus työelämän haasteisiin*, Kasvatustieteiden tiedekunnan selosteita n:o 52. Joensuu: Joensuun yliopisto.

Hutton, G. (1953). *We Too Can Prosper*. London: Allen and Unwin.

Konegen-Grenier, C. (1994). Die Anforderungen der Wirtschaft an die betriebswirtschaftliche Hochschulausbildung. Ergebnisse einer Unternehmensbefraugung. In C. Konegen-Grenier and W. Schlaffke (eds), *Praxisbezug und soziale Kompetenz. Hochschulen und Wirtschaft im Dialog*. Cologne: Deutscher Instituts-Verlag, 48-64.

Laiho, I. (1998). *Asiantuntijuuden kutsu, Yliopistojen ammatillisten erikoistumis- ja jatko-opintojen rakenteiden ja toiminnan vertailu*, Turun yliopiston täydennyskoulutuskeskuksen julkaisuja A:69. Turku: Turun yliopiston täydennyskoulutuskeskus.

Lehtisalo, L. and Raivola, R. (1986). *Koulutuspolitiikka ja koulutussuunnittelu*. Juva: WSOY.

Locke, R. R. (1984). *The End of Practical Man. Entrepreneurship and Higher Education in Germany, France, and Great Britain, 1880-1940*. Greenwich, CT: JAI Press Inc.

Locke, R R (1989) *Management and Higher Education since 1940. The Influence of America and Japan on West Germany, Great Britain and France*. Cambridge : Cambridge University Press.

Locke, R. R. (1996). *The Collapse of the American Management Mystique*. Oxford: Oxford University Press.

McGlade, J. (1995). *The Illusion of Consensus: American Business, Cold War Aid and the Reconstruction of Western Europe 1948-1958*. Unpublished PhD dissertation, George Washington University.

Nishihizava, T. (1994). The Making of Japan's Business Elites. In T. Yuzawa (ed.) *Japanese Business Success*, London: Routledge, 203-213.

Okazaki-Ward, L. (1993). *Management Education and Training in Japan.* London: Graham and Trotman.

Platt, M. (1960). The Perils of American Business Education. *Director,* 12: February, 294-299.

Sagamoto, F. (1964). *Nihon Keiei Kyoiku-shi Josetsu.* Tokyo: Daiyamondosha.

Sandström, H. (1977). *Handelshögskolan vid Åbo Akademi 1927-1977 (The Business School at Turku Academy 1927-1977), Skriftserie utgiven av Handelshögskolan vid Åbo akademi,* serie A:18. Turku : Åbo Akademi.

Sugiyama, C. and Nishizawa T. (1987). Captain of Industry: Tokyo Commercial School at Hitotsubashi, in C. Sugiyama and H. Mizuta (eds), *Enlightenment and Beyond.* Tokyo: University of Tokyo Press, 151-169.

Tiratsoo, N. (1998). Management Education in Postwar Britain, In L. Engwall and V. Zamagni (eds), *Management Education in Historical Perspective.* Manchester and New York: Manchester University Press, 111-126.

Vaubel, L. (1952). Unternehmer gehen zur Schule, Ein Erfahrungsbericht aus USA. Düsseldorf: Droste.

EXPERIENCING THE CHANGES BROUGHT BY IT AND THEIR CONSEQUENCES IN SMES

Tarja Tikkanen[1]

Abstract

The introduction of information technology has brought many changes both to work and the work environment as well as major learning experiences for many employees. This article describes how the introduction of IT has been experienced in small and medium-sized companies (SMEs). The description was made by comparing four groups, formed by cross-tabulating two age-groups, younger (below 45 years of age) and older workers (45 years and older), with two sectors, communication (service sector) and information (office) work. The data used were collected by questionnaires at the University of Jyväskylä as a part of a European research project *Working Life Changes and Training of Older Workers (WORKTOW)*. Participants were 156 employees (45.5 % women) from seven SMEs in Finland, with a mean age 40.9 years and a relatively high educational level. The IT-issues addressed were: the use of computers in daily work tasks; the effects on various matters related to work, the work environment and working climate; the difficulties encountered with IT; and IT support and information changes caused by IT during the transition period. The results showed significant separate and joint age- and sector-effects regarding IT experiences. Some findings were in line with earlier studies suggesting negative age-effects, but sectorwise analysis resulted on many occasions in no or positive age-effects. Age differences were stronger with the information sector and sector-effects among younger workers. A majority used computers to a large extent, the exception was about a third of the younger service workers. While the introduction of IT had changed work, it was only to a little or to some extent. On the other hand, rather strong effects from IT were reported on the work environment, especially among older workers and more than half in both sectors reported this as an extensive impact. Effects of IT on the working climate were commonly reported mostly among the younger workers in services, and least among the younger workers in information sector, but these effects were mainly described in negative terms. Some difficulties were faced when using IT, but again only to a little or some extent. While there was satisfaction about information concerning IT changes, the support provided for IT training was rated insufficient by most of the workers.

---

[1] The author wishes to thank the Research Assistant Tia-Maria Kenni-Lehtonen from University of Jyväskylä, Finland, for her help in collecting and preparing the data for this analysis.

Implications of the results for adult education and for learning and development in the workplace are discussed.

Introduction

Working life is currently under more turbulent change than perhaps ever before in human history. While a lot of that change comes from several general trends in society, it has been argued (Streumer & Bjorkquist, 1998) that a great deal of the changes in the workplace can be attributed, in whole or partly, to the continuous adoption of more advanced forms of technology. If we take this statement as a point of departure, it follows that the rate of adopting new technology in workplaces largely determines how much change has actually taken place in working life. Taken that 80% of all technology will be replaced in the coming decade and that we therefore become technologically obsolete about every five years (Gavigan, 2000), there is a strong push towards changes in various workplaces. As a consequence, the nature and content of jobs are changing more rapidly than before (Employment in Europe 1996).

Technology changes in SMEs

The changes that new technology creates in working life are partly based on concrete aspects, such as changing work tools. Common rhetoric implies that new technology tools are rapidly adopted in working life and in *any kind of* workplace, and that the introduction of these new tools is continuously changing working life *to a large extent*. Such rhetoric draws heavily from the situation found in large companies and in companies within new sectors, representing new occupational domains. The picture is partly supported by survey studies, which examine the workforce and work places with little attention paid to the diversity among companies when presenting the results. In terms of working tools there is a second wave of computerisation and adoption of basic-computer skills going on at the moment. The introduction of IT has meant increased use of computers for producing, storing and finding information, but also that communication in and out of companies is now more and more taking place as computer-based, electronic information networks. One basic assumption in this article is that in most SMEs, in most sectors, IT is rather novel phenomenon, and therefore, less taken for granted than in larger companies.

Available studies give evidence about general trends. Studies on Working Conditions in Finland (see Lehto & Sutela, 1998) showed that, while the rate of use of mobile phones and of e-mail has increased from less than 20 % to approximately 35 % between 1984 and 1997, the ordinary telephone (change from 70 % to 85 %) and fax (change from 30 % to 50 %) were still the most used technological equipment at work. Within the same time period the use of information technology had rapidly increased (from 15 % to 64 %), but almost always this only meant personal computer use (change from 10 % to 60 %). Approximately a half of both women (57 %) and men (46 %) reported that they work with a PC at least a half of their work time. Other studies have also shown that more than half of the Finnish population use IT in their work and that the professions in which IT is used, are growing the fastest (Asplund & Lilja, 1999; Rantanen & Lehtinen, 1998).

At a company level, however, the picture of the technology changes is more complex, depending most importantly on the size of a company and the branch or sector it belongs to. Van den Tillaart and van den Berg & Warmerdam (1998) have described how new technologies and automation have blurred the boundaries within sectors, but how they still differ in many respects: their technological development and dynamics are different, as is the degree of uniformity between enterprises and products, also production processes and networking with other sectors vary and companies differ in training traditions and in the provision of training. Adopting a sectoral approach in variety across countries and strengths in this line of studies have been emphasised by for example CEDEFOP (Warmerdam & van den Tillaart, 1998). On the one hand, SMEs can be more flexible, innovative and faster in adopting the latest technology, on the other hand they can also be much slower, due to their low resources for new investments (Lahn, Tikkanen, Lyng, et al., 1997). A nationally representative study by the Ministry of Labour in Finland (Zaminder, 1997) showed that the rate of organisational changes is higher in bigger companies and varies by sector. In office work the rate was 60 % and in service sector 51 %. The study showed also that 53 % of the organisational changes in Finland are technology-related and that the overall proportion of workers influenced by new technologies is high, although varying within the in-company hierarchy (the influence being more common among management).

These general results give some guidelines about what the situation would be like in SMEs. Yet, there are no comprehensive, comparative studies available indicating to what extent SMEs in various sectors have actually adopted new technology in practice and what kind of technology this is. Further, a great deal of the changes in working life are more relative than a concrete change of working tools. From this point of view change depends on how the workers perceive and experience the the introduction of new technology as well as to what extent they adopt the new ways of working. In this area the picture from

SMEs is even more vague and we do not know much concerning the extent to which IT has actually changed work and the work environment in the various occupational sectors in SMEs.

Technology and learning

Major technological transition periods at the workplace are also major learning experiences for the staff. Workers have to adapt to these changes accordingly, acquire new skills, and in many cases, learn to do a completely different job (Employment in Europe 1996). The learning experience gained during this process, thus, extends way beyond only learning to use and master the new tool itself, and also covers the content of work, working environments, and the social-cultural patterns in working life. Assuming that new technology is the main source of changes in the workplace, it follows that the rate of adopting new technology also sets the pace for new learning in the workplace. Further, the support provided for the adoption of new technology in companies is at the same time an important learning intervention, which is most typically provided as short training courses. A study on working conditions in Finland (Lehto & Sutela, 1998) showed, firstly, that two out of three IT-users reported sufficient support and guidance in new, complex situations with IT, women somewhat more often than men. Secondly, possibilities to develop in one's job have been increasing in Finland during the period between 1977 and 1997, especially for women, and across all ages.

A previous study (Tikkanen & Kujala,2000) with WORKTOW-data showed that about 27 % of older workers (45+) rated their possibilities to participate in continuous work-related learning as non-existent and that over 61 % of them rated their possibilities to get the necessary training to perform their job to their satisfaction as non-existing or not good. Training provision varies by company size, to the advantage of bigger companies, and by occupational sector (Agora II, 1998; Zaminder, 1997). Information (office) workers and those with higher education get more training than those in services or in manufacturing and with lower education (Zaminder, 1997). A study in SMEs (van den Tillaart, van den Berg & Warmerdam, 1998) showed that informal learning plays more important role than formal learning, but that workers are not very satisfied with their learning opportunities. Half of the workers wished to have more, informal opportunities for learning new technology by practising with new computers, hardware and software. Informal learning has been found to be the preferred way of learning rather than formal and institutional (Houtcoop & Oosterbeek, 1997), especially among the older and low-educated people (Livingstone, 2000).

Age and new technology

The existing literature typically points out that the competence in managing new technology is different between younger and older workers, with the young workers having the advantage. It is, however, not easy to grasp a comprehensive picture of these age differences, because the literature is divided by disciplines. Most of the literature concerning older workers has focused on their situation in the labour market and is sociologically oriented. In the 1980s there was a special area of research, industrial gerontology, examining the effects of the first wave of computerisation on older workers in working life (for an overview of the literature see Tikkanen, 1998). More recently the studies on effects of technology have been conducted within work psychology (Kenni-Lehtonen, 2000). Their focus has been less on age, but more generally on managing work and on stress and coping, and the results have partly been contradictory (e.g. Corbett, Martin, Wall & Clegg, 1989; Hukki & Seppälä, 1993; Korunka, Weiss, Huemer & Karetta, 1995). The technological competence and skills of younger, better-educated workers is usually taken for granted, whereas that of older workers has only recently gained more attention and duely empirical evidence is still scarce. Ilmarinen (1999) has made the following summary of the results of the Eurobarometer from 1996 concerning age-differences in mental demands of work:

- *Use of computers* (for at least half of one's work time): Men below 45 years of age use computers somewhat more commonly (25 %) in their work than those at or above 45 years (21 %). The corresponding difference was greater among women (31 % vs. 23 %), who used computers more than men in their work.
- *Tight work schedules* (for at least half of one's work time): Were more common in the work of men below 45 years of age (48 %) than of men aged 45 or older (43 %). Women worked less than men within tight schedules, and the age difference was smaller (40 % vs. 38 %).
- *Complex work tasks*: Working with complex tasks is as common among the younger and older workers, but men experience more complexity than women in their work (men 63-63 % vs. women 51-52 %).
- *Learning new things at work*: The work involved learning new things for both younger and older workers, somewhat more among younger than older workers (younger 75-78 % vs. older 70-72 %), slightly more among men than women. However, beyond no comparison, nine out of ten of the older women in the Nordic countries reported learning to be common in their work.

In general however, significant variety was found between countries in the above issues, especially between southern and northern European countries.

This is shown for example when comparing the rates of computer use between the European and Finnish data presented earlier in this text.

IT and workplace culture

Socio-cultural patterns refer to the ways intra- and inter-organisational communication takes place or has been organised and to consequent changes in the socio-cultural norms, that is, in shared rules and the ways in which these rules are formed and changed in the working places. The cultural effects of new technology have been studied less, although also in this area strong changes are taking place in the workplace as a consequence of global changes in labour market and working life (Belangèr & Tuijnman, 1997). Existing studies again show these aspects on a general level, but tell us little of the situation in SMEs and across sectors. In Finland about 70 % of workers have reported that there is an open climate in their workplaces, and 60 % open communication (Lehto & Sutela, 1998). Workers older than 45 years of age have experienced the climate more negatively (more often tense and competitive and less often relaxed) than younger workers, although very few wanted to change the climate, had they the power to do so (Jussila, Jääskeläinen & Pitkänen, 1999). Workers within industry consider their possibilities to influence their work and work environment generally low (Pitkänen & Nygård, 1999).

Purpose of the article

The purpose of this article is to describe how the introduction of IT and its consequences in the workplace have been experienced in SMEs. A basic assumption in focusing on workers' experiences is that addressing IT-changes in working life can only partly take place in absolute terms, but rather is a relative matter, depending on how the change is perceived by various actors. In order to address the effects of age and occupational sector, the descriptions were made separately in four groups, younger (below 45 years of age) and older workers (45 years and older), both within service sector and in information (office) work. Issues covered in IT were: use of the computer in daily work tasks, the effects experienced from the introduction of IT in the workplaces, difficulties in dealing with new IT, and support and information provided in the transition period.

Methodology

Data

The data used in the article represent the Finnish data from a larger European research project *'Working Life Changes and Training of Older Workers'* (WORKTOW) (Lahn, Tikkanen, Lyng, et al, 1997). The data were collected with questionnaires during March - April 1999 in seven SMEs. The companies represented three different types of work: communication (service sector), information (office) and manual work. However, since there were only eight respondents representing manual sector, in this article we have only examined the results for the part of communication and information work. Thus the total number of respondents included in the study presented here is 156. In communications work (service sector) the companies were a bank, a pharmacy, and a greenhouse-retail store, and from information work (office sector) three engineering companies and (white-collar workers in a) timber house production company. The size of the companies varied between 30-40 employees, except in a larger one with 275 employees. All the seven companies were in a transition period of adopting information and communication technology, but they varied somewhat with regard to the stage of this process they were in.

Age/worktype comparison groups

Due to sector and age differences concerning the adoption technology at the workplace, the participants were divided into four groups, which made possible simultaneous comparison of age and branch effects. The comparison groups were formed by firstly recoding age-variable (overall mean was 40.9 years) into two groups, representing below 45 and 45 years and above, and secondly crosstabulating these two age-groups with the two branches, communication (service sector) and information (office sector). As a result of this 2x2 cross-tabulation four different age/worktype -groups were formed, shown in Table 1 below.

As we can see from Table 1, the groups were not divided equally in terms of numbers of participants in the study. Out of the total of the participants, most were below 45 and represented information work. This group, referred to as INFO-45 from here on, counts for 44.2 % (n=69) from the total group. The younger workers in communication (COM-45) and the older in information work (INFO45+) both represented slightly over 20 % of the total group. Older workers in the communication sector (COM45+) formed the smallest group, 12.2 % of study participants. Table 2 further describes these four groups in terms of gender, education and type of job contract.

Table 1. Formation of the four age/worktype-groups.

	Below 45 years		45 years and older		Total	
Type of work	n	Total %	N	Total %	n	%
Communication (service work)	33	21.1	19	12.2	52	33.3
Information (office work)	69	44.2	35	22.4	104	66.7
Total	102	65.4	54	34.6	156	100

Table 2 shows that in our data work type was strongly related with gender, and education with age and worktype. While the total gender distribution was rather equal, the separate group distributions indicate a strong gendered nature of the occupational profiles in question. Not unexpectedly, women dominated within communication work (88.5 %) and men within information work (76 %).

Table 2. Description of the age/worktype comparison groups by gender, education and job contract (%).

	COM-45	COM45+	INFO-45	INFO45+	Total
Gender					***
Women (n=71)	87.9	89.5	21.7	28.6	45.5
Men (n=85)	12.1	10.5	78.3	71.4	54.5
Education[1]					***
Not at all (n=5) or lower vocational education (n=42)	51.5	50.0	15.9	30.3	30.7
Upper vocational education (n=86)	30.3	27.8	72.5	63.6	56.2
University degree (n=20)	18.2	22.2	11.6	6.1	13.1
Job contract					n.s.
Full-time	78.8	78.9	85.5	82.9	82.7
Part-time	12.1	5.3	-	8.6	5.1
Temporary	6.1	10.5	5.8	2.9	5.8
Other (agency or else)	3.0	5.3	8.6	5.7	6.4
Total	21.1	12.2	44.2	22.4	100

[1]Three missing cases; *** χ^2Sig <.001

There are three levels of education showed in Table 2: no formal vocational education (n=5) or vocational training course or program at a lower VET level (1) or at an upper VET level (a degree from an occupational training institute)

(2), or university degree (3). The overall educational level was rather high in our sample, over half (56.2 %) holding an upper vocational degree and more than 10 % a university degree. Women (40.8 %) and men (69.5 %) both typically held an upper vocational degree. There was a difference between the branches so that within the communication work a lower VET (41.2 %) and within information work an upper VET (69.6 %) was most common. While there was only a slight age-difference on the lowest level of education in the service sector, in information work the rate of older workers was double compared to younger ones at this level.

For the great majority of workers, full-time, permanent work was the most typical. No statistically significant age-differences were found, but comparison across sectors showed that in the service sector more workers held a temporary job than in information sector.

Variables describing IT-change

The questionnaire covered four aspects concerning IT in work and workplaces. Firstly, the *use of computers* in daily work was requested by asking about the degree of actual use (ranging from 'not at all' to 'to a large extent') and about the purpose of using the computer.

Secondly, the *experienced effects of IT* were covered in three areas: work itself, work environment and workplace climate. The questions concerning effects of IT on the work and about effects of IT-change on work environment were based on earlier studies on the relationship between IT and age (Ahola & Huuhtanen, 1995; Hukki & Seppälä, 1993). Various aspects of the work itself covered job tasks, pace of work, psychological experiences of work, and possibilities to use and develop one's work-competence by one's work tasks. The question about work environment focused on the extent to which the introduction of IT in the workplace was experienced to have changed it. The effects of IT on the general work climate were requested with a question used by Ahola & Huuhtanen (1995) in their study on age and well-being at work. Answers were requested with a yes/no dichotomy. In case of 'yes'-answers free, complementary descriptions of the nature of effects were requested.

The set of questions about *difficulties faced when using IT at work* was also based on the study by Ahola & Huuhtanen (1995) on age and well-being in work. Questions about the extent of difficulties experienced covered the understanding of IT-vocabulary (which for the Finns is often also presented with a foreign language), use of various functions, finding information in handbooks, learning new software, observing and correcting one's mistakes, and working speed required by technology.

Finally, we asked about whether the *information and support* (e.g. training or assisting personnel), provided in the company during the IT transition period, had been sufficient. The question about information concerned IT-changes taking place at the workplace. The question on support focused on the learning and adoption of IT among the workers in the workplace.

Data analysis

SPSS-X Statistical Package was used for the statistical analyses. The age/worktype -comparison-groups were formed by cross-tabulating formed two age-groups (below 45 years of age and 45 years and above) with the two branches, communication (service sector) and information (office sector). Data were analysed by examining and comparing percentage distributions and means differences (ANOVA) between these four groups.

Results

Use of computers

As expected the results showed that computers are used a lot at work, but also that their use varies statistically very significantly by both age and type of work. Table 3 shows that the younger workers in service work (communication) used computers the least (24.2 % little or not at all), whereas the younger workers in the information sector used them most (82.6 % to a great extent). While there was a large difference between the younger workers across sectors in using computer to a great extent (30.3 % vs. 82.6 %), this difference was rather small among the older workers (63.2 % vs. 68.6 %).

Table 3 also shows that while computers were most typically used for word processing and communication, there were major differences between sectors and also between the age-groups. In all other areas but administration the differences between age/worktype groups were statistically very significant ($p<.001$). As expected, information workers used computers much more than service sector. Within information work younger workers used computers about 20 per cent units more than their older counterparts. In the service sector (communications) age differences were in the same direction, but much smaller, except in word processing (58.1 % among younger vs. 18.8 % among older workers).

Table 3. Use of computers (%), N=156

Computer use	COM-45	COM45+	INFO-45	INFO45+	Total	χ^2Sig
Extent (%)						<.001
Little or not at all	24.2	21.2	5.8	2.9	10.9	
To some extent	45.5	15.8	11.6	28.6	23.1	
To a great extent	30.3	63.2	82.6	68.6	66.0	
Purpose (% yes)						
Word processing	58.1	18.8	80.6	62.9	65.1	<.001
Communication	10.0	6.3	82.1	62.9	54.7	<.001
Planning	6.7	6.3	69.7	48.6	44.9	<.001
Administration	13.3	6.3	7.5	22.9	12.2	ns.
(econ.)	73.3	56.3	31.3	31.4	42.6	<.001
Other						
Total	21.2	12.2	44.2	22.4	100	

Within service work, computers were mainly used for other purposes than those specified. In our data the most important areas were managing and controlling monetary transactions and goods traffic. In the bank and pharmacy computers were also used a lot as a source of information.

IT-effects in the workplace

The experienced effects of the introduction of IT in the workplace were considered with regard to work and work tasks, to the work environment and to the general climate at the workplace.

Work. The extent to which IT has had effects on various aspects of the work itself were covered in the following areas: job tasks, pace of work, psychological experiences of work, and possibilities to use and develop one's work-competence in one's work tasks. The results, presented as means differences in table 4, show some differences across age and sector.

Several observations can be made from Table 4. Firstly, while the introduction of IT had had effects on the work itself, these effects were rather modest. On average, with all respects and within all four groups, the extent of the experienced effects was rated to be between 'a little' and 'somewhat'. Secondly, the effects have been experienced strongest with positive changes, and mildest with negative ones. Thirdly, older workers in communication work reported stronger IT-effects than their younger counterparts. The two exceptions to this were that younger workers had experienced that their options for self-development and competence use had increased more. The age-effects were hardly found within information work, and in half of the issues listed, younger workers had experienced IT-effects more strongly than the older ones.

Table 4. The extent of IT-effects on work (Means), N=156

Changes in work	COM-45	COM45+	INFO-45	INFO45+	Total	Sig[1]
More interesting job tasks	2.57	2.78	2.73	2.79	2.72	*
More challenging job tasks	2.50	2.89	2.62	2.58	2.62	*
Mentally more exhausting job tasks	1.71	2.06	2.11	2.18	2.04	
Increased options for self-development	2.56	2.33	2.68	2.85	2.65	
Increased options to use one's competence	2.30	2.22	2.76	2.62	2.57	*
Increased pace of work	2.33	2.83	2.53	2.62	2.55	
More variety in job tasks	2.25	2.44	2.65	2.62	2.54	
Less variety in job tasks	1.46	1.76	1.60	1.63	1.60	*
More difficult job tasks	1.68	1.78	2.08	1.91	1.92	
Job tasks become easier	2.19	3.00	2.41	2.23	2.40	

[1] ANOVA *<.05; *Scale used:* 1= Not at all, 2 = A little, 3 = Somewhat, 4 = To a great deal

Cross-sector comparisons within age-groups showed that among the younger workers the IT-effects had been experienced stronger among the information workers in all cases. The cross-sector comparison among the older workers, however, showed a more varied picture. It was in the information sector that older workers felt their options for self-development (most of all in the four groups) and their use of competence had increased more than among the older workers in the service sector. Older service workers reported more often that job tasks had become easier, but also more challenging.

Work environment. The introduction of IT was also reported to have changed the work environment. Almost half (46.4 %) of all the respondents reported changes to a great extent, while only 15.2 % to a little extent or not at all. Older workers had experienced changes strongest in both sectors (COM45+ 61.1 % and INFO45+ 54.3 % to a great extent). Younger workers in the service sector reported the least IT-effects on the work environment (29 % 'a little' or 'not at all'). The observed group-differences were statistically significant at level p<.05.

Workplace climate. Reported IT-effects on the workplace climate are described in Table 5. Out of the total, 37.4 % of the respondents reported that IT-changes had effected the workplace climate. However, there were statistically significant differences (p<.01) between the four groups in question. Although the above results showed that workers in the service sector used less IT in their work, in both age groups they reported more often than information workers that changes brought by IT had effected their workplace climate.

Table 5. Effects of IT-changes on workplace climate (% 'yes'), N=156

	COM-45	COM45+	INFO-45	INFO45+	Total	χ^2Sig
Effects on workplace climate	60.0	47.1	23.1	40.0	37.4	<.01

Those who reported on climate effects provided free descriptions of them in both positive and negative terms. These descriptions, which have not been analysed here in all four comparison groups separately, concerned the nature and amount of work, equality, learning and competence requirements, communication and cooperation, and future expectations. Interestingly, these results showed that the descriptions drawn from actual experience (based on what had already happened in a workplace) were mainly negative, but expectations of future effects were mainly described as positive. In the beginning of the IT-change process, low mastery of the new tool and problems with the functioning of the new system had affected the pace and amount of work, which had further resulted in tensions in the workplace climate and pressures upon the work load. The expectations of IT-effects on equality were positive, but the actual experiences reported were negative. IT was reported to have created divisions between workers, because of the "pecking order" in getting computers and because of the unequal distribution/provision of the new tools (everybody does not get as powerful tools). Unequal distribution of the new IT-tools was reported to result in increasing specialisation and in selective accumulation of competence among the staff. The climate effects were feelings of inequality and increased competition. The effects on social climate were reported as positive and negative. Especially engineers reported that work had become lonelier, as the computer was almost their sole company during the day. It was generally reported that the introduction of IT had aroused positive expectations from future. However, these expectations were also mentioned to be unrealistically positive, because there had not been enough investments in collective or individual learning (training) at the workplace in how to use the new IT tools.

Difficulties faced when using IT at work

Table 6 shows to what extent difficulties had been experienced with regard to various IT use -related issues. The four groups' comparison, showed statistically significant age and sector effects with all but two regards. Generally speaking, within-sector age-differences were bigger in information work and cross-sector comparisons showed larger differences among younger than older workers.

Firstly, compared to younger workers, older workers reported IT-related difficulties to a larger extent. In all but one area these age-differences were more frequently found among the information sector workers. The only exception was in 'observing and correcting one's own mistakes', where younger workers reported having faced more difficulties and where this age-difference (not statistically significant) within communication sector was greater (0.15) than the corresponding difference among information workers (0.06). Secondly, workers in the service sector reported IT-difficulties to a greater extent than those in information work. These cross-sector differences were greater among younger workers. Thirdly, in all the groups under consideration here, most difficulties with IT had been faced with understanding text in a foreign language. The second biggest difficulty was for the communication workers to understand the technical vocabulary. For older information workers it was learning continuously for renewing software and for the younger ones finding information from manuals.

Information about IT changes and user-support

Informing about IT-changes. Answers to the question about the information process concerning IT-changes at work showed that on the average as much as 60 % of all the respondents rated it as sufficient (Table 6). There were, however, statistically significant (p<.01) differences between the four age/worktype –groups. Two observations can be made from Table 6, showing the results. Firstly, workers in information work were more satisfied than those in communication, the difference being smaller between the groups of younger than those of older workers. Secondly older workers rated information provided to be less sufficient than younger ones did. While the latter difference (age-effect) was only a slight one in the information sector, in communication work, younger workers reported more than twice as often their satisfaction in information delivery, as did the older workers (51.6 % vs. 25 % correspondingly).

Table 6. Difficulties in using IT, N=156 (Means differences)

Competence requirements by use of IT	Means				
	COM-45	COM45+	INFO-45	INFO45+	All
Understanding text with a foreign language	2.84	3.29	2.33	3.03	2.70***
Understanding technical vocabulary	2.81	3.06	2.14	2.47	2.46***
Finding information from manuals	2.77	2.64	2.24	2.45	2.44*
Learning new software	2.25	2.50	2.03	2.55	2.24*
Observing and correcting own mistakes	2.44	2.29	2.15	2.09	2.22
Understanding/remembering functions	2.50	2.53	1.92	2.26	2.19**
Speed demanded by IT	1.97	2.21	1.68	1.91	1.85

Scale used: 1 = Not at all, 2 = A little, 3 = Somewhat, 4 = To a great deal; ANOVA
*$p<.05$, **$p<.01$, ***$p<.001$

Support to learning and adoption of new IT. While overall satisfaction to informing about IT-changes in the workplace was rather high, it was less so concerning the support that had been provided at work to learn and adopt the new technology (Table 7). On average, slightly more than 40 % reported that the support provided has been enough. As Table 6 shows, there were some differences between the four comparison groups, but they were not statistically significant.

Somewhat surprisingly it was the younger workers in the service sector, who were the least satisfied (29 %) and, as we remember from above, who also used the computers least. Most satisfied with the support provided were the older workers in the information sector (56.3 %).

Table 7. *Sufficiency of information about IT-changes and of support provided to learning and adoption of IT (% 'yes'), N=156*

	COM-45	COM45+	INFO-45	INFO45+	Total	χ^2Sig
Enough information provided on IT-changes	51.6	25.0	70.1	67.6	60.8	<.01
Enough support to adoption and learning of new IT	29.0	43.8	44.6	56.3	43.8	ns.

Summary and conclusions

Summary

This article has described how the introduction of IT has been experienced in small and medium-sized companies. The descriptions addressed age and occupational sector effects, so that four groups, comprising of a cross-tabulation of two age groups (-45/45+) and two occupational sectors (services and information), were compared with each other. A summary of the results is shown in Table 8.

Conclusions

This study showed that the extent to which IT was reported to have affected work was rather modest. On average the responds to various aspects of work were 'a little' or 'not at all'. Effects termed to 'a large extent' were typically reported by around 10 %, and maximally by one third of the respondents. If we assume, as suggested in the introduction, that new technology accounts for most of the changes in working life, and that it therefore is also setting the pace for new learning, a conclusion is that the introduction of IT has not resulted in very strong overall demands for new learning and developments in SMEs, at least so far.

Besides some age-differences in the rate of computer use, there were large differences in purpose of use. In the service sector (communication work) the use of computers for communication was very low, whereas in the information sector (office work) it was high. In the service sector in SMEs, direct human communication plays a more important role than managing communication by technology. This underlines that implications for learning in working life are both less and differently technology-driven in various occupational areas. This also suggests that there is an occupational segregation of strengths and weaknesses in competence among workers of different ages.

The results also showed that the introduction of IT in the workplace had not equally increased the options to use one's competence or for self-development. These effects were seldom experienced to a large extent, however, IT had had the most impact on options to use one's competence within information work and there among younger workers, and the least within the service sector and there among the older workers. The impact on options for self-development was found to be the strongest within information work. Age-differences found were the opposite in the two sectors. While in services it was the younger workers who had felt that their options for self-development had increased more than among the older ones, in the information sector the situation was the opposite. Thus, it was the older workers in information work, who had experienced their options for self-development to have improved most with the introduction of IT in the workplace. Further studies are needed to examine whether these findings are a result from differences in nature or the content of the technological competence required in these sectors, or from an age- or career-related (life-long competence development and selection process in labour exit) differences in these options.

Age-effects in IT-experiences were studied both within and across sectors. They were mainly found within the service sector, where also the computer was less used, particularly among younger workers. In the service sector, older workers had experienced IT-effects as strongest and younger workers as weakest. A conclusion is that IT had not offered major challenges for learning and development for younger workers in services in particular. Nevertheless, they had experienced the strongest IT-effects in the workplace climate. Older workers in services used the computer more than their younger counterparts and had experienced strongest impacts among all four groups concerning IT-effects on their work and the work environment. Therefore, their challenges for learning and development in the workplace should have been strong. However, it was the least often among all the four groups in question that they had experienced their options for self-development and competence use to have increased. Within the information sector general age-effects were almost non-existent, but in the area of difficulties in using IT the age-effects were stronger than within services. These findings support the notion that the role of chronological age in managing new technology is different from one occupational sector to another.

Table 8. Summary of the age/worktype comparison concerning IT-effects in SMEs (percentages rounded to integers).

Type of work	Age	
	Below 45 years	45 years and older
Communication (service work)	- *Used computers* the least (70 % not at all, a little or some extent), most importantly to managing and controlling monetary transactions and goods traffic, to finding information and to word processing. -The least of *IT-effects on their work* (least of the 'to a great extent' and most of the 'a little or not at all' responses) - The least IT-effects on *work environment* (29 % little or not at all, 25 % to a large extent) - Reported most often IT-effects on *workplace climate* (60 %) - Were least satisfied with *IT-support* (30 %), though rather satisfied with information about IT-changes in the workplace (52 %)	-*Used computers* quite a lot (63 % to a large extent), mainly for managing and controlling monetary transactions and goods traffic, to finding information and to word processing. - The strongest *IT-effects on their work*: job tasks have become more interesting, challenging, varying, and easier (each about 30 % to a large extent); *except* least often increased options for self-development and competence use (over 50 % a little or not at all) - The strongest IT-effects on the *work environment* (61 % to a large extent) - Rather often (47 %) IT-effects on the *workplace climate* -Least satisfied with *information provided* about IT-changes (25 %) and less than half (44 %) considered *IT-support* as sufficient
Information (office work)	- *Used computers* the most in their work (83 % to a large extent), mainly for communication and word processing, but also to planning. - Least often *IT-effects on their work* to a large extent, but most typically to some extent; more variety in job tasks and increased options for using one's competence and for self-development - Rather strong IT-effects on the *work environment* (48 % to a large extent) - Seldom IT-effects on the *workplace climate* (23 %) - Most often satisfied with *information provided* about changes (70 %), but less with *IT*-support (45 %)	- *Used computers* quite a lot (68.6 % to a great extent), mainly for communication and word processing, but also to planning. - Rather modest *IT-effects on their work*; the strongest as increased options for self-development (24 % to a large extent) and as more challenging jobs (21 % to a large extent) - Rather strong IT-effects on their *work environment* (54 % to a great extent) - Rather often IT-effects on the *workplace climate* (40 %) - Most often satisfied with *IT-support* (56 %) and quite satisfied with information about IT-changes (68 %)

The introduction of IT was found to have effects on the workplace climate. The age-effect was the opposite in the different sectors. While in services, where these effects were generally experienced as strongest, younger workers reported more effects, in information work it was the older workers who did so. The descriptions showed that the experienced climate effects were mainly negative, pointing to confusion, uncertainty and a competitive atmosphere created around IT in the workplace. The results also showed that less than half of the workers were satisfied with the support provided for learning and adoption of new IT, in information work this was somewhat more so. This is less of an impact than was shown in earlier studies (Lehto & Sutela, 1998). On the basis of results in this article a conclusion is that better support to learning of IT in SMEs could play an important role, not only in learning to manage technical skills and thereby in increasing productivity, but also in improving the working climate and overall job-satisfaction. Through the latter the effects can be even wider, since improving the workplace climate has been reported to play a crucial role in making older workers to extend their presence in working life instead of retiring early (Rasku 1993).

Learning to manage new technology is one thing, but to collect, analyse and organise the experiences gained during the transition process more broadly, is likely to have an important effect on learning and on the development of individual and collective competence in the workplace. Such an approach would also enhance the development of learning organisations in a sustainable fashion. It is in this area that adult educators could have a more important role in the workplace than is the case today. Methodologically this approach also challenges most of the current approaches in adult education concerning developing new ways, forms and goals for learning in working life.

References

Agora II – "The tole of the company in lifelong learning". Report of a seminar held 17. – 18.11.1997 in Thessaloniki. CEDEFOP/EC.

Ahola, K. & Huuhtanen, P. (1995). *Ikä ja hyvinvointi työssä*. Kyselytutkimus asennus-, metalli- ja pankkityöstä. Ikääntyvä arvoonsa – työterveyden, työkyvyn ja hyvinvoinnin edistämisohjelman julkaisuja 22. Työterveyslaitos ja Työsuojelurahasto. Helsinki: Nykypaino.

Asplund, R. & Lilja, R. (1999). Teknologinen muutos ja työelämän rakenne. In P. Vartia & P. Ylä-Anttila (Eds.) Teknologia ja työ. Helsinki: Yliopistopaino, pp. 107-130.

Bélanger, P. & Tuijnman, A. 1997. The "silent explosion" of adult learning. In P. Bélanger, P. & A. Tuijnman (Eds.) *New Patterns of adult learning*: A six-country comparative study. Oxford: Pergamon & UNESCO, pp. 1-16.

Corbett, M., Martin, R., Wall, T. & Clegg, C. (1989). *Technological coupling as a predictor of intrinsic job satisfaction: A replication study*. Journal of Organizational Behavior. Vol 10, 91-95.

Employment in Europe 1996. DG for Employment, Industrial Relations and Social Affairs. European Commission.

Gavigan, J. P. (2000). *The learning imperative for Europe's ageing workforce*. http://www.jrc.es/pages/iptsreport/vol38/english/FUT1E386.htm.

Houtcoop, W. & Oosterbeek, H. (1997). Demand and supply of adult education and training. In P. Belanger & A. Tuijnman (Eds.) *New patterns of adult learning*: A six-country comparative study. Oxford: Pergamon & UNESCO, pp. 17-38.

Hukki, K. & Seppälä, P. (1993). *Tietotekniikka, työtehtävät ja ikä*. Kyselytutkimus tietotekniikan käyttöönotosta. Ikääntyvä arvoonsa – työterveyden, työkyvyn ja hyvinvoinnin edistämisohjelman julkaisuja 15. Työterveyslaitos ja Työsuojelurahasto.

Ilmarinen, J. (1999). *Ageing workers in the European Union*. Helsinki: The Finnish Institute of Occupational Health, Ministry of Social and Health Affairs, Ministry of Labour.

Jussila, K., Jääskeläinen, O. & Pitkänen, T. (1999). Ikääntyvät yrityksissä – projekti (Older workers in enterprises -project). Väliraportti 16.12.1999. Vantaan täydennyskoulutuslaitos/Helsingin yliopisto.

Kenni-Lehtonen, T-M. (2000). Työntekijöiden kokemat muutokset työssä uuden informaatioteknologian myötä. Paper presented at the Nordic conference on Adult Education, Forskning i Norden, 25-27.5.2000. Nordens Folkliga Akademi, Göteborg, Sweden.

Korunka, C., Weiss, A., Huemer, K-H. & Karetta, B. (1995). The effect of New Technologies on Job Satisfaction and Psychosomatic Complaints. Applied Psychology: An International Review. 44(2), 123-142.

Lahn, L., Tikkanen, T. Lyng, K. Percy, K., Withnall, A. & Vaherva, T. (1997). *Working Life Changes and Training of Older Workers* (WORKTOW). Unpublished proposal to the EU under the IV Framework programme on TSER.

Lehto, A-M. & Sutela, H. (1998). Tehokas, tehokkaampi, uupunut. Työolotutkimusten tuloksia 1977-1997 (Results from the 1977-1997 Studies on Working Conditions). Labour Market 1998:12. Statistics Finland.

Livingstone, D. W. 2000. Exploring the icebergs of adult learning. Findings from the first Canadian survey of informal learning practices. The Canadian Journal for the Study of Adult Education, (Forthcoming in special milennium issue).

Pitkänen, M. & Nygård, C-H. (1999). Henkilöstön kehittäminen teollisuudessa (Personnel Development in Industry). Raportti Työsuojelurahastolle 15.2.1999.

Rantanen, J. & Lehtinen, S. (1998). Tietoyhteiskunta, terveys ja työ. Publications from Sitra 164. Helsinki.
http://vakka.occuphealth.fi/tietoyhteiskunta/suomi/st21/sitra164.htm

Rasku, A. (1993). Ikääntyvä opettaja – voimavarat ja eläkehakuisuus. Ikääntyvä arvoonsa – työterveyden, työkyvyn ja hyvinvoinnin edistämisohjelman julkaisuja 9. Työterveyslaitos.

Streumer, J. N. & Bjorkquist, D. C. (1998). Moving beyond traditional vocational education and training: Emerging issues. In W. Nijhof & J. Streumer (Eds.) *Key qualifications in work and education.* Klower Academic Publishers. Dordrecht, pp. 249 – 264.

Tikkanen, T. (1998). *Learning and training of older workers. Lifelong learning at the margin.* Studies in Education and Psychology 137. University of Jyväskylä.

Tikkanen, T. & Kujala, S. (2000). Pk-yritysten ikääntyvät työntekijät ja koulutus (Older workers and training in SMEs). In P. Sallila (Ed.) *Oppiminen ja ikääntyminen.* The 41st Yearbook of Adult Education in Finland. Helsinki: BTJ Kirjastopalvelu, pp. 73 – 97.

Tillaart van den, H., Berg van den, S. & Warmedam, J. (1998). *Work and learning in micro-enterprises in the printing industry.* Thessaloniki: CEDEFOP.

Warmerdam, J. & van den Tillaart, H. (1998). Sectoral approach to training. Thessaloniki: CEDEFOP.

Zaminder, M. (1997). Enterprise flexibility and personnel training. Labour Policy Studies 177. Helsinki: Ministry of Labour.

THE LIFE-STORY IN ADULT EDUCATION

Marianne Horsdal

Abstract

In a dynamic society we both have more options and at the same time we are constantly facing new demands and challenges. Life is conceived as an individual project, preferably to be successful, rather than as a common destiny. The postmodern existence is divided into several different contexts, consequently, we do not have the same opportunities for mutual experiences over longer periods of time, as we did before. We have to tell each other about our individual experiences in order to share them. If the individual is to be able to influence his/her everyday-life and actively participate in the development of society, democracy and culture it implies new challenges for adult education towards a stimulation of reflexivity and narrative competencies. Today's focus on the life-story, narrative auto-biography exposes this issue. Through our constantly revised, reflexive interpretation of the past we try to create meaning in life, to find out where we are in order to know where we are going.

The Danish research project "Adult Education and Democracy" is trying to clarify the complex chances in the relationship between adult education, ("folkeoplysning") and democracy in postmodern society. These changes are partly deriving from individualization and globalization. In the Nordic countries adult education, ("folkeoplysning"), has been considered a precondition for democracy, but it is now changing both in character and content. Adult education is increasingly a decisive factor in the development of society, where the concept of lifelong learning is in focus. Also the relationship between the individual and the community is changing.

We have had the conviction that the Danish democracy was deeply rooted in our traditions of enlightenment and adult education, to a great extent founded on articulations of common, cultural narratives, which underlined our common identity and generated citizenship, while the actual development in the field of adult education today rather seems to focus partly on individual skills and competencies, and partly on personal development. If the common process of formation in civil education is declining, what does this mean when considering democracy?

Within this framework my research project concerns an investigation of the present conditions for personal development, identity formation, cultural and political affiliations from the individual's point of view.

Through an analysis of one hundred life-stories collected as narrative interviews, I have investigated the self-interpretations of the Danes, their conceptions of life, and their values, in order to discuss the current attitudes towards adult education, identity, and democracy and the relationship between the individual and the community.

From common destiny to individual choice

It is old news that it seems as if things move faster today than they did a generation ago. Our ancestors probably had the same feeling. The experience of an accelerating dynamic is no less valid for this reason.

For several reasons this experience has been outstanding through the last few decades. The amount of information has grown explosively. Unpredictable events have undermined the confidence in former conceptions of the world. In spite of the scientific efforts of several centuries to achieve rational control, contingency thinking is growing. The differentiation of society reduces clarity. Even in terms of the near future it is difficult to feel that our feet are on solid ground.

These dynamic factors influence our self-conceptions, our identity, and our visions of the world to a great extent, and they also effect adult education.

There have always been two decisive questions to be negotiated and determined in educational contexts:

One, how the uneducated (unlearned) can take part in education (learning), two, what kind of education, information and knowledge it is important to bring about or to gain. This is still being discussed today. The purpose and aim of education and enlightenment: Better opportunities for the individual to be able to cope with life, to participate and to contribute to the common good, is - when expressed in such general terms - by and large the same. But in more concise terms the differences between then and now become obvious, a matter that also characterizes today's debates.

Human life was always stretched between circumstances and will. But also here a lot has changed. Not only have our options increased for most of us throughout this century, but it has become a plight to chose. Life appears to be a personal project - preferably a successful one for the individual - rather than a common destiny. Additional choices imply more risks, as Anthony Giddens (1991) and Ulrich Beck (1992) noted. The consequences of the choices are hard or impossible to predict. To choose is at the same time to cut off, to include is to preclude from other possibilities. The personal responsibility for success or failure is emphasized.

Authorities to rely on do not enjoy the same confidence any more. There are competing experts and prophets on the market, and who can we believe?

Parts of our acquired knowledge become obsolete in a short time. Phrases like "learning for life" and "one never forgets one's earliest lessons" ("at lære for livet" og "hvad man i ungdommen nemmer, man ej i alderdommen glemmer") originate from a time, where the knowledge that was acquired once was useful throughout life. Today we constantly have to gain knowledge of the application of new technological "tools", and we must retrospectively revise former conceptions of the connections and significations of things again and again.

In a dynamic world life-planning is not just a matter of making decisive resolutions at the beginning of adult life, but a continuous project throughout life. "Flexibility" and "adjustment to new conditions" have become keywords, especially in working life. In a world with swift and rapid changes we are first of all challenged with a demand for radical reflexivity.

Consequently, it is insufficient to discuss the distribution of firmly established knowledge to larger groups of the population, "to enlighten the uneducated", in the traditional way known from our history of non-formal adult education, where for instance farmers and workers gained more self-confidence and autonomy through the acquirement of skills and civil education. Considering the urgent need for reflexivity, adult education faces new challenges today.

From a historical perspective we have the point of view that adult education and enlightenment in Denmark during the last 150 years established "destined communities" of different kinds through the thematizing of cultural narratives. One of those was the narrative about national identity, an "imagined community" in terms of Benedict Anderson (1983), with a notion (coming from Herder) of an intimate connection between one people with one language in one area, a narrative that was cultivated by national history, - literature and -songs.[1] The construction of these cultural narratives in the form of school-books, in the curriculum, and the repeated articulations of the narratives in classrooms, created the idea of a common destiny, a common formation of identity. Also among certain classes (e.g. farmers and workers) education provided affiliations and formation of identity through cultural narratives.

The Danes did not always feel Danes. Originally, the identity-forming affiliations were to a great extent founded on the region. People primarily identified themselves with the community they lived in, with the people they actually knew, lived with, and who shared their experiences. However, in the same way as the family narratives and traditions attached us to our ancestors, or to a large religious community, we became attached to our ethnic brothers and sisters through the metaphors of mother country and mother tongue.

The narrative of national identity certainly was not absolute. We have had parallel cultural narratives to bring about identity formation such as the Nordic Community (our Nordic brothers), a European/Occidental refined narrative about literature, classical music and art, the Christian - especially Protestant narratives, and narratives which constructed class-affiliations. After the Second World War, we have seen a distinct American influence, particularly by the new media. However, the national narrative was conceived as a precondition for the affiliation that brought about democratic citizenship.

Right now (March 1999) we witness how the national narrative is disputed and undermined. Poul Nyrup Rasmussen, the Danish Prime Minister, expressed his point of view on TV, defending NATO's bombing in Yougoslavia, that ethnic cleansing was a result of the - now erroneous - idea of a nation being an area that only contains one people with one language.

The cultural narratives which we considered to be fundamental in our adult education, because they make us stick together as a people and a nation, are now under deconstruction. Not only due to the hegemony they represent, but also because of the frequent articulation of the concepts "individualization" and "globalization", and of course, the actual experiences the concepts refer to.

---

[1] Ove K. Petersen (et al.) notice in *Demokratiets lette tilstand*, (1994) that an economic destined community in Denmark is constructed after the Second World War, which implies that "we are all in the same boat".

From earliest childhood our life is divided into many different contexts to an amount we did not know before. We constantly move about from one context to another, and when we occasionally meet our family, friends and relatives, we ask questions like "How are you?" and "What has happened since I saw you last time?" We do not stay together with the same people over very long time spans, we do not obtain extended and continuous experiences with others. We are left alone regarding the task of creating coherence in our lives, which implies that we have to *tell* each other about our experiences in order to be able to share them and to experience a meaningful coherence. We have to articulate our experiences in order to understand one another, to be able to create communities and affiliations to other people.

The degree of fragmentation, differentiation, and mobility that characterizes the present also implies that we often meet new and foreign people with whom we have to communicate and relate, both in vocational life, in leisure time, in private life, and in the areas where we live. We have to function, to cooperate, and to find a mutual understanding with people we do not know, with whom we did not share our experiences, people with a different background from ours.

Participation or marginalization

Quite a few of the people I have interviewed from the generations born before the Second World War complain of an insufficient school attendance and poor possibilities for education. The educational boom from the sixties was meant to create more equality. Democratization through education was on the political agenda as a vision and an aim. 40 years later we are still talking about marginal groups, the demands for qualifications has grown, and education has changed from being a possibility into a global competitive parameter. The ideas of life-long learning - whether the focus is on a continuous development of competencies in order to keep up to the demands of the market, or, on personal development - have resulted in several educational political efforts, which, however, nevertheless are far from attaining the aim of removing the threat of marginalization. Critical voices point out (Bauman,1998), that lifelong learning primarily is an advantage for those who are already educated, and that globalization (and individualization) are for the few, to whom the great world with all the options is open, while more and more people risk being left behind, to stay where they are, powerless, constrained by locality. Pushed to extremes, the information society does not need those without knowledge.

The threat of marginalization has serious consequences: For society, which may be less well off in the international competition, which is in danger of facing increasing social expenses, or will get the considerable problems of A- and B-teams. This will have severe consequences for democracy, and for the individual.

Seen from the individual's point of view, it appears to be harder to keep up, the faster the changes. The impotence of judgement facing the mutually conflicting "experts" makes it easier to passively just to let things pass by, covered by old habits and rituals protesting the changes that you apparently do not have any influence over.

A glance back at the history of adult education shows that it was not just a matter of acquiring vocational skills, but also of becoming self-confident which either followed from the acquired skills and the vocational knowledge as a surplus value, or the contemporary improvement from the humanistic aspects of the curriculum had immense importance. Today we are talking of "empowerment" as a result of learning. This self-confidence is first of all a matter of being able to cope, to satisfy the fundamental needs. Secondly comes the opportunity *to satisfy value-oriented needs*: To accomplish something which is important to us and thus to have a good life. There is a close connection between the possibility of influencing everyday life and active participation in the society, whether on the smaller and nearer or the larger scale.

Giddens (1991) uses the phrase "life politics", a concept he traces back to the feminist slogan of personal politics. In opposition to earlier forms of emancipation politics aiming at liberation from the ties of tradition and the claim for justice, according to Giddens, life politics is a matter of the political questions resulting from the process of self-fulfilment in a post-traditional context. Here, the effects of globalization immerse into the reflexive project of the self, and the other way round, the process of self-fulfilment effects the global strategies.

Life politics deals with the question of "How we should live?" But, in order to put forward the questions of the options and contents of a good life at all, and of what it takes for each of us to accomplish these goals as far as possible, we have to be sure that we mean something to other people, that we have some significance in a wider context.

"The reflexive project of the self" needs an interlocutor. We cannot - such as Giddens proposes - be content as individuals to relate to the systems of experts (Horsdal 1999). Also the politics of individual life styles involves relations. In this connection I find it interesting and potential to look at the definitions of democracy of Hal Kock from 1945. Hal Koch looked at democracy as an interhuman relation based on the will to the good, which ought to apply to all human kinds of relations. Democracy is a form of life to be learnt through education. Democracy is a process, dynamic, and is generated by dialogue. Based on mutual respect and understanding the dialogue will lead to an improving sense of the comprehensive interests instead of a fight between different interests.

It is my conviction that a decisive challenge for adult education involves the strengthening of the contributory influence of the individual on his or her life to oppose marginalization: Partly, by developing the capability of reflexivity, partly by strengthening the dialogue. The advancement of *narrative competencies* unites the two aims.

The life story narrative

In order to know where to go we have to know where we are. In order to know who and where we are, we need a notion of "how we became what we are, and where we are coming from"(Taylor 1989; Horsdal 1999). Giddens (1991) also points out, that a personal identity is found "in the ability to keep a special narrative going".

In a dynamic society, where major changes often shake the visions of the world we had up to now, individual narratives must be revised reflexively, and a new configuration of meaning constructed, when the established so far canonical coherence and configurations of meaning crackle or collapse.[2]

I look at narrativity as a cognitive form, our primary way of making coherence in temporality. When we link events together into a sequence with a beginning and an end, we create a configuration of meaning in retrospect.[3] We borrow and inherit plot models - configurations of meaning - from the cultural narratives, we grow up with. But we have to revise, reflexively, our understanding of coherence, when unpredicted events make the canonical narratives fall apart. The narrative of our past must create meaning in our present situation. Meaning

---

[2] Obviously this is also the case when the individual life seems devoid of meaning and absurd due to a personal crisis.

[3] Temporality, demarkation (beginning and end), selection and configuration (emplotment) are the main characteristics of narrative. A narrative sequence is thus always open for interpretation (negotiation of meaning (Bruner 1990; Horsdal 1999)).

is not a substance or an essence, but a dynamic process, created in a cultural, communicative space. The openness of a narrative - the awareness that a different interpretation and a different configuration of meaning is possible - makes narrative extremely fit for a discussion of values.

It is precisely because life today is conceived as an individual project, the individual narrative that the life story has come into focus. When everything is as usual, we interpret the sense of events automatically without reflecting the act of interpretation, but the moment we are hit by something extraordinary we become aware of the narrative element in our understanding of our experiences, of ourselves and of the world around us. The interest in the life story and the narratives is thus at the same time a *symptom* of the individualization and an *assistance* for the individual to be able to deal with life reflexively, to exchange experiences, to look for meaning in the occurrences of life and thereby find a possibility for orientation towards the future, to be able to choose the "right" options.

The alternative of this kind of reflexivity can be a feeling of powerlessness, of not being able to "keep up" and therefore "opt out" and "get off". Consequently, both self-confidence and autonomy are in danger, and the way opens to loss of meaning and marginalization. You may, of course, criticize the metaphors of movement which underlie the project-oriented and individualized vision of the world, so widespread today. However, we cannot ignore the temporal aspect of life - the incessant shift between genesis and vanishing. And it is important to point out, that life and narrative share temporality as an essential feature.

Even in my own work, the life story narratives have a double-track significance: On the one hand, I use the collected life stories in my research, as a rich material for textual analysis to procure an incredibly fascinating knowledge about actual human identity, human values, and attitudes. On the other hand, the life stories arouse interest far beyond the academic circles among ordinary people, who find sameness and difference in comparison to their own view of life confronted with the narratives of other people's lives. Finally, my occupation with life- story narratives has brought about the assumption, that it is of major significance for adult education to develop narrative competencies and create a cultural space for discussions of values.

Life-stories in research

Life-stories collected as narrative interviews are an extremely rich source of knowledge. In contrast to the traditional sociological methods using quests, questioning guides for the interviews etc. the autobiographical, narrative interview is performed throughout according to the premises of the narrator, regarding selection, content, configuration, and duration. The narrator is simply told to tell the story of his/her life from the beginning and up to the now of enunciation. The interviewer does not interfere in any way until the narrator indicates that the telling is over, for example, by saying: "And here we are today". Later the narrator is asked to affirm the validity of the written interview or make corrections as to assure that the version is acceptable (Horsdal,1999). Whereas in ordinary qualitative investigation we get information about what we as researchers find important the narrative life-story informs us about what is crucial for the narrator when he/she is trying to make sense of his/her life. We get to know about his/her values, his/her priorities, his/her interpretations of himself/herself and the world around him/her. We get information about what is directing his/her intentions and actions. The advantage is evident. We get more than we were looking for. We get new knowledge instead of self-fulfilling prophecies.

Opposed to structural analysis, the narrative methodological approach acknowledges the dynamic aspects of culture and identity, the temporality of life. We always choose to construct the past at a given time in a certain way in order to make sense of our present situation.

A decade's work with life-story narratives nevertheless revealed a very interesting general pattern in our way of telling about our lives. The typical autobiographical narrative constructs a path from context to context, from community to community. The plot of a life-story is rather a configuration of affiliations than of events. The individual is always seen and told in a social context such as family, school, group of friends, work place. Some contexts are chosen, others are not. In some context we feel a sense of belonging, we thrive and function, in others we feel discomfort or distress. This pattern exists independently of the age of the narrator. What has not changed is our need of belonging, rather the stability of the contexts we live in. And consequently we find increasing considerations of individual choice, responsibility, and a shift in function of movement and development towards being an end in itself, necessary for continuous growth, where it used to be regarded as temporary, as a means to the end: the acquisition of the final position for the grown-up individual.

The autobiographical narrative interviews are not empirical data in the usual sense. Life stories are symbolic expressions, narrative texts, interpreted visions and experiences of the "selves" and the world attempting to create a meaningful coherence, where you try to create a meaning in the situation of enunciation through the account of the route you followed from context-to-context to arrive at the place where you are today. Many significant individual life-experiences are narrated in detail and reveal information you did not think of in advance. The liveliness in the narration sharpens your sensitivity and understanding. In the analysis of the life-story narratives the chosen genre, the art of configuration, and the used metaphors are especially interesting.

Life-story narratives in adult education

Time after time, when using life-story narratives in adult education, delivering lectures about them, or reading some of them aloud, I experience how the confrontation with the narration of other people's lives make the participants start either telling about or at least reflecting upon their own lives. A similar mechanism makes people in the ordinary everyday conversation tell in turns, because "it reminds me of" or "it makes me think of this and that", whereby a new incident is narrated. We are obliged to make sense by means of analogies. The problem is abilities, competencies, opportunities, and occasions offered.

Narratives differ a lot, and we are not all of us equally favoured narrators. The narrative which comes close to a reeling off, a mere listing of events, is not particularly interesting. This can also be said of the narrative that too quickly or prematurely comes to its conclusion as well as a too circumstantial account.

Life story narratives come in different genres. Some are tragical victim-stories, others are pastorals, heroic epics, or Bildungsromans. There is an affinity between the genre of the life story narrative and the question of the latitude of the narrative.

What can we express and what has to be kept in silence? How broad and versatile is the vision of the world represented by the narrative? And how does it fit in with the self-conception of the listener and the narrator? Both parties in the dialogue can renounce or repudiate the "unseemly". Both our understanding of others and our self-narratives are influenced by our cultural and social environment. As Anthony Paul Kerby says in *Narrative and the Self* (1991, p. 6):

> *The stories we tell of ourselves are determined not only by how other people narrate us but also by our language and the genres of storytelling inherited from our traditions. Indeed, much of our self-narrating is a matter of becoming conscious of the narratives that we already live with*

and in - for example, our roles in the family and in the broader socio-political arena. It seems true to say that we have already been narrated from a third-person perspective prior to our even gaining the competence for self-narration. Such external narratives will understandably set up expectations and constraints on our personal self-descriptions, and they significantly contribute to the material from which our own narratives are derived.

We must be aware of the constraints of the cultural narratives we carry in the luggage of our traditions, and of the new ones under construction. Simultaneously, the dialogical openness is decisive, our readiness to meet the other and different, to listen and to try to understand. We need to develop our abilities to express ourselves to participate in the communication and to find meaning through articulation. Finally, we need dialogical spaces, arenas for discussions of meaning and values.

This is acutely important to day. Our networks before could be regarded as a set of concentric circles with a relative stability - mainly for the people who were property-owners and well off. To day our identity-formation takes place in multiple contexts, often of an ad hoc character, seldom stabilized of continuous shared experience. For those who feel uncomfortable with changes, the lack of stability produces an anxiety, which tempts the insecure to shut out the world and others in order to keep the illusion of control. A richer narrative understanding is a way towards a wider perspective.

Jerome Bruner is one of the few who studied the development of narrative competencies, but as he states in *The Culture of Education* (1996), none of us know as much as we ought to about how to create and develop narrative competencies. Nevertheless, he points out the importance of knowing the cultural narratives of our traditions, and the significance of stimulating imagination through fiction. Bruner emphasized, that if we want to make use of narrative as a "tool" for meaning, we must work with narratives - read them, create them, analyse them, understand their means, perceive their effects, and discuss them. He asserts the dialogical and reflexive aspects and stresses the importance of going "meta", to think about, how we think.

Albeit, *The Culture of Education* is primarily about children's leaning, but considering adult education it is an incredibly essential task to put human beings in possession of the skills to use the tools for construction of meaning available in their culture in order to be able to master the culture and eventually change it.

Thus, Bruner's proposal for a development of narrative competencies is relevant in connection with adult education. A dialogue about our fundamental values, about our visions of the good life, about the meaning of what is happening, the meaning of our lives, and about our options for action is preconditioned by acquaintance with the multiple cultural narratives which transmits those values and interpretations of existence. A "broad" narrative that integrates the complex circumstances of the present presupposes the imagination developed by fiction because we in the more refined literature meet meaning-extensive analogies, incisive expressions and complex plot models.

Last but not least, working with life-stories in adult education is significant for the development of narrative competencies, fluent articulation, understanding, and reflexivity. So we can develop mutual understanding by sharing the experiences we had apart from each other and create new affiliations. To borrow the expression of Bruner: We must read them, narrate them, analyse them, understand their means, perceive their effects, and discuss them.

References

Anderson, Benedict (1983). *Imagined Communities: Reflection on the Origins and Spread of Nationalism,* London.

Bauman, Zygmunt (1998). *Globalization,* Polity Press, Cambridge,

Beck, Ulrich (1992). *Risk Society,* Sage,

Bruner, Jerome (1990). *Acts of Meaning,* Harvard University Press,

Bruner, Jerome (1996). *The Culture of Education,* Harvard University press,

Giddens, Anthony (1991). *Modernity and Self-identity,* Polity Press, Cambridge,

Horsdal, Marianne (1999). *Livets fortællinger,* Borgen

Koch, Hal (1945/ 1991). *Hvad er demokrati,* Gyldendal,

Petersen ,Ove K. et al. (1994). *Demokratiets lette tilstand,* Spektrum,

Taylor, Charles (1989). *Sources of the Self, The Making of Modern Identity,* Cambridge University Press,

IDENTITIES IN TRANSITION: KEY INTERVIEWS AS A WAY TO ANALYSE THE TRANSFORMATION OF THE PUBLIC SECTOR

Karin Filander

Abstract

This article analyses agent-level transformations in the Finnish public sector on the basis of a single key interview. The article is part of a larger research project that includes 78 interviews conducted in 1991, 1992 and 1997 with 26 professionals living in the midst of a radical transformation of the Finnish public sector. Instead of pursuing generalizations and typical cases I examine individual key interviews for special or deviant cases that violate stereotypical generalizations and socially shared expectations. The interview that I have chosen to analyse here reveals contradictions arising from a shift in the culture of the public sector, where the employees work amid confusing transformations that are changing their traditional identities and the ethos of the field as a whole. I propose to identify and analyse metaphors as self-definitions. Metaphors serve Petra, my chosen key interviewee, as a way to describe her attitude towards the changes by using somewhat more familiar and tangible concepts. Her varying metaphors serve as a tool for analysing my materials as reflecting shifts in definitions of identity.

My aim is to highlight the fact that in research on adult education, change is all too often linked only with the strategic management of change, which does not help us to understand change as a cultural phenomenon or approach it from the point of view of agents. In this kind of system-level analysis, the confusion felt among the basic-level employees is seen largely as resistance to change, something to be overcome. In this article I am not trying to manage change but to understand it in a way that increases opportunities for re-framing the problems involved and makes possible new kinds of action. I suggest in the article that in order to be able to master the changing practices of working life and function in the other arenas where adult people are active, adult educators should construct transitional learning spaces where agents can analyse their life and the various cultural discourses that they use to situate themselves and their actions in a time of uncertainty.

Background

In the 1990s Finnish public-sector employees have been living in the midst of rapid change involving a re-evaluation of values and of administrative and professional activities. While in the past public-sector professionals tried to do their job well and properly, today the question being asked is whether they are doing things that should be done or whether their accustomed functions should be performed at all. It is less and less clear what kind of work is "proper" and what kind of expertise is needed and valued in the public sector. In a period of radical transformation different kinds of justification for action and argumentation structure operate side by side. By drawing on a variety of discourses and grammar public-sector employees define themselves, using traditional administrative or professional discourse, just as devoted public servants or experts use market-oriented discourse as their frame of reference as a kind of neo-entrepreneur or manager.

This state of radical change is marked by the severe economic depression that hit Finnish society at the beginning of this decade, increasing attempts to reassess the basic functions of the welfare state. The situation has also led to multiplied efforts to make the public sector more effective, smaller and more productive than before. These endeavours were linked with the international discussion on the modernization of the public sector, where the stress is on dismantling bureaucratic supervisory structures, improving customer service and individual services, and reorganizing service structures in accordance with the needs of the new information society.

This criticism of the traditional system of supervision has been inspired, for instance, by the market-oriented thinking of the "New Public Management" (Clarke and Newman, 1997). At its most extreme this thinking advocates the privatization of public services, argued to represent the best way to ensure, through market-oriented competition, the increased effectiveness of the public sector and a better quality of services.

From the point of view of the civil servants and professionals themselves this state of change has been a time of confusion and perplexity, characterized by the co-existence of conflicting cultural codes and discourses. While traditionally the public sector has valued reliability, predictability and long-term planning and ethical commitment to and responsibility for the citizen's well-being, in a time of market-oriented development work these self-explanatory values are being called into question. The dedicated and specialized civil servants who previously committed themselves to serve as a kind of professional benefactors (Czarniawska-Joerges, 1994, p. 200; Julkunen, 1997;

Korvajärvi, 1998, p. 78) are now being blamed for bureaucratic waste of public money and for acting in their own interests. They are expected to prioritize services, achieve greater efficiency, make cutbacks, question traditional modes of action, and adopt a new kind of entrepreneurship-oriented way of thinking based on selling one's own skills and on the internal marketing of expertise.

This transformation of the public sector undermines the traditional narratives of continuity and definitions of identity that public-sector employees have constructed for themselves as civil servants and professionals. Identity has usually been understood as a mental structure that creates continuity between the separate actions of an individual or group and integrates them internally (e.g. Erikson, 1983, p. 19), but recently the concept of identity has, as a result of the discussion on the late modern society and post-structuralist approaches in social studies, been subjected to intensive redefinitions (Hall, 1997, p. 2). The concept of a clear-cut and stable identity has been replaced by identity as a shifting and situational feature that must be negotiated case by case. Identity is seen as a socially structured and socially changing subject position, narrative and construction (Czarniawska-Joerges, 1994, p. 203) open to repeated redefinitions. Identities are negotiated using the narrative resources available to individuals and communities within their given social contexts (e.g. Ronkainen, 1999, pp. 73-74). Identities are seen as socially generated modes of self-definition that shift according to the cultural frame adopted by a person, at any given moment, to define themselves.

The market-oriented turn has given rise to a kind of crisis of identity at both the individual and the group level, creating a need to understand the questions involved in agent identity in a new way also in the public sector. The structural foundations of traditional public-sector agent identity, used by civil servants and professionals to justify their actions, are disappearing (Beck, 1995, p. 19; Giddens, 1995, p. 127). Among the social structures used as such frameworks of identity and basic elements of social organization are, for instance, professions, occupations and jobs (Casey, 1995, p. 21); in a state of change the boundaries that they create are seen as obstacles to developing the operations of the public sector. In the late modern society, market-oriented discourse invites civil servants and public-sector professionals to base their identity on entrepreneurial attitudes (Hall, 1997, p. 8), market-oriented cost-benefit thinking, and the subject position of a rationally calculating agent (see Lash, 1995, p. 169).

In this article discourse refers to institutionalized and socially shared discursive practices of a kind that not only reflect an "external" world but actively influence, through their internal conceptual repertoire - mental images, metaphors, storylines and concepts, relevant in the particular discursive practices in which each person is positioned - the way in which things and problems are though about (Davies & Harre, 1990; Aapola, 1999, pp. 67-68). It is also possible to say that discourses create the preconditions for the various shifting subject positions into which people may place themselves (Davies & Harre, 1990). The transformation of the public sector, again, refers to a situation where different kinds of meaning structure operate side by side in the work practices of the public sector, which on the agent level presupposes an ability to endure the uncertainty, unpredictability and confusion inevitably linked with such a situation.

In the last few years adult education research has similarly sought to understand the time of uncertainty linked with changing and unpredictable social reality through the debates on late modern or post-modern society (Usher, 1992; Usher and Edwards, 1994; Edwards and Usher, 1996; 1997, Edwards, 1997; Wildemeersch et al., 1998; Jansen and Wildemeersch, 1998). These debates have been inspired by social scientific research and particularly by those features of a late modern culture outlined by Giddens (1991; 1995) that suggest that the late modern society of uncertainty has lost any distinctive traditions that could serve individuals as foundations for their life.

I will now analyse just such a state of uncertainty and change, where experts like Petra are articulating, simultaneously, both traditional administrative and professional identity definitions, and market-oriented identity definitions where the emphasis is on managerialism and entrepreneurship. My aim is to find out what kind of contradictory self-definitions Petra articulates during her interview and what these definitions tell us about the cultural change taking place in the work practices of the Finnish public sector. My thesis in this article is that the metaphors found in interview texts are indicators of self-definition and are fruitful objects for analyses of agent-level change processes and everyday experiences.

Petra's Interview as a Key and Special Case

I will use a selected key interview to take a closer look at how the market-oriented turn is reflected in agent-level interpretations and explanations of the transformation of the public sector. The grounds on which I have selected this particular key interview are linked with my aim to understand the transformation, at the agent level, as an identity crisis of a kind where people find it difficult to answer such questions as who they are and what kind of objectives and values they promote through their work. A comparative approach and a longitudinal study (Filander, in press) have enabled me to select for analysis, from among 78 interviews, my latest interview with Petra, who has worked for a long time as a public-sector expert. I met Petra during our research team's 18-month training programme, based on the methods of action research and intended to promote the quality of working life and learning opportunities in the work practices of the public sector (Filander, 1996; Kirjonen et al., 1996). Petra was one of the 26 participants, who were interviewed twice during the programme. After the programme I interviewed the participants again in 1997. The present analysis is based on one of these follow-up interviews. Because of the long-term and confidential interaction between the participants and the researchers, it was possible to discuss, during the interviews, even relatively sensitive subjects with some degree of freedom. The interviews functioned as a dynamic ideas-creation occasion, where the interviewee and the interviewer together constructed new knowledge about mutually interesting subjects (Holstein and Gubrium, 1997, p. 117; Kvale, 1996, p. 42).

It was Petra's key interview that revealed most clearly the coexistence of different and mutually contradictory narratives of identity. Such an interview condenses the transformation taking place in public-sector agent identities together with the various cultural codes and arguments available to public-sector professionals in the midst of this transformation. The strategy of the special case (Billig, 1987, p. 141) or deviant case (Potter, 1996, p. 138; see also Juhila and Suoninen, 1999, p. 235) makes it possible to attempt to dismantle stereotyped conceptualizations and cultural codes taken for granted, that are here broken down during a deviant interview.

In her interview Petra violates the general expectation that people should construct themselves a relatively coherent and logical life story. According to Charlotte Linde (1993, pp. 16-17) people reveal themselves to be culturally competent when they construct their life stories on the foundation of a logical chain of causality. Constructing such a logical life story is even a kind of personal and social requirement in situations where people interact on the basis of shared common-sense reasoning. When during the interview, Petra switches to totally different forms of self-definition, she is violating this general expectation of an internally consistent narrative.

Such turning points can be called core episodes (Hyvärinen, 1994, p. 50) or epiphanies (Denzin, 1989, p. 17) that, once told, leave the narrator, who has come up against a radical change or crisis in their life, a different person. In a sense this is a question of a process of seeking and finding one's self where the myths of the self are crystallized in ways that restructure the narrator's life story. Such a core episode may be used as a key that helps a researcher to achieve a fresh reading of the interview as a whole (Hyvärinen, 1994, pp. 143-144; Denzin, 1989, pp. 67-68). In turning points of this kind people start to draw on new types of cultural frame as resources for their self-definition. This does not imply that one kind of self-definition would be better than another: in the present analysis multiple identities are an aspect of a social transformation where single exhaustive stories about stable identities do not exist anymore.

Petra in the Midst of Changes

The narrator is Petra, who has worked nearly twenty years in a Finnish central agency, employed in the administration as an expert and a senior civil servant. According to her own words, Petra's job description has completely changed in the last few years. In the new situation, decentralization and the reorganization of the administrative system have meant fundamental changes in the role of the central administration and in the position of senior administrators. The self-evident continuity of their work has been called into question. Today the continuity of an administrator's work is increasingly dependent on their personal qualities and on their own activities as enterprising consultants marketing their expert services. The foundations of the traditional supervisory and monitoring role of civil servants and the authority linked with such powers have disappeared with changes in supervisory practices involving the increasing devolution of responsibility to the basic level or to the ministries.

Petra's central agency has been done away with, there have been personnel reductions and the remaining people have moved either to the ministry or to the regional administration. From the point of view of Petra, now working in the ministry, and her work unit this means a radical transformation in their duties and position. When I ask her how her work has changed after the training programme, she tells me that her work is completely different and *I have a totally different job now* (97, 1)[1] During the interview Petra describes her old

---

[1] Later passages in italics are direct extracts from the interviews. Petra is a pseudonymous name and the reference following each extract consists of the year in which the interview took place and the page number to the interview transcript. In the longer extracts, which I call episodes, three points (...) indicate a pause , (---) indicates that I have left out some superfluous passage that I do not draw on in my interpretation or some colloquial words, such as "like" as the colloquial equivalent to "such as". Square brackets [ ] indicate that a passage has been replaced by other text in order to preserve the anonymity of the speaker and help the reader to understand the context.

and new job and the various stages, aspirations and actions that have brought her and her colleagues a new role and position. She describes how her old job at the ministry has become *trivial detail knowledge* (97, 3) no longer appreciated by the new management.

The new head of the scaled-down work unit is a political appointee not committed, as Petra sees it, to the task and expertise represented by the previous central agency, while the personnel is still committed to their old expertise. In the midst of the radical transformation the personnel of this particular branch of the administration were obliged to themselves create continuity for their own work across the divide between the old and the new and, in a sense, to survive the processes of change in one way or another. In the new situation, what Petra perceives as the hardest thing is this conflict between the values and attitudes of the new management and those of the personnel, something that she finds difficult to accept.

1. Question: When you think about this your organization around you, what seems to be the hardest thing to you and the others?
2. Well, what has been ... been rather hard is just this that there has been no understanding of the importance of the expertise that we ... our superiors have not understood that Finland needs people who know about these things or else we'll have lower standards [in this sphere of responsibilities]. And er ... (...)
3. that's the hardest thing ... Just this that when you've always been thinking body and soul that [this field] must be developed.
4. You've grown into thinking that it [the field] is important in itself and the personnel ... must not fall ill they must not [suffer any harm]
5. I mean, that's what is, like, important and I'm doing this job because it's important.
6. Then when other values emerge there alongside that you should appreciate as much.
7. For example, this that you're supposed to ensure that the producers are competitive, the other goal in market supervision, well, that's not all that easy to do in practice. (Petra 97, 18)

When the interviewer asks what has been the hardest thing about the reorganization Petra rephrases the question (what has been rather hard). In this way she avoids pointed talk and a situation where she would start to openly complain about her situation. It is not part of the discursive practice of a loyal administrator and public servant to criticize their superiors.

In Passages 3-5 Petra returns again to the interviewer's original question (the hardest thing). At first she speaks as a personally committed and autonomous public-sector professional and expert, manifesting an approach to her job that resembles a vocation (Passage 3: when you've always been thinking body and soul that [this field] must be developed). One's job is something that one takes to heart, something one does because it is important in itself and important to people and the employees. The difficulty in combining the ethos of the public-sector benefactor-professional and values with a managerial slant emerges in Passages 6-7. In her new job Petra, who defends the interests of the citizens and the workforce, is obliged to defend also the interests of the market, market supervision and the producers. The grammatical mood (should) chosen by Petra reveals her attitude towards the new goals of and the value assumptions now supposed to guide the operations of the agency. In practice it is hard to combine these conflicting interests at one and the same time.

Petra as a Flexible and Adaptable Employee

In the next episode, however, alongside the subject positions of a loyal administrator and a welfare-state professional Petra's talk already displays hints of the new subject position defined through managerial discourse. In this context she emphasizes her ability to engage in flexible and wide-ranging activities that differ from the subject position of a public-service professional committed to their job that was put into the foreground in the previous episode. When I ask her how her work unit and she herself have been able to maintain their expert position during the reorganization, her answer reveals a new attitude towards her work and its goals.

1. Interviewer: How about your own, can you speak about survival and coping strategies?
2. I don't know.
3. Interviewer: You don't?
4. Yes, I mean I don't know, well, of course ...
5. I've written something totally dumb there [referring to a pre-filled questionnaire]
6. but what I do think is that the way things are now, if you want to work here then you must have, like, an open mind for new tasks and you must, so to speak, be ready for sudden changes, too.
7. In a way it doesn't, so to speak, pay to insist on that now I'm doing this thing,
8. but instead if something new comes along then that's what you must take up, leaving the other thing aside
9. and wondering if I'll ever return to it. (Petra 97, 18)

In this episode the interactive character of the interview situation affects the way in which Petra now begins to use the cultural frames available to her and how she finally answers the question. She first intended to deny her own survival and coping strategies (Passage 2: I don't know), but the interviewer, asking an additional small question (Passage 3: You don't?), challenges her to respond in another way. Petra hesitates about the frame that she should adopt for her answer (Passages 4-5). She distances herself from her previous way of speaking with the contrasting conjunction "but" and begins a totally different narrative sequence (see also Hyvärinen, 1994, pp. 59-60). With the sentence "but what I do think is that the way things are now, if you want to work here" Petra creates a link with today and the present moment, when people act in a way that was completely different from what was done under the administrative practice of the past.

Petra uses a cliché typical of managerial developmental discourse. One "must have, like, an open mind for new tasks and you must, so to speak, be ready for sudden changes, too". When she states that "in a way it doesn't, so to speak, pay to insist that now I'm doing this thing", she is taking up market-oriented discourse as her frame. Working as a committed welfare-state expert is no longer viable and has no longer any future. Today the activities of the agency are dominated by the new instrumental and short-term rules for administrative action. The last clause (Passage 9) shows the narrator engaged in what may be called grief work. Petra has still difficulties in accepting the short-term rules of market-oriented action.

As one can see from the previous two episodes, the past and the present live side by side in Petra's speech. Sometimes Petra discusses her work from the perspective of the past, sometimes she switches to the present. In the next episodes I shall discuss a situation where Petra is recalling her past work from the perspective of the new discursive practice. Metaphors connected to market-oriented discourse open as if a new window on the experiences of the past, and previous meanings are turned inside out.

Metaphors as a Key to Understanding Radical Transformation

The metaphors that appear in human speech can be considered kinds of preconscious concepts helping people to come to grips with the experience of change, which make it possible to understand the new and strange in terms of something more familiar and concrete. Thus, metaphors articulate an emotional everyday experience otherwise difficult to grasp or verbalise. A metaphor is a vehicle for a feeling, for the "colour" of experience that people may be unable to express in words (Hirschhorn, 1991, p. 122; see also Lakoff and Turner, 1989; Vilkko, 1997, p. 140). The metaphors used in any given situation are linked with the discursive practice through which people are considering their experiences and that they draw on as their resource (Davies and Harre, 1990). They are a kind of experiential and symbolic gestalts employed by people, either consciously or unconsciously, to make sense of their lives (Lakoff & Johnson, 1980). Conscious use of metaphors is frequent in states of change involving attempts to revise norms and values and frames of reference that guide actions hitherto taken for granted. Metaphors are simple and easy to remember. For example, life can be defined as a road or as a battlefield depending on the frame of reference one is using.

A metaphor serves as a selection criterion and a mental filter with two contradictory functions: making the unfamiliar familiar and making the familiar unfamiliar (Lakoff & Johnson, 1980; Aro, 1999, p. 140). A metaphor simultaneously both reveals and conceals (Ronkainen, 1999, p. 218). When using metaphors one may draw on familiar and easily understood everyday imagery that makes it easier to understand and make sense of new things. Metaphors are, however, part of the chosen cultural framework shaping and colouring the given experience. In Petra's interview, as in most of the other interviews that I have conducted, the narrators define themselves through changing metaphors, as is seen in the episodes that I am going to analyse next.

Petra as an Assistant to the Department Head: Right Hand, Left Hand

For Petra, drastic administrative reorganization entails not only giving up a personally important job and a field of duties which is Petra's speciality as an expert and to which she is committed. The reorganization means also opportunities to achieve a new autonomous and independent agent position. The way in which administration routinely generates predictable, stable expert services that are provided for all citizens on the basis of common rules has been compared with machine bureaucracy (Morgan, 1986), where a certain facelessness and impersonality on the part of the personnel makes the reliable functioning of the overall system possible.

The interview with Petra reveals a shift from the position of a faceless and loyal expert civil servant towards a type of expertise that depends on personal competence and on marketing one's own services. As a result of the radical organizational changes, Petra gained an independent position when the administrative hierarchy was flattened. In connection with the reorganization Petra's most immediate superior had to take early retirement, which increased Petra's workload and her scope to influence things. In the next episode Petra analyses how she feels about her new autonomy and responsibility, different from the earlier hierarchical operation of the administration.

1. Interviewer: So what you say is that at that stage you gained a clearly more independent position or this kind of expert position?
2. Yes, that's it, at that stage. I mean, the things that I'm responsible for are, like, my responsibility alone.
3. I mean, I'm not the only one who signs those papers but I present their contents for discussion
4. but the person to whom I present them has no time to go into the matter,
5. so that it's my ... my responsibility and the area that I answer for, that's something that I really answer for
6. and there's no one whom I could pass a part of the blame when I make mistakes or things like that so that
7. was when things changed and actually, if you took a look at it, actually things were already changing in the final stages [of the central agency] a bit in the same direction,
8. I mean I got this independent position. (---)
9. You see, before that the way things were was that we had a bureau chief and a department head,
10. And I answered to the department head and *was his assistant, and his right, left hand.* (Petra, 1997, 5, italics by KF)

Petra repeats the concept of responsibility several times when telling me about her new autonomous position. However, she is quick to specify the limits of her action, returning to speak from the position of traditional administration (Passage 3). An autonomous right to sign official letters is the most clear and manifest symbol of administrative authority. When Petra says that she does not sign those papers alone she admits the limits of her freedom of action when working as an administrative civil servant and professional. But immediately she changes her perspective again, adopting a new kind of discourse (Passage 4). In a way she overcomes the logic of and crosses the limits set by administration. In the present system she alone has actual responsibility for real decisions. In Passages 5 and 6 Petra's discourse about responsibility gains additional emphasis from repetition. Petra is assuring herself and the interviewer that her situation has truly changed. The emphatic repetition of the words "responsibility" and "I" and "my" reveals clearly that Petra is here discussing things that are very important to her.

According to Matti Hyvärinen, repetition is one of the indicators, resembling an alarm signal, of change and crisis that make it possible to identify those core episodes of a narrative that stand for such turning points (Hyvärinen, 1994, p. 60; see also Tannen, 1979, pp. 166-179). Petra has gained an essentially more independent position whose reality even she herself still finds difficult to credit. Repetition and contrasting perspectives are ways of creating distance between oneself and the past. When Petra defines her previous agent position as an assistant to the department head, as serving as his right, left hand, she uses metaphors linked with traditional administrative discourse. She employs them to make it easier to understand the change that has taken place in her position. As an assistant to the department head and serving as his right, left hand she is part of the apparatus of administration, where she is defined mainly in terms of her position relative to the head of her administrative unit.

Petra's self-definition as an "assistant to the department head, his right, left hand" is still that of an expert loyal to the administration. She is part of the administrative machinery where she has a recognized and important position as an assistant to the head of the agency. Administrative discourse emerges also in the discussion about the authority of an administrator who presents matters for decision, continued specifically in terms of the theme of signing papers (Passage 3). The name of the presenter included in the papers is the most clear and visible symbol of authority, valued in the administration as an essential indicator of one's status. The situation seems different when Petra, in the next episode, begins to gradually move towards another kind of discursive practice involving emotionally charged talk. When the interviewer asks her whether she sees her present autonomous position as professional advancement, Petra continues her analysis of the various visible indicators and symbols of power that give her reason to assume so.

1. Yes. I do see it as advancement in the sense that even if I'm no head of office with subordinates
2. I still have this obligation to see to things
3. I mean anyhow (,) there's the money ... money er ... I'm able to influence the way that money is spent and ... and er ... I, like, am responsible for seeing that it is used and all that.
4. Interviewer: Just so, you sit on the money so to speak.
5. Yes, even if my name ... it doesn't in practice mean
6. but ... the funny thing about public administration just now is that it is naturally my superior who signs the papers
7. but he must base his decisions very largely on what his subordinates tell him,

8. that is, what I tell him.
9. I mean, like, if you argue your case well then he'll accept it
10. unless there is something that he has got elsewhere, some other argument and everything goes wrong,
11. I mean, like, not the way I've thought it.
12. Interviewer: But I suppose it is very uncommon?
13. Yes, because he has no time to go into things. How awful, I'm speaking, like, frankly, *it doesn't ... it ... how I feel*. (Petra, 1997, 6; italics by KF)

In Passage 1 Petra makes interesting use of negative sentences and comparison in justifying her affirmative answer. Petra considers that her career has progressed but she is, nevertheless, no head of office with subordinates. A negative sentence relates something that has not taken place. Matti Hyvärinen (1994, p. 59) refers to Labov's (1972, pp. 370-393) and Tannen's (1979, pp. 166-179) observations, in their linguistic analyses, according to which negative sentences reveal much more about a narrator's cognitive structures than positive sentences. Here, too, they reveal the cultural scripts usually associated with career advancement. When Petra mentions the typical symbols of advancement (managerial tasks, subordinates) she associates herself with the usual way of understanding career advancement. At the same time she defines alternative criteria that she uses to position herself. Instead of formal positions Petra starts to speak about real opportunities to exercise power, linked with decisions about how money is used. In Passage 3 the crucial function of money as a criterion of power is emphasized through repetition, additions and false starts. Petra's false starts indicate that the situation is still not quite stable, that the new criteria of power are not yet elements making up a fully established cultural discourse. The same fluidity is evident when the interviewer sums up Petra's new situation with a slight overstatement. Petra briefly shifts her perspective and returns to the official symbols of administrative power, administrative discourse, and a subject position marked by subordination rather than power (Passage 5).

However, this return to administrative discourse proves to be no more than momentary hesitation. Using the word "but" Petra quickly switches back to the new discourse of career and power, where she has authority to act and real scope for influencing the way things are done (Passage 6). At this point, signing papers ceases to be a symbol of exercising power, which it was when Petra was speaking as a loyal administrator. Here her superior appears more as a kind of figurehead whom Petra uses as she likes (Passages 7-8). The way Petra now talks reveals a new kind of self-assertiveness. Not even the concept of "subordinate", part of administrative vocabulary, seems to affect Petra here. But when Petra finally finds herself criticizing the department head for his lack of expert knowledge, she is horrified at herself (Passage 13). The switch to an emotional repertoire is a kind of turning point which leads Petra to new kinds of self-definition. Petra also begins to speak about her past in a completely new way.

Petra as an Office Girl for the Department Head

When, in the next phase of the interview, I ask Petra to describe her career as an expert working in the public administration, she first continues to talk from the perspective of administrative discourse. In a sense Petra returns to a natural cultural frame into which she has grown during her long career as a public servant. Typical of this discourse is an emphasis on the continuity and predictability of action and a gradual acquisition of the traditional administrative modes of action and adoption the identity of a public-sector employee. However, halfway through her narrative Petra goes back to the emotional repertoire she used in the previous episode and begins to define herself anew in a novel manner.

1. If you picture it as going back along the timeline, then at first the way it was that you came as a green beginner to the public administration.
2. You had to learn all those things, how public administration works, then on the other had you had to learn, make yourself familiar with all these machines and the rest and new ones were coming along all the time and you found your own field and so on.
3. Then by and by you began *to feel* that why, I actually know something and so on, but I mean there ... was, like, something ... of course it really took many years ... years before you began *to feel* that why, I actually know something.
4. and er ... uh ... um ... so all the time your expertise grew and all the time your duties became more demanding.
5. Yes, like, *there was this feeling that ... that.*
6. Then, all the time up until, which [year] was it again when things changed and these heads cleared off, up *until that I felt, so to speak, an office girl.* (Petra 97, 6-7, italics by KF)

Petra starts with a harmonious description of her career as an expert, during which she gradually found her own field and place. In Passage 3 she switches, at first as if unintentionally, to the emotional repertoire, which in the previous episode had already hinted at a break or change in her narrative. In Passage 4 she is already clearly wondering how to continue her story. There is an impression here that Petra's mind is elsewhere. In Passage 5 she returns again to feeling (Yes, like, there was this feeling that ... that). Then, in the last passage of the episode, she turns unexpectedly to a completely different discourse and vocabulary and rhetoric (Passage 6). It has no place for the self-pity and making things look better still present in the narrative of career and growth, which is based on administrative discourse. Now she is speaking from within a new kind of frame about past times, which emerge as quite different from her previous description. "Cleared off" already indicates a rather brisk judgement, which then culminates in Petra's definition of herself as an "office girl".

Considering Change: The New Perspective of the Special Case

The various and conflicting metaphors employed by Petra give a very contradictory picture of her position and her long career as an expert in the work practices of the public sector. They are difficult to use as a basis for a coherent life story where there are certain landmark events but that as a whole displays clear continuity as a life story and a narrative of identity (Linde, 1993, p. 56). Such a self-consistent narrative is exemplified by the story initially begun by Petra about how she entered the public administration as a green beginner and started to learn the things linked with her work. However, Petra's harmonious narrative breaks down as she starts to speak about her work and feelings in a completely new way. Now her talk reveals the simultaneous operation of several identities, which violate narrative continuity and reveal her situation in a totally new light (Linde, 1993, p. 101).

When Petra spoke using the vocabulary of administrative and professional discourse she defined herself as an assistant to the department head and his right, left hand. She was a part of the administrative machinery where she had a recognized and important position as an expert and an assistant to the department head , deeply committed to her work and to the objectives and aims of the public sector.

By contrast, when Petra shifts to the managerial frame and assesses her situation in its terms, she reveals a completely different scene. Her work as an assistant to the department head and his right and left hand is now seen as some 20 year of subordination and humiliation, during which the head *ruthlessly exploited people* (97, 7) and took credit for all the fruits of Petra's expertise. Petra was not given credit for her own work as an expert, something that violates the principle of justice as defined by the individualistic frame of reference of managerial discourse. Petra was no more than a kind of office girl who only later achieved a position where she could feel that *I'm something on my own* [when I earlier was only] *something as an extension of the department head (97, 8).*

The metaphor of an office girl sheds light on gendered practices not visible in Petra's previous self-definition of herself as a genderless assistant to the department head who played an important role in the overall operations of the department as the right and left hand of its head. Petra was offering a neutral description of the workings of the administrative hierarchy. She saw her own position as a natural feature of the hierarchy, as part of the way in which administration functions. Sexuality and gender are perspectives and things that Weberian administrative rationality totally excludes from its own cultural frame. They belong to the area of the personal, which fits badly in with the image of a faceless and reliable civil servant (e.g. Witz and Savage, 1992, p. 28). When she defines herself as an office girl, Petra shifts to a completely different discursive practice where the hierarchical structure of the administration is seen as gendered subordination and mental exploitation. The office girl self-definition allows Petra to examine her whole career as a time of subordination and oppression, from which only the recent organizational changes have finally enabled her to free herself. In other words, managerial vocabulary and the metaphors it brings into play enabled Petra to put into words a bitterness impossible to justify or voice in administrative discourse, in Finland marked by a tradition where gender has no place (e.g. Karento, 1999, p. 13).

The analysis made in this article enables us to better understand what the transformation of working life means on the agent level. In the field of adult education a state of change is typically seen as a rather linear and strategically managed and clear-cut change process where people move from an earlier negative situation to a new positive situation. My analysis opens up several perspectives on change. It helps to understand change as contradictory and confusing situations involving a reconstruction of social and cultural reality. In this way it becomes possible to conceptualise everyday experience, originally one of the most central key concepts in the field of adult education research (Usher, 1992, p. 201; Olesen, 1996, p. 65). Everyday experience is here analysed through metaphors, which enable a researcher to create preconditions for new ways of seeing things and for reframing traditional research questions (e.g. Morgan, 1993, p. 285). An examination of agent-level interview materials opens the possibility of approaching change as what may be called a kind of riptide situation, where the past, the present and the future are manifested in the different kinds of discursive practice that people adopt (Filander, in press). Such research can also help people living in the midst of change to better understand themselves and the various alternative avenues of development that emerge when working life enters a state of change.

Looking at the Findings: The Perspective of Adult Education

A lively post-modern debate on the changing, disintegrating and multiplying identities characterizing the present time of uncertainty is going on in the field of international adult education research. At times the debate covers the discipline of adult education as a whole, seen as suffering from a crisis of identity and facing a paradigm shift (Finger et al. 1998, p. 17, Edwards and Usher 1998, p. 27; Collins 1995, p. 71). At times the focus is on the identity crises of the people operating in the field. Adult educators lack shared cultural narratives, an established knowledge base and professional codes that would help them to situate and define themselves (Alheit 1995, p. 153; Edwards and Usher 1996, p. 225). At times the debate on identity crises in adult education is linked with civil society, democracy, and the erosion threatening the public sphere and the new kind of communicative spaces needed to prevent it (Welton 1998, p. 187), and aesthetic communities that create organic solidarity between people (Jansen et al. 1998, p. 237). In Giddens's terms, it could be argued that these debates function as a context where adult educators are searching for a role of their own and a relationship with life politics in a society where various communal ties have weakened, leaving the individual to face the uncertainties of their life more naked and alone than ever (Roos & Hoikkala 1998, pp. 9-10).
This article is an attempt to go beyond these general discussions and undertake an agent-level analysis of the changes of identity taking place in working life. In order to help research on changes in late modern society, my aim has been to develop methodological approaches where cultural, social and political transformations are read through the lens of individual interpretations. The most important feature of my approach is that speech and language are analysed as social action that does not reflect some underlying "objective" reality but that, instead, serves as the medium where the agents' reality is being constructed all the time. People like Petra, living amid drastic change, exist at the intersection of different cultural frames and discourses, drawn on by them as resources for their definitions of professional identity. They often find it difficult or nearly impossible to construct a coherent biography or assess the role that the different change trends and cultural discourses play in their own life.

In such situations of drastic change, if they are to be able to master the shifting practices of working life and function in the other arenas of their life, they need interpretative communities and transitional learning spaces (see Filander 1992;

1996; in press) where they can pull their disintegrating selves together and make sense of their lives, despite events that are constantly changing and are difficult to master. In such interpretative communities they can meet "significant others" who help them to stop and reflect on the rapidly changing situations and look for alternative lines of action. Transitional spaces of learning are intended to support agents' ability to survive, in the midst of various upheavals and breaks in continuity, as functioning people capable of perpetual change who are able to build bridges between the different phases of their discontinuous careers and divergent narratives of identity.

Caught amidst the pressures and tight schedules of various structural changes, the requirement of multiple expertise and the reality of temporary jobs, public-sector agents are, in a time of uncertainty, looking for preconditions for an identity that would enable them to find the resources that they need in order to change and assess and compare different alternative perspectives on the future. The transitional learning spaces represent spaces and communities that make communicative action possible. These are spaces and communities where people negotiate for a shared understanding of how things hang together, where work organizations and society are going, and how agents should consider the changes that are taking place. Such a definition of the task of adult education is one possible response to the identity crises from which the field is suffering at a time when traditional adult education institutions and professionals search for a new place and task in a changing social reality. A definition of this kind allows adult education to retain its critically oriented role as a type of action where space is made for different voices, counternarratives and alternative ways of understanding a state of change. In these deconstructive spaces (see Lather 1994, pp. 123-124) agents can draw on different language codes that open up a world of alternative knowledge. Such spaces enable them to negotiate new meanings and develop new ways of perceiving things. In these contexts, the aim is not to achieve more efficient transfer of information but to help agents to analyse the world that surrounds them.

References

Aapola, S. (1999). *Murrosikä ja sukupuoli. Julkiset ja yksityiset ikämäärittelyt* [Puberty and gender. Public and private age definitions]. Helsinki: SKS.

Aro, J. (1999). *Sosiologia ja kielenkäyttö. Retoriikka, narratiivi, metafora* [Sociology and language use. Rhetoric, narrative, metaphor] (Acta Universitatis Tamperensis 654). Tampere: Tampereen yliopisto.

Alheit, P. (1995). "Patchworkers": Biographical constructions and professional attitudes - Study motivations of adult education students. In P. Alheit, A. Bron-Wojciechowska, E. Brugger, P. Dominicé (Eds.) *The biographical approach in European adult education* (pp. 151-171). Wien: Verband Wiener Volksbildung.

Beck, U. (1995). Politiikan uudelleen keksiminen: kohti refleksiivisen modernisaation teoriaa. In U. Beck, A. Giddens, S. Lash, *Nykyajan jäljillä. Refleksiivinen modernisaatio* (pp. 11-82) (L. Lehto, Trans.). Tampere: Vastapaino. (Original work "Reflexive modernization. Politics, tradition and aesthetics in the modern social order" published in 1994).

Billig, M. (1987). *Arguing and thinking. A rhetorical approach to social psychology*. Cambridge: Cambridge University Press.

Casey, C. (1995). *Work, self and society. After industrialism*. London: Routledge.

Clarke, J. & Newman, J. (1997). *The managerial state. Power, politics and ideology in the remaking of social welfare*. London: Sage.

Collins, M. (1995). Critical commentaries on the role of the adult educator: From self-directed learning to postmodernist sensibilities. In M.R. Welton (Ed.) *In defense of the lifeworld. Critical perspectives on adult learning* (pp. 71-97). New York: State University of New York Press.

Czarniawska-Joerges, B. (1994). Narratives of individual and organizational identities. In S. Deetz (Ed.) *Communication Yearbook/17* (pp. 193-221). Newbury Park, CA: Sage.

Davies, B. & Harre, R. (1990). Positioning: The discursive production of selves. *Journal for the Theory of Social Behaviour 20* (1990): 1, 43-63.

Denzin, N.K. (1989). *Interpretive biography* (Qualitative Research Methods Series, Vol.17). London: Sage.

Edwards, R. & Usher, R. (1996). What stories do I tell now? New times and new narratives for the adult educator. *International Journal of Lifelong Education 15*(3), 216-229.

Edwards, R. & Usher, R. (1997). University adult education in the postmodern moment: Trends and challenges in adult education. *Adult Education Quarterly, 47*(¾), 153-168.

Edwards, R. (1997). *Changing places? Flexibility, lifelong learning and a learning society?* London: Routledge.

Edwards, R. & Usher, R. (1998). Modern field and postmodern moorland: Adult education bound for glory or bound and gagged. In D. Wildemeersch, M. Finger, & T. Jansen (Eds.) *Adult education and social responsibility. Reconciling the irreconcilable?* (pp. 27–56) Frankfurt am Main: Peter Lang.

Erikson E. H. (1983). *Identity. Youth and crisis* (Reprint). London: Faber and Faber.

Filander, K. (1992). Siirtymätila aikuiskoulutuksen itseymmärryksen välineenä [Transitional spaces as a tool for self-understanding in adult education]. *Aikuiskasvatus-lehti 4*, 216-220.

Filander, K. (1996). Agents of change at an uncertain time - Discourse, action, learning. In S. Papaioannou, P. Alheit, J.F. Lauridsen, & H.S. Olesen (Eds.) *Community, education and social change* (Anogia Workbooks Vol 2, pp. 131-159). Roskilde: RUC.

Filander, K. (in press). Experts in uncertainty. A study of changes in ethos and agent identity in the public sector. In K. Weber (Ed.) *Lifelong learning and experience. Papers and presentations of the 1st International Summer School on Lifelong Learning and Experience, Roskilde University, Graduate School in Lifelong Learning, August 1999.* Roskilde: Roskilde University Press.

Finger, M., Jansen, T. & Wildemeersch, D. (1998). Reconciling the irreconcilable? Adult and continuing education between personal development, corporate concerns and public responsibility. In In D. Wildemeersch, M. Finger & T. Jansen (Eds.) *Adult education and social responsibility. Reconciling the irreconcilable?* (pp. 27–56) Frankfurt am Main: Peter Lang.

Giddens A. (1991). *Modernity and self-identity. Self and society in the late modern age.* Cornwall: Polity Press.

Giddens, A. (1995). Elämää jälkitraditionaalisessa yhteiskunnassa. In U. Beck, A. Giddens, S. Lash, *Nykyajan jäljillä. Refleksiivinen modernisaatio* (pp. 83-152) (L. Lehto, Trans.). Tampere: Vastapaino. (Original work "Reflexive modernization. Politics, tradition and aesthetics in the modern social order" published in 1994).

Hall, S. (1997). Introduction: Who needs "identity"? In S. Hall, & P. du Gay (Eds.) *Questions of cultural identity* (pp. 1-17). London: Sage.

Hirschhorn, L. (1991). Organizing feelings toward authority: A case study of reflection-in-action. In D. A. Schön (Ed.) *The reflective turn. Case studies in and on educational practice* (pp. 11-163). New York: Teachers College Press.

Holstein, J.A. & Gubrium, J.F. (1997). Active interviewing. In D. Silverman (Ed.), *Qualitative research. Theory, method and practice* (pp. 113-129). London: Sage.

Hyvärinen, M. (1994). *Viimeiset taistot* [The last battles]. Tampere: Vastapaino.

Jansen, T., Finger, M. & Wildemeersch, D. (1998). Reframing reflectivity in view of adult education for social responsibility. In D. Wildemeersch, M. Finger & T. Jansen (Eds.) *Adult education and social responsibility. Reconciling the irreconcilable?* (pp. 237–248) Frankfurt am Main: Peter Lang.

Jansen, T. & Wieldemeersch, D. (1998). Beyond the myth of self-actualization: Reinventing the community perspective of adult education. *Adult Education Quarterly* 48(4), 216-226.

Juhila, K & Suoninen, E. (1999). Kymmenen kysymystä diskurssianalyysistä [Ten questions about discourse analysis]. In A. Jokinen, K. Juhila & E. Suoninen (Eds.) *Diskurssianalyysi liikkeessä* [Discourse analysis on the move] (pp. 233-264). Tampere: Vastapaino.

Julkunen, R. (1997). Työyhteiskunnan tulevaisuus - tosiasiat, projektit ja optiot [The future of labour society - facts, projects and options]. In Julkunen, R. et al., *Kuusi esseetä työn ja työyhteiskunnan tulevaisuudesta. Valtioneuvoston tulevaisuusselonteko eduskunnalle. Osa II. Oheisjulkaisu 1* [Six essays on the future of work and labour society. The Council of State Report on the Future to the Parliament. Volume II. Supplementary publication 2) (Valtioneuvoston kanslian julkaisusarja 1997/5). Helsinki: Prime Minister's Office.

Karento, H. (1999). *"Olen tehnyt parhaani". Tutkimus naisista valtion ja kuntien johtajina ja vaativissa asiantuntijatehtävissä* ["I have done my best". A study of women as senior civil servants and municipal managers and in senior expert positions] (Acta Universitatis Tamperensis 718). Tampere: Tampereen yliopisto.

Kirjonen J., Heiskanen T., Filander K. & Hämäläinen A. (1996). *Tila ajattelulle. Asiantuntijatyön kehykset julkisella sektorilla* [Space for thinking. Frames of expert work in the public sector]. Jyväskylä: Institute for Educational Research, University of Jyväskylä.

Korvajärvi, P. (1998). *Gendering dynamics in white-collar work organizations* (Acta Universitatis Tamperensis 600). Tampere: University of Tampere.

Kvale, S. (1996). *InterViews. An introduction to qualitative research interviewing*. London: Sage.

Labov, W. (1972). *Language in the inner city. Studies in the Black English vernacular*. Philadelphia: University of Pennsylvania Press.

Lakoff, G. & Johnson, M. (1980). *Metaphors we live by*. Chicago and London: University of Chicago Press.

Lakoff, G. & Turner, M. (1989). *More than cool reason: A field guide to poetic metaphor*. Chicago and London: University of Chicago Press.

Lash, S. (1995). Refleksiivisyys ja sen vastinparit: Rakenne, estetiikka, yhteisö. In U. Beck, A. Giddens, & S. Lash, *Nykyajan jäljillä. Refleksiivinen modernisaatio* (pp. 153-235) (L. Lehto, Trans.). Tampere: Vastapaino. (Original work "Reflexive modernization: Politics, tradition and aesthetics in the modern social order" published in 1994).

Lather, P. (1994). Staying Dumb? Feminist Research and Pedagogy with/in the Postmodern. In H.W. Simons, & M. Billig (eds.) *After Postmodernism. Reconstructing Ideology Critique.* (pp.101-132) London: Sage.

Linde, C. (1993). *Life stories. The creation of coherence.* New York: Oxford University Press.

Morgan, G. (1986). *Images of organization.* Beverly Hills, CA: Sage.

Morgan, G. (1993). *Imaginization. The art of creative management.* London: Sage.

Olesen, H.S. (1996). Experience, life history and biography. In H.S. Olesen & P. Rasmussen (Eds.) *Theoretical issues in adult education. Danish research and experiences* (pp. 65-86). Roskilde: Roskilde University Press.

Usher, R. (1992). Experience in adult education: A post-modern critique. *Journal of Philosophy of Education. Vol. 26*, No. 2., 201-214.

Usher, R. & Edwards, R. (1994). *Postmodernism and education.* London: Routledge.

Potter, J. (1996). Discourse analysis and constructionist approaches: Theoretical backround. In J.T.E. Richardson (Ed.), *Handbook of qualitative research methods for psychology and the social sciences* (pp. 125-140). Leicester: British Psychological Society.

Ronkainen, S. (1999). *Ajan ja paikan merkitsemät. Subjektiviteetti, tieto ja toimijuus* [Marked by time and place. Subjectivity, knowledge and agency]. Helsinki: Gaudeamus.

Roos, J.P. & Hoikkala, T. (1998). Esipuhe [Preface]. In J.P. Roos & T. Hoikkala (Eds.) *Elämänpolitiikka* [Life politics] (pp. 7-19). Tampere: Gaudeamus.

Tannen, D. (1979). What's in a frame? In R.O. Freedle, (Ed.) *New directions in discourse processing* (pp. 137-181). Norwood, New Jersey: Ablex.

Vilkko, A. (1997). *Omaelämäkerta kohtaamispaikkana. Naisen elämän kerronta ja luenta* [Autobiography as a meeting place. Narrating and reading women's lives] (Suomalaisen Kirjallisuuden Seuran toimituksia 663). Helsinki: SKS.

Welton, M.R. (1998). Civil society as theory and project: Adult education and the renewal of global citizenship. In D. Wildemeersch, M. Finger, & T. Jansen (Eds.) *Adult education and social responsibility. Reconciling the irreconcilable?* (pp. 187-219) Frankfurt am Main: Peter Lang.

Wildemeersch, D., Finger, M. & Jansen, T. (Eds.). (1998). *Adult education and social responsibility. Reconciling the irreconcilable?* Frankfurt am Main: Peter Lang.

Witz, A. & Savage, M. (1992). The gender of organizations. In M. Savage & A. Witz (Eds.) *Gender and bureaucracy* (pp. 3-62). Oxford: Blackwell

AUTONOMY AND COMMUNALITY IN SELF-DIRECTED OPEN LEARNING

Leena Ahteenmäki-Pelkonen

Abstract

Self-directed learning is often connected with open learning. This kind of learning environment both demands and facilitates self-directed learning. But does the lack of face-to-face contact automatically inspire the student's self-directedness? How do the students themselves experience this learning environment? In my research, these issues are based on the research material consisting of 65 essays written by students of adult education in the basic part of the degree programme (15 study weeks) at the Open University. Self-directed learning is understood as a main concept consisting of four categories: autonomy, communality, critical reflection, and integration to reality. In this article the relationship between autonomy and communality is discussed. The essays reveal forms of self-directed learning that can be called self-study and self-direction. Both forms are very individual - the turning point seems to be the nature of the dialogue: does it lead to more individualistic utilization of others as learning resources or to communality in which dialogue and solidarity are combined?

Introduction

Self-directed learning is one of the most essential goals of adult education. However, it is a very complex and fuzzy concept. This confusion on the conceptual level also causes confusion on the practical level: when we are talking about self-directed learning, to which phenomenon do we actually refer? These facts and questions were the starting points of my research.

Self-directed learning is often closely connected to distance teaching and open learning. Distance teaching demands self-directed learning, at least the learners' ability to learn independently (Moore 1983). My interest is to develop a better understanding of how the students themselves experience the possibilities and realities of self-directed learning within distance education. I have asked 65 distance students to write an essay about this theme. These students study adult education at the Open University in the basic degree programme, this course is 15 study weeks. Their essays have at the same time formed their distant assignments, and they have been used for research purposes with the students' permission.

The structure of these essays has been the conceptualization of self-directed learning which were developed with grounded theory and methodology from the definitions of self-directed learning (Ahteenmäki-Pelkonen 1992). According to this structure, the concept "self-directed learning" consists of four main categories whose subconcepts are mentioned in brackets: autonomy (self-initiative learning, emotional independence, authenticity), communality (solidarity, dialogue), consciousness (reflection, commitment), and integration to reality (reflected adjustment, intentionality). This structure was introduced in an article "Objektista subjektiksi" [From object to subject] that was part of the course material.

The essays are one part of the course "Didactics in adult education" (two study weeks). During this course students had face-to-face contact in lessons (10-20 hours), tutoring and independent learning by designing their learning assignments. The instruction for the essay contained two tasks:

1. Evaluate how your self-directedness (defined according to the categories and concepts in the article) has been fulfilled during your studies in adult education.
2. Evaluate how the main categories (autonomy, communality, consciousness, and integration to reality) have been emphasized in your studies of adult education.

Most students completed this learning assignment in the middle of their 15 study weeks. So they did not have experience of the whole course, but they already knew the structure of the system very well and their own way of learning and working in this context. It must also be mentioned that I had been their teacher in many courses in their degree, so the evaluation also concerned my work as a teacher. They were, however, used to critically discussing many kinds of issues, which they also mentioned in their essays, so there is no reason to presuppose that my role as their teacher can have overly influenced their essays.

This article concentrates on two first categories, autonomy and communality, and the relationship between them. My aim is to understand more deeply how the individual and common aspects of self-directedness are linked. The method of the analysis has been qualitative, deductive content analysis. The results of the analysis are outlined in this article and are illustrated with direct quotations from the research material.

Autonomy

Self-initiative learning

The first concept, self-initiative learning, has its roots in two classic or traditional views of adult learning. According to Allen Tough, about 80 % of adult learning is mostly planned by the learners themselves. Learning processes (or learning projects, as Tough calls them) take place in the natural contexts and life situations of the adults, like in moving to new surroundings, starting a new job, divorcing or having a baby. In these situations adult learners use different kinds of human or material help, but the learners have the main responsibility for the learning process. Only about 20 % of adult learning takes place in educational institutions in which most of the learning process is designed by teachers or other professional helpers (Tough 1979, 1982.).

Tough's results from the 1960s and 1970s are clearly not out-of-date. Informal learning, learning by experience, and activating tacit knowledge are very usual ways for adults to learn nowadays. One must also remember that Tough's findings were obtained at a time before the Internet or other possibilities that high technology has opened to self-help in learning. Now you can reach professionals from your own home, and the resources for planning and implementing learning without the teacher's presence or control are much richer than previously.

The other source for the concept of self-initiative learning is Knowles' well-known definition of self-directed learning: "In its broadest meaning, 'self-directed learning' describes a process in which individuals take the initiative, with or without the help of others, in diagnosing their learning needs, formulating learning goals, identifying human and material resources for learning, choosing and implementing appropriate learning strategies, and evaluating learning outcomes" (Knowles 1975, 18). According to Knowles, self-initiative learning is the most essential point of self-directed learning. From his definitions of teacher-directed and self-directed learning you can also conclude that the adult learner should be very active and take the initiative especially in the planning and evaluating process in order to direct the learning according to his/her own interests and needs (Knowles 1975, 1980).

Many factors in distance teaching, especially in the open university are settled and made ready on behalf of the students: the aims, main contents and materials are determined in the degree requirements of the faculty. In these settings the teacher has the autonomy to emphasize the aims and the contents in his/her personal way, because of the freedom of academic teaching. This freedom is realized for example in the design of the learning assignments. It would seem that there are not many opportunities for the student to participate in the planning process. Perhaps this is the case, but students can still see their possibilities to influence in this situation. Most students think that self-initiative learning is not impossible but rather restricted:

> *"There is a lot of space to have one's own learning style **within** the ready-made frames of education."*

There can also be impediments that come from traditional attitudes, so that it is difficult to take self-initiative in the evaluation of one's own learning process. The final reason for not taking personal responsibility can just be the habit to study in the situation in which the teacher traditionally has taken care of all phases of the learning process:

> *"Evaluation is often seen as the task of the teacher. It is easy to be content with the evaluation made by the teacher, and trust their expertise. And when this kind of evaluation happens continuously, one easily gets used to it. It would be an extra struggle to question and criticize the teacher's evaluation."*

There seems to be both external and internal impediments to self-initiative learning. The open university system contains many demands and requirements. The student's self-initiative learning must be in the framework of these ready-made plans. Currently, studying for adult education degrees begins by making an individual curriculum. The students are helped to clarify their own interests and needs which then can be emphasized in their studies. The students are also encouraged to conduct self-evaluation in the different stages.

Emotional independence

Emotional independence as a part of autonomous learning comes from Moore's (1983) idea, and means that the student does not seek acceptance or approval from other persons. They are studying for their own sake, not for fulfilling other people's expectations. The student's value as a human does not depend on success in learning and on other people's judgements. The distance education situation limits the student's possibilities to get feedback from the teacher and peers. Because of indirect communication the education process is different from the traditional face-to-face situation, and the teacher also has to rethink the planning process.

In this type of learning situation the important people are the teacher, other students, parents, spouses, children, and neighbours - perhaps the significant others in one's near surroundings can influence the open learning situation more than in the traditional learning situation since the learning process happens in the midst of everyday life. So encouraging comments by one's wife or husband, as well as the envy of the neighbours can be very motivating - and even necessary if the student has not internal motivation to the learning process.

However, this does not seem to be the case. On the contrary, the students show clear emotional independence, but for many different reasons:

> *"Students' interaction concerning the learning assignments has been very open: there have been many kind of opinions and conceptions, and all have been accepted. The teacher has created an atmosphere of mutual respect and encouraged us to see different aspects of the issue. So everyone's conceptions and opinions have been justified in some way and this has reduced the stress to seek approval for your own conceptions."*

> *"In distance education, you don't get so much help for preparing the learning assignments that you would become emotionally dependent on the teacher or other students!"*

> *"At the beginning of the studies, other people were just a mass without faces and I really longed to know them - in spite of the danger of becoming emotionally dependent on them! Later during the studies it was easier to enter into the learning situations not knowing anyone. Then I knew that it is just my own, internal motivation that makes me study and gives me the confidence I need in different learning situations."*

In the interpretation of these answers, one must still bear in mind that being emotionally independent is more socially acceptable than the opposite. This difference in attitudes and values has perhaps influenced the students' answers. If this speculation is right, then one must examine the students' emotional independence still once more, from another perspective. We must also remember that the emotions involved in the learning process and especially in learning interactions have not scarcely been researched, so we do not have many concepts or terms with which to discuss them.

Authenticity

The third subconcept of autonomy is called "authenticity". It is not easy to express the meaning of this concept by one word. The original idea comes from the Nottingham Andragogy Group which consisted of experts in social work, human relations and group dynamics, who defined andragogy as an approach "aimed at enabling people to become aware that they should be the originators of their own thinking and feeling" (The Nottingham Andragogy Group 1983, 2). This definition emphasizes the adult's capacity to be conscious of his/her own thinking and feeling and to express these in his/her own way.

This idea of the originator-idea is identified here with the term "authenticity". It refers to free self-expression and creativeness in the learning process. The authentic self-directed learner does not want to imitate anyone or prepare his/her learning assignments according to some model. The self-directed learner uses his/her own thinking and feeling generatively, and sees their connections with the subjects or theories of the learning process.

The analysis of the first concept, self-initiative learning, showed us that in the degree studies at the Open University there is not much space for self-initiative in planning or evaluating the learning process. But what about the authenticity of the student's self-expression? The students comment on it in this way:

> *"The learning assignments are not too strictly formulated, so everyone can construct the answer in his/her own way. Especially in adult education where the students come with different experiences, for instance from different occupations, they see the same issues in quite different ways. Then the students learn very much from each other."*

> *"To work with a good learning assignment is a creative learning process where you do not have to follow the contents of some book, but where you can combine the subject with your own experiences. When the answers are various, original and individual, the learning assignment has fulfilled its task and the teacher can be content with it."*

> *"I started to study after a long break in my 40s and, partly because of these studies, partly because of my ageing and maturation, I have begun to 'use my own voice' even in everyday situations - by analysing, criticizing, questioning and by looking for different solutions - by being myself."*

In most essays, authenticity is combined with the concrete learning situation and especially with the learning assignments. It is easy to understand this connection, because the learning assignments especially leave space for the learner's self-expression in this formal education. They mostly demand some kind of application in which the student must combine theory and practice, theory and experience. The connection of authenticity and ageing in the last quote is very interesting and would call for further research about the transfer of learning across different contexts.

Communality

Solidarity

In this connection, solidarity means a sense of jointness. It is commitment to mutual learning, both emotionally and in action. It can be seen as cooperation when preparing learning assignments. Solidarity also finds expression as mutual support when experiencing different learning difficulties, e.g. lack of motivation, disappointments in learning (Ahteenmäki-Pelkonen 1992, 44).

The students did not see solidarity as an essential feature of their studies. Partly it depends on the few face-to-face contacts, partly of their own lack of interest. There was a possibility of participating in a study circle, guided by a tutor, but only a few students were present. Adult learners have other commitments which demand their time and motivation: work life, family, other studies and hobbies. The students write:

> *"I think that solidarity is not very essential in these studies. I also attend other studies elsewhere and they demand my commitment. Because there are not so many face-to-face learning situations, the students become estranged from each other."*

> *"In a face-to-face situation you can sense the solidarity: we belong to the same group, but outside of these situations we are not dependent on each other."*

> *"I have felt solidarity in the study circles. We have supported and encouraged each other, and studied the materials together. The feeling has been warm: we share the same situation. In groups we have had a common task to which everyone has been committed. We have felt solidarity also in mutual phone calls, which can be very motivating and help you through difficulties."*

The social form of studies seems to be very important to the feeling of solidarity. In informal study circles, it is possible to feel strong solidarity and a sense of jointness. Still there are many students who do not participate in study circles because of their other duties, and so the lessons become the only face-to-face contact with other students. The solidarity can also grow also during lessons, especially in group tasks, but it is often forgotten as soon as the lesson is over. The solidarity of the study circle is informal, and therefore it can perhaps continue in other informal contacts.

The essays very clearly reveal that the students were not used to having contact by e-mail or that they were not familiar with the Internet. By using these methods it would have been possible to work together and also have contacts outside the lessons. However, the solidarity does not seems to be an important concept in these studies. The term "solidarity" is not easy to define, and it also has political connotations which can make people cautious in expressing it. It can also be difficult to draw a borderline between solidarity and emotional dependence. Altogether, the students do not seem to even miss the feeling of solidarity because the studies are only one part of their lives and they find their own reference groups elsewhere.

Dialogue

The concept "dialogue" comes from the ideas of Paulo Freire, Malcolm Knowles and Jack Mezirow. Each of them has contributed to this concept in his own way. For Knowles, a dialogue is a learning resource, which helps the student reflect on his/her own ideas in comparison to those of others and thus get new information, ideas and visions. Participating in a dialogue is also an area of self-expression: one must appreciate his/her own knowledge and experiences in order to share them with others (Knowles 1975, 1980). According to Freire, dialogue is a common process in which the teacher and learners orientate to the subject, which is not only an academic subject but also an expression of the prevailing reality. Mutual respect and reciprocity are the essential elements in the interaction of dialogue. The opposite of dialogue is antidialogue which is based on oppression and the silence of the oppressed (Freire 1972, 1985). To Mezirow, a dialogue is a means to self-reflective, transformative learning which can foster transformation of one's personal frame of reference, i.e. meaning perspective (Mezirow 1981, 1991, 1997).

> *"In the examination the teacher often expects one right answer which the student should know. In a way this is natural, because the examination can be seen as a control of quality in learning and therefore the criteria*

must be commensurable. However, it is often possible to express one's own, well-argumented opinions and conceptions, too."

"There has been a possibility for an open dialogue all the time during these studies. In my thoughts I participate very eagerly in the debates, but in practice I used to listen to others and their ideas. In that way I have learned very much. I am wondering if I really appreciate my own knowledge and resources enough to share them with others. Maybe I do, maybe not."

"Often only a few students participate in the dialogue and others mostly listen to them. This is of course against the aim, but if you are not quick-witted and feel a little unsure about how to express your idea, then you willingly stand aside and are silent. Consequently, minimal learning occurs."

The essays clearly show that the role of an active, participating adult learner can easily be recognized in the expectations of the teachers and the whole system. A good adult learner is always ready to discuss whatever issue and see it from various perspectives. Contrary to Freire, the prevailing situation is not "the culture of silence", but "the culture of talking". As long as the group discussions are the most usual way to activate adult students, we are captured in the culture of talking and at the same time leave many other aspects of learning aside. Brookfield (1986) has criticized the research of self-directed learning of being limited to middle-class, educated white men - a position and role which are very familiar to the researcher himself. This critique is no longer totally true. But we can ask if the role expectations for the adult learner are as one-sided and supply only one role model, i.e. the role most familiar to the teacher?

Adult education is a very generative subject in starting an open-ended dialogue. Many essential concepts - like self-directed learning - are defined in various ways, and it is easy to begin an open discussion on them. However, the teacher should also pay attention to the argumentation that is used in the dialogue. When the concepts and issues are fuzzy, it is easy to limit the discussion only to opinions and experiences.

Conclusions

The essays draw a picture of a busy student who works very much by himself/herself, attends lessons and participates in dialogues during them, is willing to learn both from the teacher and from peers, but who is not very committed to cooperation or emotional ties with other learners. One can clearly notice their self-directedness, but also its limitations.

Many students show self-directedness that could be called **self-study**. They are able to work independently on their distant assignments and prepare themselves for their examinations. In this case, the students focus on the external framework of distance education to the extent to which they need advice or have particular demands. Aside from that, students try to fulfil their role by studying independently and conscientiously according to the demands. Working with this attitude can depend on, for example, the lack of time or their unwillingness to do more than is demanded. This may also reflect a sort of obedience to institutions and the authorities. In a way, it is a very natural attitude in formal learning settings.

Self-study is not the only form of self-directedness that the essays reveal. The students have their own interests and ideas concerning all of their studies and especially the subject matter. At least some of them are conscious of their own aims and follow this polestar during their studies, relating the tasks and the contents to this idea. These students form their own attitudes towards the ready-made factors in learning, and in doing so evaluate their relevance according their own aims and intentions. In this way, they also participate in the planning and evaluation process, but this is often silent work in private, and the teacher or other students do not know of this process. This kind of learning is called **self-direction**.

There are no serious problems in students' autonomy, which many mention as the most important category of self-directedness. "Self-study" and "self-direction" are realized in their studies, at least after some guidance. But do we see self-directed and very individualistic students who advance their studies and even their inner learning on the basis of their own interests and intentions? How do these students use their knowledge in cooperative common learning situations, such as these demanded in worklife and learning organizations?

The dialogues seem to be fragmentary, and the students have not internalized the idea of dialogue as a common orientation to reality. Perhaps the learning assignments or face-to-face contacts do not emphasize this aspect enough. Or how do the teachers and tutors see the function of studies and the essence of the learning process? Is their sincere purpose to help every individual to be successful in his/her studies and learn as much or as deeply as possible? Is the learning group the only possible way for them to handle many students at the same time? Does the learning group mean more for the teacher or for the students? Is it also a tool for learning, and more than a tool, a context providing cooperation and common tasks like many others in the society?

Surprisingly, the concept "dialogue" seems to be very important in self-directed learning. The conception of self-directed learning as independent, solid learning has mostly been repelled. For instance, Knowles uses the term "self-directing interdependence" which I have argued as one of the most generative in the idea of self-directed learning (Knowles 1975, 1980; Ahteenmäki-Pelkonen 1994). This combination of the individual and the social aspects of self-directed learning forms a genuine dialogue in which there is space for every individual and in which the learning results are based on cooperation and on the sense of jointness.

The dialogue is also the turning point: do the learners retreat into their inner worlds, even to self-reflection, or do they open themselves to their surroundings? Mezirow claims: "One must look to the nature of interpersonal communication of the theoretical assumptions and educational implications of self-directed learning" (Mezirow 1985, 142).

The nature and meaning of dialogue has changed with today's technology. One must learn to read and interpret different kinds of signs and symbols in order to understand the message. This situation creates new demands and new possibilities for the dialogue between the learner and the material, and between the learner and other learners (Walthers 1996; Tella and Mononen-Aaltonen 1998). In reality, how open are our learning environments?

In my design, communality consists of two concepts: dialogue and solidarity. Dialogue can be mutual, but it can also be used as a learning recourse by listening to others' experiences and conceptions without giving anything of oneself. The latter form of interaction is not dialogue because it lacks reciprocity. One student expresses his/her knowledge and experience perhaps in a very authentic way, and the other makes use of them for his/her own learning process. In this case the dialogues are one-sided resources for learning, but they are not genuine dialogues, for they are not common enterprises in understanding the reality and its representative, i.e. the subject matter to be studied.

It seems that both dialogue and solidarity belong together very closely. What is the nature of a dialogue without solidarity? Can there be solidarity without dialogue? The essays reveal that there is not much solidarity among the students and they do not miss it either. The dialogues - when they occur - are during the lessons and function as learning resources, and the jointness that is perhaps felt in them is mainly forgotten after the lesson. So the role of peers in the learning process becomes an important question which should be researched more in different learning contexts.

It would be comfortable to dismiss the category of communality and be content with the students' abilities for self-study and self-direction. However, it is not possible, because the surrounding society and its demands force us to face the question of common responsibility and the learning situation cannot live in isolation outside of society. What is learnt should be meaningful and relevant in different contexts. The learning situation is a mirror of society, a micro-system where you can see the regularities and norms of the macro-system in a more concrete way.

As a mirror of the prevailing circumstances, the learning situation is also a possibility to analyse and understand them and to seek alternatives to the prevailing situation. Critical theory has especially emphasized this intention. In his critical view of self-directed learning, Mezirow sees the **communicative action** as the essence of adult learning. Mezirow uses Habermas' term "communicative action" to mean a critical discourse in which equal participants analyse their norms and conceptions, seek alternatives to them and research the arguments that legitimate them (Mezirow 1991, 1997; see also Ahteenmäki-Pelkonen 1997). Mezirow sees the meaning of discourse and education:

> *"... education may be defined as the process of fostering the deliberate effort to extend one's ability to make explicit and elaborate, contextualize, validate and/or perform upon some aspect of one's engagement with the world. [...] In discourse, we suspend our a priori judgement about the value of an idea and let the weight of evidence and the better argument establish or negate its validity" (Mezirow 1985, 142-143).*

Is there any space for communicative action in educational contexts? Is communicative action just an ideal, too unobtainable to research in the everyday world of adult education? Do the adult educators want to commit to it? What would it mean in practice? It would perhaps be very demanding to analyse huge social problems at macro-level in formal education. But what about the micro-level? In the studies of adult education there is always an educational system and learning context present - also as an object of analysis and change. The students are used to react to ready-made plans and give feedback to them during the last lesson. But would it be possible for them to be also proactive in planning the common learning effort? Would that even be essential subject matter for studying adult education?

In the analysis of the concept "self-initiative learning", the students mention that they have struggled in order to organize the appropriate time for studying and combining studies with work life and family life as well as possible. They have been very active and creative in constructing the optimal infrastructure for their studies in their own environments, but they have not been able to influence so much the aims, contents and methods. They have made initiatives in their environments in order to adjust to the system. They do not relate uncritically to the system, but they often lack power and courage to express their discontentment. Some of them mention only in passing that they have not had the possibility to participate in the planning of their studies. Even then their comments mostly concern the external arrangements of the studies.

There can be many reasons why we are not able to take communicative action in our learning context and educational situations. Maybe the students are not willing to accept this new way of learning? What about the teachers and tutors - which attitudes and opinions do they (or we) have towards this change? The question still remains, and it leads us to see other questions concerning - educational values. Do we want to emphasize the student's individual efforts in self-study and self-direction? In which way are the individual intentions connected to communality in learning and in other contexts? Do we encourage the students with our educational aims and didactic solutions to privacy or to shared responsibility?

References

Ahteenmäki-Pelkonen, L. (1992). Objektista subjektiksi. [From object to subject]. In I. Hein & R. Larna (toim.) *Lähellä, kaukana, yksin, yhdessä.* Helsingin yliopisto: Lahden tutkimus-ja koulutuskeskus, 41-52.

Ahteenmäki-Pelkonen, L. (1994). From self-directedness to interdependence? An analysis of Mezirow's conceptualization of self-directed learning. In *Social Change and Adult Educational Research. Adult Education Research in Nordic Countries 1992/93.* Trondheim: Tapir 1994, 173-183.

Ahteenmäki-Pelkonen, L. (1997). *Kriittinen käsitys itseohjautuvuudesta. Systemaattinen analyysi Jack Mezirowin itseohjautuvuuskäsityksistä.* [A critical view of self-directedness. A systematic analysis of Jack Mezirow's conceptions]. Diss. Helsinki: University of Helsinki, Department of Education, Research Report 157.

Brookfield, S. (1986). *Understanding and facilitating adult learning.* San Francisco: Jossey-Bass.

Freire, P. (1979). *Pedagogik för förtryckta.* Tionde upplagan. Stockholm: Gummessons.

Freire, P. (1985). *The politics of education. Culture, power and liberation.* Massachusetts: Bergin & Garvey Publishers.

Knowles, M.S. (1975). *Self-directed learning: A guide for learners and teachers.* Chicago: Association Press Follett.

Knowles, M.S. (1980). *The modern practice of adult education: from pedagogy to andragogy.* Revised and updated. New York: Cambridge: The Adult Education Company.

Mezirow, J. (1981). A critical theory of adult learning and education. *Adult Education (USA)* (32) 1, 3-24.

Mezirow, J. (1985). Concept and action in adult education. *Adult Education Quarterly.* (35), 3, 142-151.

Mezirow, J. (1991). *Transformative dimensions of adult learning.* San Francisco: Jossey-Bass.

Mezirow, J. (1997). Cognitive processes: Contemporary paradigms of learning. In P. Sutherland (ed.) *Adult learning: A reader.* London: Kogan Page, 2-13.

Moore, M. (1983). The individual adult learner. In M. Tight (ed.) *Adult learning and education.* London: Croom Helm, 153-168.

The Nottingham Andragogy Group. (1983). *Towards a developmental theory of andragogy.* University of Nottingham. Department of Adult Education. Adults' Psychological and Educational Perspectives 9.

Tella, S. & M. Mononen-Aaltonen. (1998). *Developing dialogic communication culture in media education: integrating dialogism and technology.* Helsinki: University of Helsinki, Department of Teacher Education, Media Education Centre.

Tough, A. (1979). *The adult's learning projects. A fresh approach to theory and practice in adult learning.* 2nd ed. Ontario: The Ontario Institute of Studies in Education.

Tough, A. (1982). *Intentional changes.* Chicago: Follett Publishing Company.

Walther, J. (1996). Computer-mediated communication: Impersonal, interpersonal and hyperpersonal interaction. *Communication Research* 23: 3-43.

GRUNDTVIG´S EDUCATIONAL IDEAS
- On tying bonds and cutting knots

Ove Korsgaard

Abstract

Previous research on Grundtvig´s ideas has mostly been concentrated on his pedagogical ideas and the folk high school. A third category must be added - Grundtvig´s ideas regarding enlightenment. These ideas can be understood only in light of the main complex of problems which occupied Grundtvig throughout his entire life, viz. what does it imply to be a person, a member of society, and the world? The assignment is to "develop a complete enlightenment of man" containing a treble effect, viz. to enlighten: "The Immediate Everyday Life," "People´s Life through Centuries" and "Human Life through thousands of years." Grundtvig wanted to establish a school system based upon two columns: the people and mankind – a folk high school and a university.

We now live in the era of the school – resulting in an individualization of man which may become dangerous if there is no agreement on "the common good." Only true enlightenment will result in the triad between the individual, the people, and mankind. The folk high school was to enlighten the people. The university was to be "a spiritual workshop" striving towards a universal understanding and clarification. Grundtvig´s university was never established. However, in this time of globalization the need is as great as ever for research into Grundtvig´s ideas of enlightenment.

Most of the numerous books and articles about Grundtvig´s educational ideas can be divided into two main categories: *Grundtvig's Pedagogical Ideas*, and *The Grundtvigian Folk High School*. For decades in the latter half of the last century K. E. Bugge and Roar Skovmand, both professors at the Royal Danish School of Educational Studies, were authorities, each in their own field. Thus, in the authoritative work, *Grundtvig og grundtvigianisme i et nyt lys (Grundtvig and Grundtvigianism in a New Light,* 1983, not translated), Professor Bugge writes about "Grundtvig´s Pedagogical Ideas," and Professor Skovmand describes "The Grundtvigian Folk High School."

There is a necessity to add a third category, "Grundtvig´s Ideas on Enlightenment." As a result of the pedagogical and the historical school approach there are aspects of Grundtvig´s ideas about enlightenment that have not been seriously illustrated. The following is a short presentation of the two well-known categories.

Grundtvig's Pedagogical Ideas

According to K. E. Bugge, the prevailing concept of the principal content of Grundtvig's educational ideas can be summed up as follows:[1]

1. Emphasis on *youth* - opposed to childhood - as the optimal period of schooling,
2. Emphasis on *oral* teaching, in particular the inspiration to be derived from the stimulating "spiritual" lecture,
3. Emphasis on the Danish-Norse cultural tradition as being the best foundation for education, in contrast to the classical-Latin tradition,
4. Emphasis on the fact that these ideas are in some way linked to a *Christian attitude towards life.*

However, K. E. Bugge makes reservations concerning the fourth point, rejecting - against the background of Kaj Thaning's work - that Grundtvig directly involves Christian matters of faith in the determination of the aim of education.

K. E. Bugge considers the concept of "Interaction" as being the key to understanding what is unique about Grundtvig's ideas concerning education and upbringing. Interaction is the basic category, permeating his pedagogical ideas. The folk high school was to be based on living interaction between students and teacher, mutually between the students, and between life of the people in the past and present. The education was to be historical and poetic in order to create a living interaction between the past and the present. In short, it can be said that according to Grundtvig, poetry is connected with creation, and history is connected with development. Poetry is an imitation of the order of creation, and history is a development towards a re-establishment of this order. The historical-poetical method has in particular given a distinctive character to Grundtvig's pedagogical ideas.[2]

---

[1] K. E. Bugge. "Grundtvigs pædagogiske tanker." In: *Grundtvig og Grundtvigianismen i nyt lys.* Ed.Christian Thodberg and Anders Pontoppidan Thyssen 1983:210-224 ("Grundtvig's Pedagogical Ideas". In: *Grundtvig and Grundtvigianism in a New Light* (not translated)).

[2] Cf. K. E. Løgstrup's view that the Grundtvigian folk high school is a historical-poetic school. "Such is its nature. It stands or falls with it". K. E. Løgstrup "Højskolens nye fronter." In: *Højskolen til debat*, ed. Johannes Rosendahl. (The New Battle Lines of the Folk High School. In: *Debating the Folk High School*, not translated).

The Grundtvigian Folk High School[3]

Roar Skovmand begins his account about "The Grundtvigian Folk High School" with the establishment of Rødding Højskole in 1844. However, Rødding was no immediate realization of Grundtvig's pedagogical ideas, although especially Professor Christian Flor was much influenced by Grundtvig's ideas. Grundtvig continued to have high hopes of establishing a kind of "people's college" at the Academy in Sorø. His intention was that this "college" should apply not only to future civil servants but also to broader circles. It was therefore a great disappointment to Grundtvig when, in 1848, the newly elected government dropped the plans for a folk high school in Sorø.

During the period from 1844 to 1864 there were no clear indications that Grundtvig's name was to be inseparably tied together with the folk high school. Most of the 14 "folk high schools for peasants" that existed in 1862-63 were, in fact, continuation schools for boys. It was not until after Denmark's defeat in the 1864 war against Prussia and Austria that the folk high school movement was enhanced. The establishment of Askov Højskole in 1865 initiated "the great age" of the folk high schools. During the following ten years approximately 50 folk high schools were established - most of them Grundtvigian.

Folk high schools were established not only in Denmark, but also in Sweden, Norway, and Finland. By 1900 the folk high schools in the four Nordic countries all had their distinctive national character. "However different they were, their principals and teachers sometimes gathered at Nordic folk high school meetings to confirm their solidarity and acknowledge the inspiration from Denmark and the Grundtvigians there or from Grundtvig himself."[4] During the last century schools were established in many other countries. These were inspired by Grundtvig and the Grundtvigian folk high school.

The folk high school has fascinated many educators all over the world; this has contributed to the fact that Grundtvig's educational ideas and the history of the folk high school almost grew together to become two aspects of the same matter. The folk high school was considered to be a successful institutionalization and materialization of Grundtvig's pedagogical ideas.

---

[3] A folk high school is not a high school. The word folk (common people), is the most important. The first folk high school was established in 1844 as a school for adults who wanted national education. The concept was created by Grundtvig.

[4] Roar Skovmand. "Den grundtvigske højskole." In: *Grundtvig og grundtvigianismen i nyt lys,* 1983:334 (The Grundtvigian Folk High School. In: *Grundtvig and Grundtvigianism in a New Light,* not translated)

It cannot be denied that there is a close connection between Grundtvig's ideas on enlightenment and the Grundtvigian folk high school. However, it is subject to discussion whether the folk high school is a realization of Grundtvig's complete educational programme.

Grundtvig's Three Spheres

It is important to be aware that Grundtvig was not occupied with pedagogy in a narrow sense of the word. He was not a theoretical pedagogical philosopher, developing his own pedagogical system. Nor was he a practical pedagogue, although he held a series of lectures at the Marielyst Folk High School during the years 1856-71. Grundtvig's pedagogical ideas were, so to speak, a by-product of his work with national and political affairs.

It is therefore no coincidence that Grundtvig, in his first political article - *Politiske betragtninger med blik paa Danmark og Holsteen*, 1831 (Political considerations with a view on Denmark and Holsteen) advocates the need for a "folk high school for the scientific and civil education" of the common man.[5]

Grundtvig's thoughts regarding the folk high school are, however, only a part of a more comprehensive programme of enlightenment, the content of which was determined by the basic problems of humanity with which he worked his entire life.

1. What does it imply to be a human being?
2. What does it imply to be a human being in society?
3. What does it imply to be a human being in the world?

Grundtvig's ideas regarding enlightenment are based on his ideas concerning a universal historical triad between: "The Individual," "The People," and "Mankind." In other words, the connection between the individual, the nation, and the universal forms the basic structure of Grundtvig's educational ideas. According to Grundtvig, the task is to "develop a complete enlightenment of man" containing a treble effect, viz. to enlighten:

- "The Immediate Everyday Life"
- "Life of the people through Centuries"

---

[5] *Udvalgte Skrifte*, 4:XIX.

- "Human Life through Thousands of Years"[6]

According to Grundtvig, everyday life is inscribed in time dimensions reaching beyond "the immediate;" it is both a part of life of the people and life of mankind. However, while life of the individual can be counted in decades, life of the people can be counted in centuries, and life of mankind in thousands of years. To Grundtvig the universal is first and foremost synonymous with the world-historical, and last, but not least, the religious perspective.

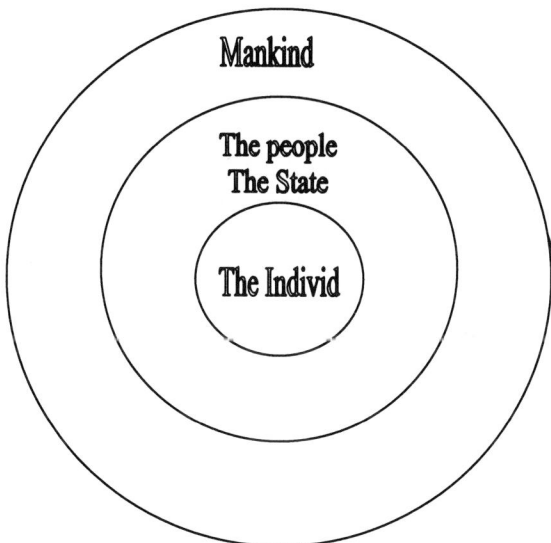

Grundtvig's Two Institutions

Grundtvig's extremely ambitious plan was to establish a school system based upon two columns: the people and mankind. One column to support the folk high school, the other the university. Between them there were to be both differences and coherence which to Grundtvig are the reasons for the intense relations between the national and the universal.

The two institutions - the folk high school and the university - do not refer only to two formally different educational levels; they are also based upon different

---

[6] Grundtvig. *Statsmæssig Oplysning* 1983:45 (Grundtvig *On State Enlightenment*, not translated).

horizons of comprehensibility, one more based on the common man "folkelig", and the other, a more universal horizon of cognition and life.

In his writings, Grundtvig uses various names for the two types of schools he was dreaming of establishing, a Danish folk high school and a folk high school of Sciences and Letters - the folk high school in Soer (Sorø), and the university in Gothenburg, the "School for Life" and the "School for Lust."

A subject index can be outlined for the two types of schools as follows:

Sorø	Gothenburg
The folk high school	The university
Folke-lighed	Menneske-lighed
People's enlightenment	Scientific and scholarly enlightenment
The national	The universal
School for life	School for lust

At this point I must draw attention to the expression "folkelighed" and "folke-lighed". There is an untranslatable play on words as the Danish word for equality is lighed, so in fact, the word folke-lighed means equality among people/folk. Likewise the expression menneske-lighed means equality among individuals/human beings.

Nordens Mytologi (Norse Mythology, 1832), and Om Nordens videnskabelige Forening (On the Academic Union of Scandinavia, 1839), as being the manifesto of the folk high school and the university respectively. However, important aspects of Grundtvig's programme of enlightenment were developed already in the Danne-Virke publications from 1816-19. Without the background of these publications his later ideas about scientific and scholarly enlightenment become almost incomprehensible. In Danne-Virke he develops his views about science and enlightenment on which his ideas concerning a university are based. Characteristically, one of Grundtvig's publications is called "*Om Mennesket i Verden*" (*On Man in the World*, 1817, not translated).[7] The title indicates that in this publication Grundtvig is especially concerned with "man in the world;" viz. the relationship between the individual and the universal. Thus, the perspective in *Danne-Virke* is far more specific in its universal philosophy of life than in Grundtvig's later works. Especially after 1832 he occupies

---

[7] Danne-Virke II 1817:118-206. Optryk i: Ove Korsgaard (ed.). *En orm - en Gud*, 1997 (Danne-Virke, a Danish periodical, edited by Grundtvig. Reprinted in Ove Korsgaard, ed. *A Worm - A God*, not translated).

himself mainly with "man in society", i. e., the relationship between the individual and the people.

Consequently, Grundtvig's educational ideas have often been reduced to dealing with two spheres only: the individual and the people. However, such a reduction shows a misleading understanding of his programme of enlightenment, because after 1832 there are still three spheres in his programme of enlightenment, although the universal perspective fades at times.

Grundtvig's complete ideas concerning education and school are especially expressed in the draft *Statsmæssig Oplysning* (*On State Enlightenment*, 1834, not translated) which was not published until 1983 when it was edited and published by K. E. Bugge and Vilhelm Nielsen. The publication is a draft of a complete school programme in which the two central institutions are the folk high school and the university. And, as Vilhelm Nielsen states, the publication especially illustrates the later publications on education and schools as "a number of topics were never said more sharply and clearly in other folk high school publications than they were here."[8]

In the manuscript the crucial problem is the relationship between the individual, the State/the people, and mankind. Grundtvig talks about the individual, not only as a special individual, but also about the age of the individual as a certain era in the history of the world. He uses the expression "the age of the individual" in connection with his description of the New Age, and he connects the beginning of this New Age with Columbus - and with the Renaissance.[9]

Like many other great universal historians Grundtvig regarded history according to the figure three. The history of mankind goes through three great eras of mutually corresponding time, and he uses different concepts to describe these eras. He talks of a mythological, a theological, and a historical era, of the era of the Father, the Son, and the Holy Spirit, of the era of the Church, the State, and the School. In Grundtvig's terminology the era of the School is also the era of the individual. In Antiquity the State is the most important institution, in the Middle Ages it is the Church, but in the era of the individual it is the School.

---

[8] Grundtvig *Statsmæssig Oplysning* 1983:79 (Grundtvig *On State Enlightenment*, not translated).

[9] Grundtvig. *History of the World,* Vol. III, 1843 (not translated).

Compared with Antiquity and the Middle Ages the individual in the era of the school appears on the stage of history in quite another way and to a higher degree than earlier. Grundtvig considers this individualization, symbolized by Columbus, to be an important but also extremely dangerous phase in the development of universal history - the French Revolution in 1789 shows how dangerous. During the revolution the relations between the individual's urge for freedom and the State managing the common good were destroyed with fatal results.

The rising self-assurance in "the age of the individual" results in new conditions for the creation of society as enlightenment now plays a far more important role than earlier in the relationship between the individual and society. According to Grundtvig, absolute individualism is incompatible with the notion of a society. To be member of a society means to undertake a responsibility for its common life. Each society depends upon the bonds between the individual and the State. Creating a society always depends upon a certain agreement concerning the common good; "for, where such a basic harmony cannot be traced there has never been established a civil society, but only two contrasting classes, masters and slaves. This may all together *be called* a state, still it is not necessarily so, for in such a society it cannot be denied that the superior force is the fundamental law."[10] If there is not a certain agreement upon "the common good," the relation between the individual and the State will end in becoming a Gordian knot. Therefore, according to Grundtvig, a main issue is whether it is possible to avoid such a knot. And, if such harm has been done, will it be possible to cut the knot with means other than the sword?

Here, the school enters as a new and important institution. According to Grundtvig, the historical task of the school is to cut the Gordian knot with means other than the sword.[11]

"This is the knot, the Gordian knot, in the development of mankind. Until now it has always been cut with the Alexander-sword, however, it is necessary to be

---

[10] Grundtvig *Statsmæssig Oplysning* 1983:59 (Grundtvig *On State Enlightenment*, not translated).

[11] Grundtvig often uses *the knot* as a metaphor of both the personal and interpersonal relations. When the personal is the issue he recommends to cut the knot, when the issue is interpersonal relations he recommends to be lenient and patient. Cf. "Om Kirke, Stat og Skole". In: *Danne-Virke* IV 1819:319 ("On the Church, the State, and the School." In: *Danne-Virke* (not translated) and "Om Mennesket i Verden". In: *En Orm – en Gud* 1997:186 ("On Man in the World." In: *A Worm – a God*, not translated).

lenient and patient if we want to save the State, and want the true enlightenment of man to proceed till the end of days."[12]

To loosen the knots between the individual and the State, state enlightenment was to substitute the sword. Later Grundtvig preferred to talk of people's enlightenment and the people. However, there is no great difference. The State and the people are in the same sphere in the universal historical triad. When Grundtvig talks of state enlightenment or people's enlightenment, he believes this enlightenment is meant to serve the superior purpose of "cutting the knot," of solving the problems - without loosening the ties - between the individual and the State/the people.

What is Enlightenment?

In 1784 Kant asked the famous question: Was ist Aufklärung? Grundtvig asks the same question in *Statsmæssig oplysning*. He asks whether there is only one kind of enlightenment, or whether there are various kinds. Is enlightenment only singular? Or plural? And is it possible to talk of true enlightenment if there are many kinds?

Grundtvig does not deny that it is difficult to clearly define enlightenment. "It is a very difficult matter to discuss enlightenment." When you begin to think of the word enlightenment it is easily concluded that there are "as many kinds of enlightenment... as there are heads with eyes."[13] In other words, there are just as many kinds of "enlightenment" as there are people. In fact, each individual - his own light.

Does this make sense at all? To Grundtvig it does, "for, just as I was despairing over the countless kinds of 'enlightenment' it occurred to me, of course, that it so happens that I myself also have a head with eyes, thus I am helped and know very well what I say myself when I talk of enlightenment of the people, I do know that first and foremost I think of their *own enlightenment.*"[14] Enlightenment of the people is from beginning to the end *enlightenment of*

---

[12] Grundtvig *Statsmæssig Oplysning* 1983:31 (Grundtvig *On State Enlightenment*, not translated).

[13] Grundtvig. *Statsmæssig Oplysning* 1983:67f. (Grundtvig *On State Enlightenment*, not translated).

[14] Grundtvig. *Statsmæssig Oplysning* 1983:68 (Grundtvig *On State Enlightenment*, not translated).

themselves.[15] In modern terms it can be said that enlightenment begins with self-enlightenment, viz. individualization.

To Grundtvig there is a close connection between enlightenment and individualization. The true follower of enlightenment is individualization. However, this makes enlightenment a two-edged sword. Because, how is it possible to ensure the necessary bonds between the individual and fellowship when enlightenment always results in a rising individualization? Therefore, enlightenment "is a very ambiguous word," says Grundtvig.[16] Enlightenment has a Janus head. Indeed, the State may be "destroyed by enlightenment."[17]

According to Grundtvig, this is due to the fact that in reality there is both true enlightenment and false enlightenment. False enlightenment is an enlightenment which "constantly acts according to the interests of the individual."[18] This form of enlightenment is dangerous to "the civil society at all times and under all skies," because every society is based upon a certain "awe of a higher justice than that of the individual."[19] If enlightenment undermines the sense of fellowship and the common bonds among people, the very foundation of society is threatened.

On the contrary, true enlightenment is based on the condition that we, as individuals, exist *only* by virtue of fellowship; "such enlightenment, extending to all *human life* and showing the deep cohesion between the individual, life of the people, and all generations, such an enlightenment develops a way of thinking which is desirable for all conditions of society."[20]

---

[15] Grundtvig's confidence in "own enlightenment" is based upon the conception that every man – through *the word* has access to enlightenment on life. In the "small" word every man has part in the logos of the "great" word. The most important text in Grundtvig's word-theology is the prologue to St John's, Grundtvig's entire enlightenment and "clarification" programme is based upon the introduction to this Gospel.

[16] Grundtvig. *Statsmæssig Oplysning* 1983:26 (Grundtvig *On State Enlightenment,* not translated).

[17] Grundtvig. *Statsmæssig Oplysning* 1983:31 (Grundtvig *On State Enlightenment,* not translated).

[18] Grundtvig. *Statsmæssig Oplysning* 1983:28 (Grundtvig *On State Enlightenment,* not translated).

[19] Grundtvig. *Statsmæssig Oplysning* 1983:27 (Grundtvig *On State Enlightenment,* not translated).

[20] Grundtvig. *Statsmæssig Oplysning* 1983:31 (Grundtvig *On State Enlightenment,* not translated).

Thus, Grundtvig's educational ideas contain the idea of a form of enlightenment which is able to illustrate the universal historical triad between the individual, the people, and mankind.

"Folke-lighed"

Grundtvig's folk high school ideas are based on the concept of folk/people. To Grundtvig a folk, or a nation, is a group of people with an inner consciousness that they belong together by virtue of a common language, common history, common traditions and habits. The people do not exist by virtue of itself; it obtains its existence only through reflection. Thus, self-reflection and existence are two aspects of the same matter. It is reflection that creates the experience of co-existence, of a common room, of a collective identity.

The two most important elements that constitute a folk are *the language* and *the history*. Grundtvig was deeply influenced by Herder's trail-breaking view that there is identity between language and people. In both Herder's and Grundtvig's opinion the language defines a people/folk and a nation. The language boundary is the border of the people and the nation. Each nation speaks the way it thinks and thinks the way it speaks. The language is the epitome of the spirit and mind of the people. Language is the medium which enables people to be conscious of themselves; at the same time it is the key to understanding our surroundings. The language also ties us to the past by revealing the ideas, feelings, and prejudices of former generations. Thus, the past is deeply rooted in human consciousness, at the same time - helped by the language - conveying the past and the present into the future. In this way, language expresses a living growth in history, and we receive our heritage through our native languages and history. According to Grundtvig and Herder, all who have an historical and linguistic tradition in common constitute a folk or a nation. Few ideas have had such great widespread political impact as this.

Grundtvig said it is the task of the folk high school to enhance the linguistic sense of community. Each individual must be aware of his/her own culture. The means are first and foremost to search for the memories of the people - memories that have left their traces in myths, poetry, proverbs, etc., thus enlivening the language of the people.

Almost by definition the people form a particular unity, an exclusive party, as the people must necessarily exclude the others to be able to identify themselves. It can be said that the people basically express an ethno-political dimension of significance. The people are always ethnically, religiously, nationally, linguistically, historically, geographically, and politically determined. Expressed in this way the people are always placed on a scale between a biological and a political determination.

In his thesis, *Grundtvigs historiefilosofi* (Grundtvig's Philosophy on History, 1999) Ole Vind has clearly demonstrated that Grundtvig founds his understanding of the concept "people" on outdated views. He calls Grundtvig's nationalism a biblical nationalism, for Grundtvig always based his views on the ethnocentric story of the creation in Genesis, 10:11.[21] However, because Grundtvig founds his understanding of the concept of people on outdated views does not imply that his ideas concerning the people as a connecting link between the individual and the universal are outdated. The people do not cease to play a constructive part in developing a society just because a certain way of interpreting the people is outdated. The ability of establishing connecting links between the individual and all mankind still forms the basis for the creation of a society - in both small and great matters.

"Menneske-lighed"

As mentioned above, Grundtvig's educational ideas are based on a basic distinction between life among people and human life. While the folk high school is based on the people, the national, the State, the university is based on the universal; "A university - which conforms to its name and purpose - must contain, nourish, and comply with *universal ideas* only, whereas the State is bound to the *partial and temporary* so that learned and civic enlightenment can only contain an obscure unity in the *popular* when pertaining to feelings and only corrupt each other by being willingly and obviously connected."[22] There must be a difference between the people's school and the school for human life, between the school for enlightenment of the people and the school for scientific and scholarly enlightenment, between "The School for Life and the School for Lust" which both, each in their own way may be good but do not bear to be confused."[23] The university - *The School for Lust* - is also partly a "School for Fun" as only time will show which distorted and crazy ideas and imaginations of the world will last. It is not decisive whether you hit the right thing in one

---

[21] The first time Grundtvig based his views upon the ethnical Story of the Creation was in *Verdens Krønike* (*Chronicle on the World*, not translated), 1814.
[22] Grundtvig. *Statsmæssig Oplysning* 1983:65 (Grundtvig *On State Enlightenment*, not translated).
[23] Grundtvig. *Statsmæssig Oplysning* 1983:65 (Grundtvig *On State Enlightenment*, not translated).

century or another because "the School for Lust has plenty of time - right up to the end of the world."[24]

Grundtvig asks whether it can be imagined that the State supports a university where the education reaches beyond the particular interests of the State. Would the State consider "The School for Lust" to be superfluous and unnecessary, perhaps even dangerous and harmful? Certainly, we do not know. However, Grundtvig believes that the State will find it profitable to support an institution that is devoted to working with "man in the world." After all, there is a tradition to continue; for many years the states in Germany and the Nordic countries have supported the "Faculty of Philosophy," which to all appearance is useless and unprofitable.

When Grundtvig wrote his educational publications in the 1830s and 1840s he was particularly engaged with the folk high school, and life of the people constitutes his horizon of understanding. However, the university and human life do not disappear completely from his field of vision. In his publication *Til Nordmænd om en Norsk Høi-Skole* (*To Norsemen about a Norwegian High School*, not translated, 1837), he asks the question, How does the general education and culture of people interact with "profound scholarship and true scientific spirit?" The folk high school is not able to manage both. Consequently, a new university must be established. Grundtvig is convinced that as soon as the Nordic countries each get their folk high school, the result will be the establishment of a *"large scientific and scholarly high school...for the benefit of the development and explanation of human life, in all its enigmatic profundity and wonderful diversity, in short a university."*[25] It is impossible to solve the mystery of the people at their own national level of description. To solve the mystery an institution is demanded where people, with wit and curiosity, are occupied with the deepest universal and historical subjects.

In Grundtvig's last important publication concerning schools, *Det Danske Dummehoved og Den Danske Højskole* (*The Danish Fool and the Danish Folk High School*, not translated, 1847), he is absorbed with the relationship between the people and the human being. In these books he expresses a strong belief that the Danes are not "infatuated with their own affairs", but appreciate "the so-called strange and unfamiliar...in order not to miss the common human where everything "folkeligt" will find its object and explanation."

---

[24] Grundtvig. *Statsmæssig Oplysning* 1983:66 (Grundtvig *On State Enlightenment*, not translated).
[25] *Grundtvigs Skoleverden* bd. II, 1968:77 (*Grundtvig's School World*, not translated).

Grundtvig seriously develops his university ideas in the publication, *Om Nordens videnskabelige Forening* (*On the Academic Union of Scandinavia*, not translated, 1839), where he suggests a large common Nordic university in Gothenburg. Three hundred scientists and scholars above the age of 30 were meant to work there for the benefit of nothing less than "honour, profit, and joy for all mankind."[26]

The university in Gothenburg was meant to be a "spiritual workshop" where people, through combined efforts, strive towards everything which is all-embracing and common - towards the universal. This should be done by "adapting and working on all human knowledge according to the interests of life."[27]

Grundtvig maintains that each individual and each people are a part of a greater universal history. The universal history must ensure that the people maintain a universal-historical horizon so that one never forgets that life is by no means able to manage its mystery through the characteristic experiences of each individual or people, but always only "through thousands of generations, as a divine experiment, showing how spirit and dust permeate each other and are explained in a common divine consciousness. This is the way man must be understood when the aim is a spiritual, scientific, and scholarly character on earth."[28]

In other words, the task of the university is to place the limited reality of the individual and the people in a connected whole, exceeding the particular. Scientific and scholarly enlightenment must throw light on the deep coherence between the individual, the people, and all mankind. This was the background for Grundtvig's proposal for a Nordic university.

Grundtvig's Educational Programme

However, Grundtvig's educational programme was implemented only to a limited and reduced degree. The folk high schools were developed and based upon the concept of people/folk; the large common Nordic university in Gothenburg was never established - this university which should have been

---

[26] Grundtvig. "Nordens Videnskabelige Forening" In: *Grundtvigs Skoleverden* II 1967:148 (*The Academic Union of Scandinavia*, not translated).
[27] Ibid. p. 149.
[28] From "Nordens Mytologi". In: Udvalgte Skrifter 5:408 (Norse Mythology. In: *Selected Writings*, not translated).

based upon science and the humanities. There is no doubt that Grundtvig considered the common Nordic university to be the crown of his educational endeavours.

There are strong historical reasons why only half of Grundtvig's educational programme was implemented. The folk high school was supported by the "folkelige", national currents of the nineteenth century - currents, which seriously appeared after the disastrous defeat in 1864. It was this defeat which made the country the nation state of which we are so proud, and which made the Grundtvigian folk high school the unique school in which we also take pride.

However, now at the beginning of the twenty-first century, the world is very different. The European and global movements through the last decades have put a heavy strain upon traditional Grundtvigian self-perception. Common problems due to growing individualization and globalization, are still more difficult to solve within the framework of a traditional Grundtvigian philosophy of life.

At the same time it is evident that as people we still need "connecting links" between "the individual" and "the global." We must be able to identify ourselves by a "we," forming a particular unity between the individual and the entity. There is evidently a basic need to be able to enter into particular connections whose existence and history can be symbolized and told.

Therefore, according to Grundtvig, it was a decisive issue how a "we" can avoid the danger of withdrawing into itself. The reason why he did not write a proper history of Denmark, but several histories of the world, is due to the fact that he wanted to give the national story a universal historical perspective.

The need for a universal historical understanding of the development of the international community is greater than ever. Therefore, there is every good reason to be interested in the general view of Grundtvig's educational programme, that is to say, the universal historical triad: the individual, the people, and the universal. In Grundtvig's own words it is desirable to promote enlightenment which is able to "show the deep coherence between the individual, the people, and the life of all generations."[29]

---

[29] Grundtvig. *Statsmæssig Oplysning* 1983:31 (Grundtvig *On State Enlightenment*, not translated).

As a result of the pedagogical and historical school approach to Grundtvig´s educational programme, the universal dimension has not been seriously examined. However, the time is evidently now ripe for a closer study of Grundtvig´s educational ideas in their entirety.

References

Allchin, A. M. (1997). *N. F. S. Grundtvig. An Introduction to his Life and Work.* Aarhus University Press.

Borish, S. M. (1991). *The Land of the Living. The Danish Folk High Schools and Denmark's Non-violent Path to Modernization.* Grass Valley, California.

Bugge, K. E. (ed.) (1968). *Grundtvigs skoleverden i tekster og udkast,* I-II, Copenhagen.

Bugge, K. E. (1993). "The School for Life. The Basic Ideas of Grundtvig's Educational Thinking". In A. M. Allchin. et al. (ed.) *Heritage and Prophecy.* Aarhus.

Grundtvig, N. F. S. (1816-19). *Danne-Virke,* Copenhagen.

Grundtvig, N. F. S. (1983). *Statsmæssig oplysning,* edited by Bugge, K. E. and Nielsen V. Copenhagen.

Henningsen, Hans (1993). "The Danish Folk High School". In: *Heritage and Prophecy.*

Jonas, Uffe (2000). "Det individuelle, det folkelige, det universelle". (Not published).

Korsgaard, Ove (ed.) (1997). *En Orm – en Gud. Om mennesket i verden.* Odense.

Korsgaard, Ove (1998). *The Struggle for Enlightenment. Danish Adult Education during 500 Years.* Copenhagen.

Løgstrup, K. E. (1961)."Højskolens nye fronter". In Johannes Rosendahl (ed.) *Højskolen til debat.* Copenhagen,

Skovmand, Roar (1983). "Den grundtvigske folkehøjskole". In Christian Thodberg and Anders Pontoppidan Thyssen (ed.) *Grundtvig and grundtvigianismen i nyt lys.* Aarhus.

Vind, Ole (1999). *Grundtvigs historiefilosofi.* Copenhagen.

SOCIAL PARTICIPATION AS A CHALLENGE TO LIFE-LONG LEARNING IN EUROPE

Anja Heikkinen and Kristiina Laiho

Introduction

This article is based on the experience and reflections of a Finnish research group (University of Tampere), which participated in a Socrates studies and analysis project "Effective Processes for the Acquisition of Qualifications for Life-long Learning" - Lifequal - carried out in 1998-1999. The project was coordinated by the University of Bremen (Germany) and the other six partners were BETA/Cra-Céreq of the University of Strasbourg (France), the Institute for Employment Research of the University of Warwick (UK), the University of Patras (Greece) and the OCTO Institute of the University of Twente (Netherlands). In order to clarify the title of our paper, we briefly describe the project in the context of the dominating European education policy discourse, represented and supported by the European Commission programmes.

Why have so many projects emerged studying education in terms of "effective processes" - or "best practice" as it soon became interpreted in Lifequal? Why have European researchers for years been only focusing on the challenges of "knowledge society", "learning society" and "life-long learning" as if they were natural and inevitably emerging states of the world and not deliberate political, economic, cultural programmes and projects, which "challenge" us to perceive our research topics in certain discursive manners and practices. The Lifequal project is a concrete example and consequence of such programmes which have led us into our recent discursive realities. It is one of the many projects which have been set up under the European Commission programmes in order to implement the educational ideology which was explicitly presented in the 1995 White Paper on Teaching and Learning, aiming at the making of the learning society and the promotion of life-long learning in the EU member states. In studying "effective processes for acquisition of qualifications for life-long learning", Lifequal in fact aims primarily at reflecting the implications of the programmes for policy development at both EU and member state levels. Despite its appearance as a research project, Lifequal is clearly one tool or instrument in the implementation of the dominating educational policy of the EU.

During the first year of the project, the partnership decided to develop a more critical approach to the dominant discourse of life-long learning, which was considered to be limited to the recognition of a need to develop a flexible workforce which responds to the needs of industry and economy and linked to competitiveness in a so-called "global economy" (cf. Attwell 1999). It was also questioned whether the policies and discourses of life-long learning are consistent with each other. Even inside the dominant discourse of life-long learning, the Lifequal project identified varying types, like the skills growth model, the personal development model, the social learning model and the learning society model. It may be argued that even the previous international attempts, e.g. during the 1970s, to develop policies of recurrent and alternating education, failed to proceed from rhetoric to the practical level, and this may be the case for recent endeavours as well.

During its second year, the Lifequal project agreed on studying and analysing following topics (Attwell 1999):

1) competing discourses about life-long learning in Europe,
2) policy platforms facilitating life-long learning in different ways (in different meanings of life-long learning),
3) the influence of different research genres in looking at support and in implementation of practices of life-long learning in member states,
4) models of teaching and learning facilitating life-long learning (examples of effective and appropriate practice),
5) practice of education supporting commitment to life-long learning.

All topics were primarily considered in vocational education and training.

The Finnish group in Lifequal decided to bring social participation to the fore as an alternative to the dominant discourse of life-long learning. We found it fruitful to ask how to integrate the development of trans-national research perspectives on life-long learning into learning from national perspectives, and how individual partners could contribute to this. We believed that the shared or trans-national perspective could be found only if we become familiar with the national and cultural traditions and realities of education which are relevant for life and life-long learning. In the following sections we will reflect first on what social participation might mean as an educational category, second on why we find social participation a crucial issue in discussing the meaning of life-long learning. We ask why social participation is a challenge for life-long learning, especially in the European context. Third we describe examples of alternative practices to the dominant conceptions of life-long learning, responding to these challenges at national level. Finally we ask about the possibility of developing alternative discourses in life-long learning: who should recognize social participation as the challenge in Europe?

What is social participation as an educational category?

One central point of dominant policy of promoting life-long learning, adopted in the Socrates programme in studies and analysis is combating social exclusion. During the second year the Lifequal project discussed some potential European alternatives to the dominating discourse of life-long learning in the member states, which are not only opposing the policy developments but also the very concept of life-long learning, considered by critics to represent a new form of social control and social exclusion. Partners brought into discussions other initiatives in the EU, which aim at preventing social exclusion in Europe, mainly supported under the ESF-programmes. However, most of these action-programme type interventions in fact promote developments where vocational education is conceived of as part of social or labour market (employment) policy. In most member states, interventions are limited to diagnosing the problem groups for competitiveness as countries develop infrastructure for trans-national economy. The focus has been on people who are at risk of being excluded or becoming non-productive and thus constituting a potential threat to social and political stability and economic growth. As in other EU member states, such politics in Finland, too, are materialized in massive programmes and initiatives targeted towards groups of young (ESF-supported apprenticeship and workshop training projects) and elderly people (ESF and nationally supported programmes "for the aged", "ageing and society"), who are opting out of educational or labour markets. Minor attention has been paid to the rules and practices in the mainstream logic of labour market and educational systems, which may be in total contrast with the quasi-participatory initiatives.

Unfortunately and typically for many EU-funded projects, most partners hardly searched for any alternative conceptions or initiatives of life-long learning. The partners from the UK and the Netherlands especially emphasized employability as their starting point, on which they already had completed evaluations for their governments and in other EU projects. Because Germany was represented by an English researcher, the German contribution remained at the level of discussing the modernization of the dual system. Referring to the lacking tradition of systematic vocational education and of societal or academic discussions on life-long learning, the Greek partner concentrated on carrying out and describing a survey about the demand for vocational education. The Finnish and the French partners tried to be more consistent in preparing critical discussion papers and focusing on social participation. Thus the French opposed the adoption of the concepts "effective" or "good" practice in (vocational) education, which promotes polarized definitions of the good and the bad in education and society. However, the project never managed to discuss these issues.

The papers of the British partner concentrated, on the one hand, on teaching-learning processes, which would promote transfer of skills and knowledge from one learning or work situation to another. On the other hand, he presented central topics in British policy discourse on life-long learning, which stress creating learning opportunities for poorly educated young people and for adult workers, who are changing jobs or are unemployed, in order to improve their employability. The papers gave some general recommendations - developing methods for collecting " a learning passport", creating work-sites with learning opportunities - but they gave no concrete examples nor did they discuss the British situation from a wider cultural or political perspective. The paper from the Netherlands was based on a national evaluation of the latest educational reforms. It concentrated on structural features like decentralization and modularization of vocational education, which may promote its responsiveness to the demands of local enterprises and of students with disrupted paths of learning. The Greek paper contextualized the relations between work and education in the country's economic and industrial system well. This is based on small family enterprises and often informal work and where improvements have been greatly influenced by EU policy and support. Among the most interesting findings in the Greek demand survey among employers, employees, the unemployed, education providers and unions was that employment training seldom promotes employability, on the contrary, it may stigmatize the "life-long learner" and make him/her even less employable. However, it may provide psychological and social support for life mastery. Also, though work-based learning has minor potential as a solution for obtaining occupational skills, the involvement of unions can make it more effective in raising people's consciousness of their role and situation in working life. The French partner brought the PAQUE programme into the discussion as an example of public initiative of "acquisition of qualifications for life-long learning". The PAQUE programme, which was abandoned because of its high costs, supported young people with little or no qualifications to achieve occupational qualifications by flexible and group-based methods. The cultural importance of public recognition and status of qualifications was stressed.

The Finnish group tried to start by clarifying that the concept of "participation" and "social participation" in the Finnish/Nordic popular education context does not restrict itself to combating (social) exclusion or promoting (social) inclusion. This is due to the peculiarity of educational thinking (philosophy) of Finnish/Nordic education, which is so often ignored in considering the relevance of the heritage of Nordic popular (adult) education. Especially among researchers of industrial and labour history, the Nordic tradition of popular (populist) educational policy has been widely criticized as a hindrance to modernization policies carried out by the elite in these countries (e.g. Korsnes 1998, Kettunen 1997). However, the typical characterizations of the polarization and divergence of the forms of education are typically based on dichotomous functions of education and work, and the division of educational work, focusing on "academic" or "general" and on "vocational" or "specific/ applicable" knowledge. Only by reflecting the cultural heritage can it become understandable that these polarizations in the Nordic countries in forms of knowledge, skills and competence cannot be conceived of as only between academic and vocational, but between popular, academic and vocational conceptions of education.

Historically and culturally, life-long learning should be contextualized at least in relation to cultural forms of education and to the timing of educational interventions in an individual's life-course. Because the aim of Lifequal was also to discuss and draw conclusions at European level, reflections should also extend to questions about whether and in what respect the concept and political slogans of life-long learning are trans-culturally defined or definable, or whether it actually maintains divergent meanings in different cultural contexts.

As mentioned above, it is typical for European reflections on education to only discuss polarization between "academic" and "vocational" forms of education. In Finnish (Nordic) educational thinking, the cultural forms of education and growth must since beginning of 19th until 1950s-1960s be structured in three major categories, related to their political functions and typical conflicts between them. (cf. Heikkinen 1995, 1997).

1) The first form of education is **folk (or popular) education** as education for citizenship (with its changing connotations), consisting of initial folk education in folk school (later comprehensive school) and of liberal adult education or folk enlightenment. The basic pedagogical idea in folk education has been the promotion of participation in the life of the family (households), community and nation-state. Life used to be conceived of in a holistic way, thus participation also included various forms of work and occupations. Later folk

education was increasingly transformed into initial or basic general education and adult education for civilized leisure-time activities.

2) The second form of education is **encyclopaedic education** in *gymnasia* (grammar school) and universities. The guiding pedagogical principle has been to promote participation in bodies and the production of knowledge, which is organized into disciplinary structures and practices. It implies transcending and overcoming the boundaries of specific forms of working life and occupational life. Still, until recently, encyclopaedic education has also included a certain kind of idea of "citizenship", which considers the good of the people, communities and nation (or nations) from a more universal perspective.

3) As a third form of education, **vocational education** has emerged. Though it has progressed step-by-step and it is distinguished by its distinctive pedagogical ideas, it has come to focus on participation in the world of work. This is in the context of an occupationally structured society with specialized skills, technical expertise and trade (livelihood), which constitute people's occupational identities.

When proceeding to trans-national discussions on social participation, we pointed out in Lifequal project about respecting the cultural specificity of educational thinking and concepts: the Finnish (Nordic) popular adult education heritage differs fundamentally from e.g. the British concept of "liberal adult education" in its understanding of relations between the individual and the community: the Finnish concept of civilized adulthood recognizes personal fulfilment only as a counterpart to the demands and limitations rising from the community, which in fact may greatly limit the options of "personal flourishing", which are so characteristic for the British liberal education ideals. It is a fact that - as has happened in most European countries - there has been a (political, middle-class programme) tendency to transform folk education into preparation for encyclopaedic forms of education, to overtake occupational elements of education with encyclopaedic elements. In the face of concrete educational challenges, educationists have always had to remember the ideas of popular and vocational education.

Secondly, the cultural and historical meaning of social participation is related to the question, which has been raised several times in the Lifequal project, about "how long is life-long" in life-long learning, because most of the endeavours in the life-long learning-movement seem in the end to restrict life-long learning to both ends of our lives. The question is a more general concern for the Lifequal project, but can also be addressed in the Finnish context. The institutions which intervene in individual growth processes during the course of life have been differentiated and integrated in various ways. When considering the meaning of life-long learning in the perspectives of the different forms of education described above, we might, on the one hand, start from an assumption that individual growth processes should lead to personal integrity, and question whether the various forms of education have been separately or mutually supportive of such an aim. On the other hand, we might accept that the differentiation of forms of education corresponds to the inevitable differentiation of spheres of life, inside individual life-courses and between individuals. Although commitment to either of these assumptions is an essential and permanent issue of education, we can historically evaluate educational institutions in respect to their promotion of differentiation or integration of personal growth processes. From the perspective of the **timing of educational intervention** in the forms of education, the need for "life long learning" was first recognized explicitly as the promotion of citizenship (folk education), i.e. participation in the life of the community and the nation state. The main forum of life-long learning has until the 1970s been liberal adult education, carried out by non-governmental or semi-governmental organizations. In encyclopaedic and vocational education, conceptions of the preparatory or 'once and for all' character of education has dominated, to be followed by self-education in the later phases of life. The possible need for later educational interventions based on abnormal courses of life, failures and mistakes in individual cases. Until the 1980s, the interventions aiming at the promotion of learning of individuals in the work process or work organizations received marginal attention as educational measures.

Considering the transformation of the Finnish (Nordic) heritage of educational thinking, the main tendency has been, on the one hand, the hegemony of the encyclopaedic form of education, e.g. in the construction of the comprehensive secondary school since the 1960s and the reform of vocational education since the late 1970s. The other side of the coin has been the politics of relevance of all forms of education for industry. Until the 1960s, popular adult education was rather a national or Nordic concept. Ever since the discourse has been transforming according to global trends (cf. Husen 1964, 1985, Botkin et al. 1979, Coombs 1983, KM 52/1973) The changing vocabularies were adopted from international organizations, who were looking for alternatives for building educational systems and interventions in the third-world countries in educational provision of various non-formal economic, political or non-governmental associations. These impacts were also important for the Finnish policy-makers in adopting the concept of life-long learning as democratization (humanization) of society and working life. Another interpretation became stronger through the initiatives of the OECD. The concept in use during the 1970s was recurrent education and training, focusing on improving the efficiency of production and work by reducing initial education interventions, which were not necessary, especially in the field of vocational education. Although the political initiatives did not materialize into radical reforms in the Finnish educational system, vocational adult education and personnel training in big companies and organizations of the public sector increased remarkably. The status of popular adult education was maintained, but it started increasingly to transform into promoting leisure activities and individual self-expression, on the one hand, and into alternatives of vocational education in non-established work tasks on the other. Thus losing its function of promoting participation in civic (or political) life.

Since the turn of the 1990s, **life-long learning** has started to dominate global educational policies both in educational and economic organizations (UNESCO, OECD, EU etc.). In Finland, the basic policy documents were commission reports "National education (civilisation) strategy" (KM 36/1993), "National schooling strategy" (KM 1/1994) and "Life-long learning in the knowledge society" (KM 13/1995, KM 10/1996), the most representative one being the report "The joy of learning: a national strategy for life long learning" (KM 14/1997). Although education was replaced by schooling - representing an instrumental, credentialist conception of education - already in the reform vocabulary of secondary education in the 1970s, the most recent documents defend the policy of promoting learning. Instead of formal schooling, working life, leisure and civic associations are central if not the most influential platforms for learning. The responsibility of educators and teachers for educational interventions is disappearing, when life-long learning is delegated to the various "learning environments" of everyday life.

According to policy-makers and planners, the contribution of new educational thinking to life-long learning is, that "the narrow school-centredness has now transformed into a wider strengthening of learning". (Lampinen 1998) Formal education and schooling are now conceived of as "springboards", where people proceed to the continuing training procedures of working life. This implies that the educational system is radically reduced to an educational service industry, satisfying the learning needs of (potential) employees, defined by 'working life', represented by leading employers and professional organizations. The promotion of national industries as a component of the construction of an occupationally structured, coherent nation-state, is replaced by providing optimal infrastructure for industrial clusters, which occasionally operate in a certain national socio-political and educational environment. A leading proponent of the latest educational policy education from the Ministry of Education expresses this as follows: "Schools should co-operate closely with industry. Teaching in schools should be based on an update perception of the needs of the industry. The organisations in industry should also be able to use the educational system to carry out their current training tasks... The theme of life-long learning has become prevalent in the political discussion on education... it can serve as a wide slogan for educational policy, stressing learning outside the formal system of schooling. As such, it can maintain the attention of companies and public organisations regarding their constant need to grow and develop through learning" (Lampinen 1998, pp. 149-151).

The Finnish Lifequal group identified typical meanings given to life-long learning in Finnish research genres. Two of them confirm the dominating policy discourse: one is based on social and psychological constructivism, focusing on individual informal learning biographies, another starts from the principles of rational choice, economic utility and effectiveness, focusing on human resource development and management practices in companies (Finnqual report 1999). The only critical genre was found in the sociology of education (e.g. Silvennoinen & Tulkki 1997, Rinne & Salmi 1998). This criticizes the universalized model of life-long learning as misleading: e.g. assumptions of rapid and continuous change, increasing complexity and challenge are true only for some areas and positions in working life, for many people work remains routine or depressing. The ideology only suits groups for whom the integration of the life-long learning concept into economic utility and effectiveness is correct. The warnings of obsoleteness of skills and education uphold general alertness about life-long updating one's labour-market value. Because in fact certain forms of learning allow themselves to be commodified more easily, people search for such education and training which has a higher labour-market value, whether they substantially need it or not. This is related to the new accreditation and certification systems, which would differentiate education and training provision: the suggested "competence passport" implies that some organizations will have the right to control what is included. As a conclusion on the criticism, one could claim that the dominating concept of life-long learning is promoting the middle-class, which needs new forms of differentiation, with the expansion and inflation of ever-higher level educational credentials. People who are not positive to continuous learning will be themselves responsible for their failures and problems in life. Furthermore, from employment policy perspective, life-long learning can actually be considered as non-voluntary storing or hiding of the unemployed.

The continuation of the policy of promoting life-long learning is confirmed in the latest statement of the Council for Adult Education (Aikuiskoulutusneuvosto 1999). The elements of dominating European discourses of life-long learning, identified in Lifequal partnership, are clearly present.

Accordingly, what life and life-long learning means is primarily
* working life or life of an employee - for example "informal learning" is explicitly equated with on-the-job learning
* training for work and employability after initial vocational education
* polarization: expanding (prolonging) the educational provision for people in mainstream education and working life and creating special provision for people who are non-productive, and a potential threat to social and political stability and economic growth.

The national and trans-national power-field of education will change, when the organizers, examiners and certifiers of education and training obtain increasing influence which has not been discussed through democratic processes. When trying to define trans-national educational challenges from the perspective of life-long learning, the Finnish Lifequal group questioned how the pressure for continued change, uncertainty, economic effectiveness is threatening the continuity and sustainability of human and non-human life at individual, community or global level and what context are decisive for it. From the educational perspective, the right and ability to participate in processes which are constructive for the sustainability of life, can be characterized as adulthood. The core of (humane) adulthood should not only be the individual and self-directed process of self-construction, but ethical commitment to constructive (social) participation in sustaining life and the conditions of life. When considering the heritage of Finnish (Nordic) popular adult education, we found the revitalization of its idea of adulthood as constructive social participation to be important. However, in its further elaboration, the transformation of the context of adulthood as social participation must be analysed. We believed that only by reflecting on the educational challenges in Europe, could the Lifequal project proceed to discussions about what kind of learning is worthwhile during the life-course of individuals and for organizations, communities, societies during their histories.

Why would social participation be a challenge for life-long learning?

In Lifequal project, alternative discourses of life-long learning were expected to be based on a critique of the values and purposes of education and training and should especially question whether the task of VET is to reproduce the skills required by the (hegemonic) European economy, or whether it has a wider commitment to empowerment, participation and social justice. In looking at Finnish alternative discourses on life-long learning, we cannot ignore considerations of the substitution of both the vocabulary of "education" and the metaphor of "school" by that of "learning" in the dominating discourse of life-long learning. Tentatively, it may be argued that the transformation in the rhetoric of life-long learning is indicative for all education. The educational and management discourses increasingly intermingle (cf. Geissler & Orthey 1996, Jacques 1996, Heikkinen 1998). Hand in hand with the quasi-pedagogical transformation of organizations (meaning, in fact, companies) goes the transformation of pedagogy into consultation and management of human resources development. When learning and change, life-long learning and permanent change become interchangeable, the rest of the vocabularies of work and education (learning) become mixed.

Table 1. Mutual penetration of educational and work discourse

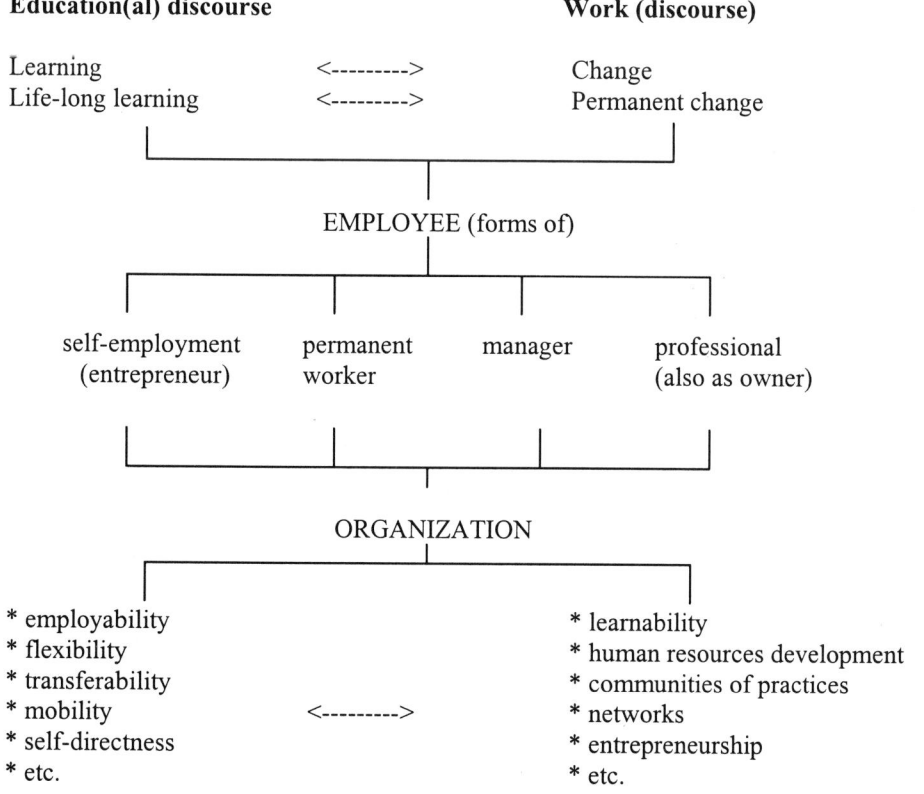

The mutual penetration of educational and management discourses, indicative in the rhetoric of life-long learning, are by no means restricted to the "lowest" categories of workers or social actors, but dominate the entire spectrum. This concerns permanent workers, managers or professionals or even professional owners, not to mention researchers as people, who are responsible for detaching, decontextualizing, disembodying the knowledge needed in learning processes, which basically does not discriminate age, sex, race, culture, in the world of post-modern culture and globalization of production-consumption systems. The conceptions of people in education as life-long learners, are increasingly, though not explicitly recognized (e.g. in esoteric courses in philosophy of education), geared towards what P. Fitzsimons characterizes as counterparts or functions of companies acting on global markets, i.e. self-interested utility-maximizers, detached from their personal, embodied knowledge and understanding, embedded in a certain cultural context. (Fitzsimons 1997). What the various versions of the dominating discourse of life-long learning share is the economic reduction of people and life: characterizing people as life-long learners and life as a platform for learning or as a provider of learning environments are parallel indicators of the subsumption of education under the logic of economics (calculative rationality).

At the moment, there are few educational alternatives for life-long learning in Finland. The critical commentators of the discourse of life-long learning only state negatively that it is "not indicative of a radically new way of conceiving learning and education, but of profound changes in the social and economic context, where educational policy is being developed and implemented" (Silvennoinen & Tulkki 1997). The discussion seems clearly to be preconditioned by a new configuration of the national production-consumption system, occupational and educational order, which are defined from the perspective of "clusters of industry (or work)" in a global setting. Learning is a central metaphor in this reorientation, related to the metaphors of "knowledge" or "information society" - learning which is primarily conceived of as a characteristic of an organization and society. Similar confusion is identifiable among the proponents of adult education elsewhere, when many of the ideas they still found progressive and radical in the 1970s have lost this potential, as well expressed by Peter Jarvis: "Continuing education (i.e. life long learning - AH) has become incorporated into the mainstream provision of education... The idea of adult education itself appears to be an almost outdated concept - after all, it was a product of the Enlightenment. There is almost certainly no future for it as a separate form of educational provision. Many of its ideals have been achieved and introduced by right-wing governments..." (Jarvis 1997). The metaphor of learning has replaced those of education and growth (or becoming educated), meaning learning in life, which in turn means predominantly learning at work. In searching to remain in their progressive role, some educational thinkers commit themselves to ideas like "options of cultivating work" or "educational options of work", in order to have a role in the argumentation on life-long learning. However, that which is at stake now is not even what H.-E. Tenorth characterized as the historical trend in education, i.e. the "Scholarisierung" of life and society (Tenorth 1988). What is essential now, is no longer becoming educated because of learning for life or for work-life, but evaluation of life or work itself in relation to its potential or contribution for learning as such. "Die Frage... lautet nicht mehr: Was hast Du für diese Tätigkeit gelernt? Sie heisst dann zukünftigt häufiger: Was lernst Du in dieser Tätigkeit" (Geissler & Orthey 1996, p. 73).

In the trans-national or global discourse, the language of the utopia of a learning society strongly opposes those of education and training, as well expressed by such leading figures as Longworth and Davies (1996, p. 145): "What we have tried to describe... is the end of the age of education and training and the beginning of the era of lifelong learning. As a necessary companion to the age of information it will allow us to understand better its implications for the lives of everyone of us and allow the human race to develop its potential in more positive way than hitherto..." As the prototype of the learning organisation is the company (cf. Ruohotie 1998, Simons 1998): the ideal learning society would be equal to one universal global company. What such a change means in practice is well characterized by Phil Hodkinson, who in the UK context has shown the contrast of connecting the utopian (post-modern) and neo-liberalist rhetorics of life long learning to the actual strengthening of neo-Fordist practices of personnel policy and training in companies. (cf. Hodkinson 1998)

It is exactly here that we could recognize the potential of the critical revision of the Finnish (Nordic) concepts of popular adult education. In the context of mutually penetrating vocabularies of work and education, the heritage of Finnish (Nordic) popular adult education is very interesting, because "originally" it was characterized by this very penetration. The factual developments in global economy can hardly be affected by educational criticism. Still, analysis of the heritage of popular adult education in Finland (Nordic countries) could be fruitful in searching for alternatives to the dominating discourses of life-long learning. Comments have been made that the kind of approach presented in this paper imply a radical jump away from the original thinking in the Lifequal project and also from "typical" thinking about vocational education. However, in a historical and wider cultural perspective the jump should not be considered especially radical at all: e.g. originally "popular education" in Finland (Nordic countries) was most closely linked to work and the promotion of industry as the main components of community and civic life. In the following table, the different aspects of adulthood as social participation are characterized in the historically changing context where adulthood is being defined.

Table 2. Contribution of the popular adult education heritage to identifying educational functions of life-long learning

Context for educational challenge	Adulthood as participation: changes and/or layers of participation
Community and people ("folk")	Member of life-community (holistic participation, based on obligation and reciprocity)
Nation state, based on national industries structured by occupational system	(State) citizenship, having a place in the system of occupations and society (political and occupational participation)
Trans-national economic and political blocs, industrial clusters and organizations	Competent life-long learner in permanently changing communities of practice (participation as work-force)
The globe, humanity?	"World-citizenship"? (participation in LIFE)

The context of emerging Finnish popular adult education was agrarian communities, which were the basic units for people in the mobilization for nation-formation. In the nation state, adulthood was democratic citizenship and participation in occupationally structured national industry. The transformation which we are experiencing now is the replacement of this context by transnational economic and political entities and the new ways of utilization of people as work-force. Without historical and critical interpretation, the vocabulary of life-long learning has only a legitimizing function. In order to envisage alternative futures, we need interpretations which are sensitive to the historical layers in our mentalities and social practice. The importance of communities of livelihood and holistic participation do not disappear with the commitment to national cultural and political entities or to occupational forms of life. Nor is it necessary for people to accept the offer of post-modern culture, which legitimizes their utilization as mobile work-force, who only have identity as members of changing organizations. The recent trans-national educational challenge of adulthood is, what does participation in this context of life means and how is it promoted. A further challenge is whether and how adulthood and participation could or should be conceived of in an alternative trans-national context, which is more holistic in relation to human and non-human life. It may also be that without analysing the limits and controversies of the heritage of popular adult education, there is a danger of replicating them in the new situation.

The Finnish group suggested that the Lifequal project should start from the view that there are culturally meaningful and important traditions in every partner country which would be worth remembering and important in promoting a trans-national (European) alternative discourse of life-long learning. In the Finnish (Nordic) tradition we wanted to note the aspect of social participation, no matter if it was represented as a genuine form of education or as a component to other (vocational or encyclopaedic) forms of education. The idea of participation was not only for the socially excluded or for certain periods of life. It was a holistic principle, which was linked to the ideas of encyclopaedic and vocational education, which in the mainstream Anglo-American and continental heritage have exclusively been conceived of as the only alternative forms in education. However, the Lifequal project was never able to enter this level of cultural and comparative reflection.

Examples of alternative approaches to life-long learning

The Finnish research group wished to bring examples from alternative approaches to life-long learning into the Lifequal project, which would make the suggestion of social participation as an alternative to the concept of life-long learning into something concrete, by revisiting the category of adulthood and utilizing the heritage of Nordic popular adult education.

As an example of ways of responding to the challenge of social participation in the context of the dominant discourse of life-long learning we presented two examples from the report of the "Good Practices of lifelong learning" (Suurla & Markkula 1998). The 20 examples in the report are evaluated based upon the criteria, which were set according to "The joy of learning: a national strategy for lifelong learning" (KM 1997;14) and implement the dominant discourse with the object of "the learning society" and "knowledge society". These initiatives are said to conclude the methods by which strategies will become concrete in the future. In this way, life-long learning has become a "knowledge society" project, which evolves from early childhood and is still strongly present during retirement. However, the most significant are the employed people and their continuing training and education. It is expected that once learning is found to be pleasant and once this is perceived, it will be difficult to separate learning either at work or in leisure time.

Both of the examples presented were funded by the European Social Fund, which is a common feature in all of these initiatives, emphasizing the markedly international involvement and importance of network development. The first example is an IT-based Youth Workshop Project and the second a network supported by European Commission programmes, i.e. development projects for villages in the Kainuu area (scarcely populated area in north-east Finland). The role of youth workshops in Finnish education and labour market policy is controversial. Workshops are targeted at young people who are unemployed and at risk of social exclusion. The employment authorities address the participants and a youth workshop is a workplace. They aim to make it easier for the participants to access further education, to gain experience of vocational education and training in practice and to help to plan future studies. Learning by doing for half a year instead of unemployment is one of the positive functions. Also, new ways of support, guiding and motivation are found in the workshops (Paakkunainen 1996). So far, workshops have no formal status either in education or employment. Perhaps this is one of the reasons why youth workshops are seen as positive learning experiences for young people who may have difficulties in finding a place in society. However, workshops located between the formal education system and employment activities have the role of being administered and controlled by both the ministries and are a means to promote active labour market policy instead of being new ways of organizing education.

What might be the potential of youth workshops as alternatives in promoting life-long learning? Firstly, workshop activities provide an opportunity for those young people who have left compulsory education with or without a certificate and who are uncertain of what they would like to do in the future. Workshops give time and space to make plans for the future, be it education, working life or private life. Secondly, they have given general experience of social participation instead of having being forced into temporary employment, employment courses or unemployment. The feeling of security, permitting failure and still being accepted and the chance for positive social contacts have been considered to be the most important outcomes. Finally, a workshop period is one way to keep young people in continuous learning outside the formal system. The learning experience which the young themselves regard to be the most important aspect may be different from the official aims of the workshops, i.e. vocational skills or effective employment. Participating, learning to be with others and having others around one are reasons why young people have also come to regard the workshop as a positive experience (Paakkunainen 1996). How far the aims and practices of youth workshops really are or can be an alternative to dominating concepts of life-long learning, is still an open question.

The Kainuu project has given rise to a cooperation network extending beyond the levels of officials, developer organizations and villages. The objectives and actions of the projects differ, but the target group is the same, i.e. the village and its environment, services, residents and enterprises. The core idea has been that people involved in different projects and activities should benefit from one another's know-how instead of competing and trying to gain ground from one another. The basic tenets of life-long learning will be realized in the development of the villages: learning shared responsibility and individual responsibility, cooperation skills and personal growth. In this example the EU-funding is a catalyzer instead of being meant to build a project for a problem group, i.e. for middle-aged women with few opportunities to obtain meaningful work. Secondly, the individual characteristics of the villages are strengthened like the status of women in this area. In the search for multidimensional impact, the village project may have been successful.

What are the alternatives inside the "knowledge society"? As alternative approaches we presented The Nature School, The Food Circles and the Pro Ahvenisto Project, all activities in the town of Hämeenlinna (42 000 inhabitants) and initiatives of informal learning. In the Nature School the aim of the activity is to support the development of the personal relationship with Nature. The learning method is experimental learning, beginning from single experiences and progressing to ethical questions with the ideas of Agenda 21 as a starting point. The aims of the activity vary depending on the target group, children or adults. The Food Circles are an alternative way to provide daily food for one's family. The circle has a direct contact with the farmer(s) to order daily food. The essential prerequisite of the success of the Food Circle is that people become engaged in the activities and want to learn other daily habits in providing, cooking and eating.

The Pro Ahvenisto project has the aim of protecting and revitalizing a beautiful area. Ten years ago a group of volunteers decided to renovate the area which includes forest, a small lake, a swimming pool, a sauna and some other buildings. It was and is typical of the group that it consists of people of very different ages: young people who wanted to have a place for sunbathing, adults who wanted to have a clean and safe beach, older people who remember and respect the memory of the 1952 Olympic Games (swimming and shooting were held in Hämeenlinna). The starting point was also to take care of the rare natural environment. Nowadays the Ahvenisto area is again lively and in fairly good condition. The Pro Ahvenisto group has active cooperation with the association of the unemployed. Skilled workers led the repair projects. The local authorities have slowly woken up to provide some support for the materials, likewise the Ministry of the Environment.

Both the members of the Food Circle and the Pro Ahvenisto Project were surprised at the questions on learning; they had not considered their action as learning but only normal everyday doings or voluntary work. When they took the viewpoint of learning they all found many aspects which they could call learning. And, as they said, a kind of learning that could not have happened in school. The very names of the examples of best practice indicate how different they were. Matters pertaining to people's everyday routine do not easily lend themselves to the parlance of learning and education. Such learning remains unconscious. If it is not recognized as such or if it is classified as of lesser importance, it lacks prestige and status. However, matters related to the protection of the environment, for example, affect the well-being of everyone, and contemplating them and appreciating them occurs through knowledge and action, by learning and understanding. If this type of learning is not noticed by researchers, however, and receives no appreciation, we are also ignoring an area of life which is still one of the most important for us all: living and learning outside work.

For whom is social participation a challenge?

The dominant expectations and arguments about life-long learning are contradictory in many ways. On the one hand, life-long learning of a certain kind (supported by "good practice") is assumed to solve social and economic problems which individuals, communities and countries are facing in Europe. On the other hand, despite the celebration of informal learning as a component of individual life-politics, and almost hostile criticism of formal learning and educators, the demands to develop authentic learning environments can only be targeted at educational institutions and educators. Consequently, parts of the vocational education system are increasingly perceived as socio-political and employment political interventions, targeted at groups, which have been diagnosed as problems because of non-productivity or being socially excluded, being in need of social and political control. The separate actions and programmes guarantee that the mainstream forms of education or working life are not challenged to change or question the problems of social participation as their own problem.

Furthermore, if the criticism of formal learning and the idealizing characterizations of learning societies are constituted by informal learning processes in all spheres of life and through the life span, the educational challenges should not be primarily targeted at schools and educators in formal education. The long-lasting glorification of informal learning as the core of life-long learning, which would primarily take place at work, does not seem to lead to constructive educational alternatives. Even if we recognize (once again) that people learn and have to learn for life outside formal education, this does not imply that formal education is not important or valuable. On the contrary, the conclusion might be that educators should (as always) have the right and responsibility to ensure holistic support for the life and livelihood of individuals, communities and humankind. Instead of developing "second chance" ("second class") solutions for the problem groups, this would imply a more universal and general change of educational institutions and collaboration among educationists in different spheres of life. Beside initiatives for developing alternative forms of education for problem groups or for mobilizing grass-root democracy, there are also some signs in the formal education system of revitalizing some aspects of popular education in Finland. However, it may still take time before the suggestions of profiling teaching in comprehensive schools in a more educational and holistic direction expand to other stages and forms of education.

What could and should the role of European researchers be in developing alternative discourses and promoting alternative practices for the dominant ones? As we learned from the Lifequal project, despite some promises of critical reflections, it ended in a collection of papers which respond to the political goals of the Socrates studies and analyses programme. Increasingly educational research functions as a subcontractor for policy-makers in diagnosing, planning, forecasting and evaluating reform strategies at the European level. However, like the research which is used to legitimize the dominating discourses of life-long learning the research on alternative discourses likewise has no consequences, if it does not somehow promote their recognition and legitimization. A crucial question is whether there are alternative platforms for mobilizing people in alternative discussions. Until now, even critical researchers in Finland and the Nordic countries have primarily allied with the (potentially) progressive, education- and democracy-friendly state and searched for discursive platforms in alliance with the state. However, in the recent context, where policies, economies and industries are deliberately being developed trans-nationally, the nature of the state as an ally may have changed: in their commitment to promoting the development of optimal operational infrastructures for trans-national industrial clusters, nation-states with their neo-liberal programmes may only force the educational and research communities to serve as instruments for the hegemonic global projects in politics, economy and culture.

Researchers alone cannot develop alternative platforms where alternative discourses, policies and practices of life-long learning can be discussed, whether they focus on the sustaining of life and adulthood as social participation at individual, communities, nation-states and globe or not. The following picture characterizes the various fields of education, where new potential platforms for alliance and for alternative discourses for life-long learning could be developed.

Figure 1. Collaborative forums, educational policy platforms among actors in different fields of VET

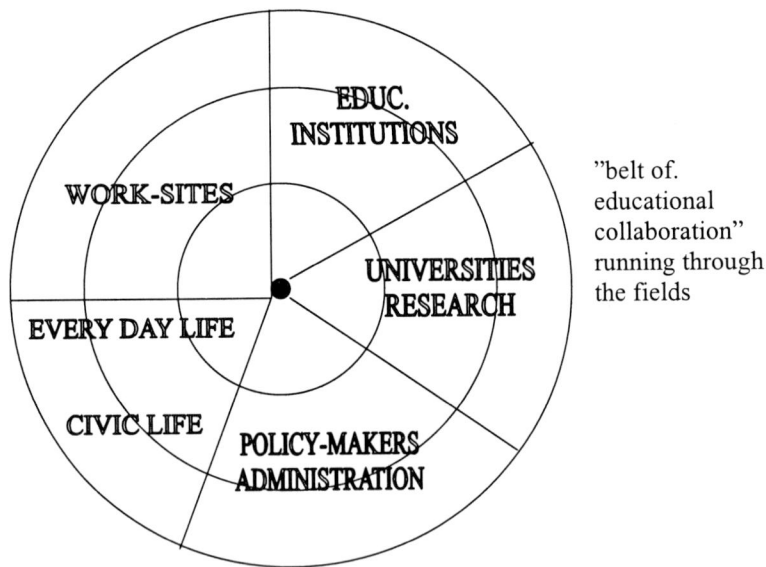

"belt of. educational collaboration" running through the fields

If researchers as co-constitutors of education are responsible for recognizing and being sensitive towards the educational challenges of their time, could they and should they be active in defining and explicating the varieties, complexities and tensions of the arenas of learning - not only in schools and educational institutes, but on work-sites, in structures of educational administration and policy making, in universities and research institutions and in practices of everyday life? Should and could researchers explicate the potential of belts and networks of people with an educational commitment in different arenas of learning, which could be mobilized into an educational community developing an alternative discourse for life-long learning? Do researchers or academics (of education) have a special or any role at all in such mobilization as they have been believed to have had at least during certain periods of history, especially during the construction of nation states - or have they already become too conformist and corrupted to support any alternatives, which might endanger their own status as handmaids of the powerful? Whatever the answer is, researchers cannot escape the question of their commitment and alliances in confirming and legitimizing certain discourses (and policies and practices) of life-long learning.

References

Aikuiskoulutusneuvosto (1999). *Aikuiskoulutuspolitiikka 2000-luvulla.* Helsinki.

Attwell, G.(1999). *Notes and minutes of Socrates Lifequal project meetings 1998-1999.*

Botkin, D. & al. (1979). *No limits to Learning.* London.

Committee-reports
* KM52/1973. *Vuoden 1973 koulutuskomitean mietintö.* VPK. Helsinki.
* KM 36/1993. *Kansallinen sivistysstrategia* (National civilisation strategy)
* KM 1/1994. *Kansallinen koulutusstrategia* (National schooling strategy)
* KM 13/1995, KM 10/1996. *Elinikäinen oppiminen tietoyhteiskunnassa* (Life long learning in knowledge society)
* KM 14/1997. Oppimisen ilo: *Kansallinen elinikäisen oppimisen strategia* (The joy of learning: a national strategy for life long learning)

Coombs, P.H. (1983). *The World Crisis in Education.* Oxford University Press.

Coffield, F. (ed) (1999). *The Learning Society.* ESRC: The Policy Press.

Fitzsimons, P. (1997). The Politics of Self-constitution. In *Journal of Philosophy and Theory of Education* 1/1997.

Friman, M. & Heikkinen, A. & Laiho, K. (1999). *For Life or Work-life?* Presentation in the LIFEQUAL Workshop Seminar in the University of Jyväskylä 11.-12.3.1999.

Friman, M.& Heikkinen, A. & Laiho, K. (1999.) *FINNQUAL.* Finnish interim report for LIFEQUAL project. 11/1999.

Geissler, K. & Orthey, M. (1996). Wandern bildet - Heimweh. In Wittwer, W. (hrsg): *Von der Meisterschaft zur Bildungswanderschaft.* Bielefeld.

Heikkinen, A. (1998). *The Making of a European Employee.* Paper presented at Learning and Work conference, September 1998, Zurich.

Heikkinen, A. (1999). *Dominating and alternative discourses on life-long learning - views from Lifequal project.* Paper presented at Forskning i Norden conference, Tampere 27.-29.5.1999.

Heikkinen & al (1999). *Elinkeinon edistämisestä koulutuspalvelujen laaduntarkkailuun.* Tampereen yliopisto.

Hodkinson, P. (1998). Technicism, Teachers and Teaching. In *Journal of Vocational Education and Training.* 2/1998.

Husen, T. (1986). *The Learning Society Revisited.* Oxford: Pergamon Press.

Jacques, R. (1996). *Manufacturing the employee.* Sage.

Jarvis, P. (1997). *Ethics of education for adults in a late modern society.* NIACE.

Kettunen, P. (1997). *Työjärjestys.* Vastapaino.

Korsnes, O. (1998). *Pitfalls of comparative research on VET.* Paper presented in VET and culture network conference, August 1998, Bergen.

Lampinen, O. (1998). *Suomen koulutusjärjestelmän kehitys.*Gaudeamus.

Longworth, N. & Davies, W. K. (1996). *Life-long Learning.* Kogan Page.

Paakkunainen, K. (1996*). Nuorisopaja: Tehdashallin hämärästä autonomiseen oppiin teoksessa* Aaltojärvi, P & Paakkunainen, K. (1996). Nuorten työpaja – sosiaalinen peli, palkkatyö vai varasto? *Nuorisotutkimus 2000* 2/1996. Helsinki.

Rinne, R & Salmi, E. (1998). *Oppimisen uusi järjestys.* Vastapaino.

Ruohotie, P. (1997). *Osaamalla menestykseen.* Edita.

Silvennoinen, H. & Tulkki, P. (1997). *Elinikäinen oppiminen.* Gaudeamus.

Simons, R.- J. (1998). *VET institutions as Learning organisations.* Paper presented in TSER-FORUM workshop, Evo, Finland, June 1998.

Suurla, R. & Markkula, M. (1998). *Elinikäisen oppimisen hyvät käytännöt.* KM 14/1997, Liite.

Tenorth, H.-E. (1988). *Geschichte der Erziehung.* Juventa.

A FUTURE FOR LIFELONG LEARNING? SOME COMMENTS ON A NORDIC SCENARIO PROJECT

Gunnar Grepperud and Odd Einar Johansen

Background

Typical to the 1990s, primarily the final half of this decade, is the keen and renewed interest in knowledge and competence, and thus also lifelong learning. Bearing this in mind, there is good reason to claim that we are living in a period of strong knowledge optimism (Grepperud, 1999). In the Nordic countries and elsewhere this has manifested itself in a number of studies, reports and specific measures primarily aimed at raising the general level of competence in the adult population.

There is reason to point out that having faith in knowledge and education is not new in itself. Our entire education system as we know it today is based on the idea that one form or another of formalized knowledge transfer constitutes the basic underpinning of social development. Moreover, in all the Nordic countries we find examples during particular periods of time where training, education and non-formal education have been assigned particular great importance.

Similarly, lifelong learning, both as a perspective and as a concept, has earlier generated both inspiration and vision. In the transition from the 1960s and the 1970s this was a vital topic in education policy debates within UNESCO (lifelong learning) as well as in OECD (recurrent education), and in the same way as thirty years later, a number of ideas and proposals were launched, breaking radically with established thinking on education and conditions for education. Even if this "wave of optimism" brought about a revitalization of adult education, as instantiated in the Norwegian Act relating to Adult Education from 1976, interest cooled, visions vanished and focus was turned to other matters. When reading reports and articles based on the knowledge optimism of the 1990s, striking similarities may be found on more than one point with the rationale and proposals of the 1960s and 1970s. A review of the Norwegian report "Ny kompetanse" (New Competence) (NOU 1997:25) shows that most of the proposals launched here have seen the light of day more than once before. Indeed we can follow them from report to report throughout the 1970s and 1980s, for example both the right of the individual to be granted leave from work for education purposes and the promotion of a far more liberal and open attitude to non-formal learning.

In this historic pespective, and partly in spite of the knowledge optimism, a degree of doubt with respect to future development also creeps into the picture. Could history repeat itself? Could visions of lifelong learning "disappear along the way"? Might we (once again) fail to lay the groundwork for the learning society in spite of the many measures of the 1990s (understood as something more and different than education policy glibness)?

The research question, purpose and focus of the project

Bearing in mind what history can show us (which in this case is simplified and merely outlined) and the ambiguity we currently sense with respect to the future development of this field, our aim, and that of the Nordic Council of Ministers which supports the project, has been a desire to peer into the crystal ball. Is it possible, based on today's situation, and also casting sidelong glances at the historical development, to state something about how this issue will develop in the years to come?

Having said this, we hasten to add that we fully endorse the Danish poet Piet Hein's wise words that it is difficult to predict, *particularly* about the future. This was more than evident in the Norwegian project "Scenarier 2000" (Scenarios 2000), launched in 1987. At a summary conference in the autumn of 1999 the original scenario group assessed their three models. The main conclusion was that none of them had proved true, and that on entering the new millennium only a limited number of the sub-aspects of the three scenarios could even be recognized. Thus any ambition to predict the future is an uncertain task at best as in part it is impossible to include all the conditions that impact social developments, and in part it is impossible to predict sudden and dramatic changes that drive development in an entirely different and unexpected direction. The main problem thus derives from the fact the we often create our future visions on the basis of references to the past, on what we know something about, not on what will come, and what we only vaguely can discern. On the other hand, the uncertainty of the future may also induce us to predict a quicker pace of change, perhaps even assuming far more radical and fundamental changes than what actually occurs. In this respect we find that the education sector in a historical perspective is an area where major qualitative breaks from the status quo are not common phenomena. In our assessment, changes that have come about in the education system seem to be more connected to problems of scope rather than to fundamental and radical changes.

Our work aims to arrive at one *realistic assumption* of what will be typical of lifelong learning in 20 years. The main aim of our work is to suggest a possible direction of development as the underpinning for raising awareness of and increasing discussion on *what we want* and whether *we have an intention* behind our focus on lifelong learning in the years to come. More than providing accurate answers, the scenario aims to inspire the necessary questions that beg asking for further development. Thus the scenario appears more as a planning tool, a qualitative approach to the future by developing *mindmaps* or visions that will capture some of the complexity that escapes more quantitative approaches.

Our approach to lifelong learning has been to work with the scenario based on a broad understanding of the field. Hence we are not only concerned about adult learning but also about lifelong learning as an overarching philosophy for the future structure and development of the learning society. Bearing this in mind, lifelong learning is about all forms of learning, all learning arenas and all forms of insight and perception.

The scenario is based on the situation in 20 years' time, i.e. in 2020. Eleven main themes have been identified on which the scenario is based:

- Lifelong learning as a topic of social debate.
- The degree to which the learning society has been realized on various levels.
- The role of the central authorities in the learning society.
- Rationales for lifelong learning.
- The role of non-formal education.
- The relationship between the actors in adult education (including further education).
- ICT as a tool and impact factor.
- Knowledge and learning philosophies.
- Competence and equal rights (gender, geography, ethnicity, socio-economic background, profession).
- The situation for primary and upper secondary school.

Research strategy, method and publishing form

The *scenario study approach* is our starting point. This is an expert-based scenario process where a group of selected experts work in a relatively closed process before publishing a report. This report is then used as the groundwork for planners. Based on the so-called "Delphi technique", 15 persons, three in each of the Nordic countries, have been interviewed about their assessment of future developments based on the 11 themes outlined above. In our case the most precise description of the method is to call it a "virtual Delphi strategy." In place of written interviews we chose in the first round to conduct oral interviews based on a comparatively open interview form. The interviews were conducted as a combination of research interviews and "in-depth conversations" (Mellin Olsen, 1995).

As lifelong learning can also be understood as a series of sub-fields, it was emphasized that the interviewees, seen together and across national borders, would need to cover as many areas as possible (see the appendix for an overview of participants). It was, moreover, emphasized that expertise should not only be understood in relation to field and nation, but should also be connected to position. As the basis for our work we defined three important positions:

- The practician, i.e. the person who on a daily basis needs to realize/implement the visions.
- The politician, i.e. the persons who outline the visions and facilitate framing conditions.
- The researcher, i.e. the person who contributes to insight and improvements with respect to goals, framing conditions and practices.

As with the Delphi technique, the scenario project has a number of phases. In Phase 1 strategies and research questions have been clarified and instantiated and the interviews have been held. In Phase 2 a first scenario draft will be written. In contrast to the Delphi technique this writing should not attempt to create a picture that might be called representative for the total contribution of the participants. The interviews are primarily used as the foundation for the design of our own scenario. It must therefore be pointed out that the designed scenario is our responsibility alone, and that the interviewees cannot be held responsible for the assessments and conclusions that are drawn. However, great emphasis will be placed on the interview and the interviewees as experts. We therefore have a Phase 3 where our original scenario will be sent to all participants for their comments and elaboration. Phase 4 will therefore consist of a revision of the first draft, if necessary, based on the feedback that we receive.

Preliminary reflections on lifelong learning in the Nordic countries in 2020

Referring to the four phases, it is too early to give a comprehensive presentation of the final scenario. We shall nevertheless outline some of the (preliminary) reflections we have made with respect to future development.

- **Lifelong learning as a theme in the public debate**

The debate on lifelong learning will, even in 2020, primarily be linked to players in the education sector and working life. However, it will have a strong position as education policy rhetoric. In 2020 challenges connected to financial development and raising competitive ability will continue to be a stated rationale for lifelong learning. The growing degree of migration leads to learning needs not only for the well-educated "global riders", but also for persons from other continents with minimal education. These will make up the bulk of immigrants into the Nordic countries in the future. Changes in the composition of the population and improved general health conditions will mean that relatively speaking we will have many well-to-do elderly persons who also wish and demand meaningful learning activities. As the majority of adults will also have more leisure time we shall find that traditional hobby courses will boom again, in part in completely different areas than we currently find them in.

To some extent the debate on lifelong learning will re-ignite when the reforms introduced in the late 1990s' are assessed, but this debate will not be part of a greater social policy context. The assessment efforts, which exclusively examine parts of the total effort, primarily focus on effect and much less on basic values and choice of direction. In the short term the assessments have little impact on development in the field, but will primarily serve as the basis for sustaining a certain degree of debate on the field. For the final part of the period initiatives will be taken for some new studies, for example to adjust the course in relation to the developments that have specifically occurred. The worry in relation to an education policy perspective will be that differences in competence are equally prominent features as the levelling out of competence. Even if overall there has been some rise in competence, the competence gap has in fact been strengthen by the emphasis on competence in working life.

In addition to the traditional knowledge players, i.e. the education system, influence will be exerted by actors in working life, primarily private business and industry, impacting ideas and the debate that still exists. In some large, knowledge-intensive companies learning will appear as a basic perspective, i.e. as a manner of understanding and explaining the world and everyday affairs. For the main part of small and medium enteprises, education and competence is still determined by the state of the marked.

While the evolution of democracy had an important place in the debate on lifelong learning in the 1970s, this will be virtually absent in 2020. This does not mean that the democracy debate will become less important, but rather that this debate and the growth debate will run parallel to each other and with few points of contact. The concern with gradually retreating political involvement in the population will result in a greater focus on training in democratic participation in the compulsory school. This democracy training will be carried out in a form that can be placed under the umbrella of "civic education", and which prior to the turn of the century was described through comparative studies (Torney-Purta et al., 1999). Sadly this does not lead to a revitalization of individual social involvement.

- The visions of the learning society and the learning organization

The visions about the learning organization and the learning society will be high on the rhetoric agenda, also in 2020. The financial powers in our Nordic countries will sustain this discourse, which will be propelled by the expressed growth motives. The situation will thus be quite different than the 1970's wave of lifelong learning. At that time adult education was motivated by the distribution policy, the desire to level out wage differences and the realization of the Nordic democracy model (cf. above).

Over time a paradoxical conflict between the learning organization and the learning society, understood as the democratic society, will arise, because the development of organization and society partly builds on different values and because the various arenas have varying degrees of importance and impact. While in working life (both private and public) the development of competence is, and will be, based upon adaptation, efficiency and financial value creation, the learning society assumes that each citizen will be heard, where no social group dominate and where everybody will participate in a number of discourses and will develop genuine critical competence.

Even though adult education will be defined more and more as the development of competence in working life, developments over time will show that recognition of competence as a decisive input factor for economic value creation has not quite gained general acceptance. In many companies competence will continue to be a boom-time phenomenon, i.e. something that may be given priority when business is good. This especially applies to small and medium-sized companies, and this will in all probability be the situation more for companies on the periphery than in the centre. Furthermore, the discussion in working life will focus on very specific approaches, primarily discussions on accreditation schemes, surveys of competence and individual career planning. In some knowledge-intensive companies and some larger enterprises, however, a number of good examples show how learning for the individual employee is dealt with (i.e. as more than short or long education programmes). For example, we will see that these organizations utilise and develop in an exciting manner the work forms that have been important in non-formal education contexts. Groups such as Statoil, Nokia and Ericsson will not only develop this for their own employees, for example through corporate universities, but they will also sell their learning products to others.

Even though working life seen as a whole contains many differences, we shall be influenced by and join the symbolic actions of the learning society. This will be brought about by using the competence and quality labels to make belonging in the learning society more explicit. A hot-dog factory may become "the competence company of the year", and in the future we might be invited to spend our holidays in "the competence city of the year", or "NN the learning community". These labels will also be actively used for marketing purposes.

While knowledge optimism will lead to the setting of values for education-defined knowledge in the financial sphere, silent knowledge – non-formal learning - will be assigned greater importance in the learning organization. The learning organization will have room for a substantial number of persons with "merely" non-formal learning. At the same time the concept of the learning organization has been developed in close association with the idea of organizations that must compete to survive, and such organizations must seek to make the best players join their team. It is thus reasonable to conclude that some, but not all, may join the "winning team" – the learning organization. Thus such a learning organization may work selectively, excluding large groups of people from participating in the lifelong learning course.

The learning society, as described in OECD and EU documents, should strive for lifelong learning *for everyone*. Again we see the outline of a paradoxical landscape. A "learning society" can paradoxically enough not only consist of "learning organizations". The authorities must therefore play an active role, working for lifelong learning for everyone.

- **The importance of the state for lifelong learning in the Nordic countries**

The trend towards internationalization, primarily developments within the EU, will dominate education and working-life policy in all the Nordic countries. The homogeneity that has been typical of the individual Nordic states after the war will dissolve in a more varied European context. By this time both Iceland and Norway will be member of the EU. Even though the Nordic countries attach importance to co-ordinating and improving their collaboration with the EU, it will become more and more difficult to speak of a "Nordic dimension". The national geographical centres in all the Nordic countries will orient themselves more and more towards Brussels, while the mental and cultural distance between the geographically peripheral areas and their own national centres and Brussels will grow. For this reason a growing number of binding regional cooperation groups will be found, along similar lines as the Øresund region, across national boundaries. This will apply to Sweden, Finland and Norway in particular. This will in turn create a greater feeling of regional identity and undermine national identity to a certain degree.

The employment and business policies will gain greater importance for lifelong learning than education policy. This will be a consequence of a growing emphasis on financial rationality in the whole education sector, combined with the conscious effort to move "learning arenas" for adults from school as an institution and into working life and business and industry. In 2020 the central authorities will also have reduced their role compared to the "total" role they currently play in the entire education sector. This feature is a symptom of a development whereby the welfare state (in the sense of state responsibility) is de-escalated and the idea of the welfare society (the responsibility of each and every person) is strengthened.

In the future public authorities will primarily finance obligatory primary school and upper secondary education. Basic higher education will generally be publicly financed. Other types of financing, both of research and teaching, will nevertheless gain increasing importance. In 2015 funds allocated directly for the operation of universities in the Nordic countries will constitute slightly more than 60 % of the total resources. What currently is called continuing education and non-formal education will be financed entirely by non-state sources. This means that there will be stronger integration, or possibly a complete merger between the traditional education field and adult education/non-formal education. Special programmes for adult groups with special needs will, however, continue to be financed through public funds. The role of the state as the guarantor of welfare will be reduced, but the state will nevertheless retain power in the education sector, primarily through legislation, provisions and regulations. This will apply more to lower levels than to higher levels, more to institution education than the "classic adult education field". In the future, school will not substantially increase its importance for lifelong learning. The paradox will now be the following: The Nordic obligatory school is as good as it can be, and it will continue to contribute to creating inequality in society.

- **Nordic non-formal education**

The volume increase in lifelong learning ensures that even in 2020 there will be room for non-formal education organizations in the Scandinavian countries, but the activities of these organizations will be substantially reduced. Non-formal education will no longer be considered a "semi-state" sector. This leads to simplification of legislation in this area, and financial state support will disappear, with the exception of financing for education of special groups.

It is probable that in 2020 we shall see a counter-reaction against the financial rationality philosophy that permeates the entire society. New groups will emerge that on an ideological or religious basis will perform awareness-raising work, and global, informal and formal networks will be created. Action groups engaged with ideologically based studies probably will increasingly work in regions and transcend national borders, also in the Nordic countries.

People with different functions in society will now also be assigned different qualities. The education of the people will, with the growing degree of position change in society in 2020, ensure that education activities that we associate with non-formal education will take place throughout all phases of the life course. Questions may be raised as to whether character is formed during upbringing, whether it stays more or less unchanged for the rest of a person's life, or whether the *self* to a certain extent also becomes more "flexible" in late-modern society (Giddens, 1991).

- **Dominant actors in the adult education of the future**

The entire education system will attain a greater degree of liberation. There will be fewer centrally issued curricula and regulations on all levels. The public education system will, for example, be allowed to receive payment for its services in a completely different way.

A growing number of national and international actors will also establish themselves in the area of further and continuing education for working life, not least in what we currently call ICT-based education. Higher education institutions will be far more active in this field than today, which will cause changes in the relationships between education providers in general and between higher education institutions in particular. Development will be in the approach of increased competition. The shift to a market-oriented direction will also cause the higher education institutions to develop more as unified organizations with stronger management and a greater degree of control. The academic staff will come to be regarded more as employees in a knowledge company than as independent and autonomous professionals. There will be a higher degree of network building and binding collaboration between higher education institutions and private business and industry. These relations will be established both within each country and between countries. One of the most powerful networks being built in a Nordic context is an international syndicate comprising the Business Management Colleges in Norway, Sweden, Finland and Denmark, the Norwegian School of Management, Norsk Investorforum and the Wallenberg group. The goal is to establish a leading global position in economic and management subjects. Developments also force a number of mergers between universities and colleges. Similar restructuring will also be witnessed in other areas of the adult education sector. In a Norwegian context, the merger between large distance-teaching institutions and a part of the Open University's and the Worker's Education Association's largest urban departments is particularly interesting. The new unit will be called "The Flexible Academy".

The so-called "young elderly persons", i.e. those over 55 years of age who have ample resources, will be a new and large target group for the study organizations in 2020, especially with respect to study circles of short duration with elements of cultural experiences leading to informal learning. Folk high schools and study organizations will focus their activities on small groups with special needs, for example immigrant groups, which will receive public funding for such non-formal education. The financing is entirely based on tender.

- **ICT as a tool and impact factor**

Technological development during the initial 20 years of the new millennium ensures that what we currently call ICT will be an integral part of everyday living. Thus ICT will also become an increasingly important dimension when developing education programmes. The question is no longer <u>whether</u> to use ICT, rather <u>how</u> to use it. A comprehensive programme of net-based programmes will exist, both short courses and long study programmes. During this period such programmes will come under growing critical scrutiny, but it turns out that a great many students and/or companies find accessibility to be more important than quality. Absolutely decisive in this context is that such courses are less cost intensive, as they are cheaper and the high cost of hiring substitutes is avoided. Net-based programmes will also make many companies attempt to privatize learning, i.e. make it the individual's responsibility, inducing him or to take it outside working hours, for example by covering expenses for ICT equipment in their employees' homes.

Institutions offering teaching via the Internet will develop more flexible solutions with combinations of physical meetings for participants within a number of themes. On the other hand, the traditional "classroom teaching" of established education institutions will also undergo change to comprise Internet-based transactions with users when teaching given topics. The actors that will dominate the "net-based marked" t will be global providers.

In working life the situation will also be that very few companies will be able to assess the quality of the programmes offered. Only major companies will be able to give priority to their own employees to quality assure the programmes they are using. Accordingly there is a danger that the learning society will not necessarily be the learned society. A broad focus on ICT-based education may also generate a more superficial relationship to knowledge and insight. This will be reinforced by a tendency by some to look upon *learning* and *information without a meaningful direction* as being equal.

Technical developments may also open for increasingly enhanced two-way communication using text, sound and images. In 2020, communication and direct interaction between persons mediated via digital solutions will be more important than software development in a learning context. However, a significant number of learning software applications will have been developed for a variety of reasons, not least for simulation purposes. ICT development will also lead to a certain rejuvenation of self-studies, for example based on electronic learning aids.

English-language textbooks/learning aids will be more common in the Nordic countries, but not as total solutions. Some programmes at universities and scientific colleges will be exceptions in this context, as universities will be internationalized much more than today. Furthermore, we will be offered a higher number of programmes from education institutions abroad given as net-based programmes comprising especially adapted teaching material.

- **Teaching, learning and knowledge**

In a society with many and shifting interests, priorities, and parallel and conflicting development traits, the definition of relevant knowledge will be ambiguous and shifting. In part it will change over time, but it will also be connected to various social and interest groups. As the learning of adults will be so strongly linked to working life, instrumental/operational knowledge will continue to have a dominant position. This knowledge is the gateway to new or better jobs. The demand for shorter courses at tertiary or higher levels will increase, particularly in the poly-technical field. In the future it will probably also become more common to acquire a number of degrees through a lifelong learning process.

During the last decade up to 2020 questions will also be raised as to a one-sided instrumental approach to knowledge and competence and it will be claimed, also by employer and employee associations, that a broader understanding of "useful knowledge" is required. It will be asserted that the ability of individuals to be flexible requires a more general and basic foundation. This will be evidenced by the fact that the composition of knowledge types in working life will span a wider range than previously.

In the course of this period private businesses will recruit persons with higher education to a far greater extent. The reason will primarily be that a smaller number of candidates with such training are employed by municipal authorities and particularly by "the new state". The development shows that while two-thirds of candidates with higher education found employment in public administration at the start of the millennium, only one-third will do so in 2020. Such an influx of persons with competence from higher education will, to a certain degree, change corporate ideas about what is useful expertise and also corporate attitudes to higher education. However, in addition to academic competence, more practical competence connected to job performance, organization culture and context will be needed. This "practical competence" can only be developed by and through the work a person does. The importance of this competence will increase in the course of the indicated period of time. When being hired by business or industry, persons with high formal education will be required to show that they have acquired non-formal learning of value for the company as a "learning organization". For this reason much work is being done to survey and document such competence.

Parallel to this we will see that demands will be increasing in other sections of business and industry that are not engaged in extensive knowledge-based operations for persons who do not require formal education beyond the level of compulsory school.

Rhetorically it is pointed out a need to change the focus of education policy from a school-based didactic strategy to an "enabling strategy" that will enable all adults to learn in many more contexts than what has been the case in many countries.[1] It is said that facilitating a learning in working life that will allow all employees to follow technological developments must be a social responsibility. Programmes must be designed for the necessary training of persons of all ages who lack the required reading, writing and mathematical skills to cope satisfactorily on their own in modern society. This strategy will also build upon the aim that each individual is responsible for contributing personally to developing his/her own lifelong learning. This is supported by the fact that importance is attached to the necessity of changing our perspective from an emphasis on teaching to learning. These recommendations are not realized. Our traditional school-based vision, needless to say, has teaching as the teacher's responsibility, but the authorities behind the new strategy wish to underline that learning is the responsibility of each individual, admittedly with society's assistance.

In connection with the use of ICT a number of new visions will be launched about "new teaching" and "new learning". This will not be manifested in the programmes offered to any large degree. The main rule will continue to be that new elements will be found in technological development, while educational aspects will lag behind.

- **Competence and equality in access to knowledge**

The equality of competence will appear as an important goal in 2020. A strong belief will continue to exist that knowledge and competence will be "help for self-help" in line with the OECD's "opportunity-based strategy for lifelong

---

[1] The concept "enabling strategy" in contrast to "didactic strategy" was launched in 1998 at the conference *How Adults Learn* that was arranged by the OECD and the U.S. Department of Education in Washington DC, and this shift in strategy was also confirmed in March 1999 by the OECD's Employment, Labour and Social Affairs Committee.

learning for everyone". The idea behind this is to prevent some persons from being rejected and who would otherwise need to be defined in more costly social-welfare categories. The results of this new deal in lifelong learning nevertheless contribute little to the attainment of a greater degree of equality. The area where the greatest success will be attained will be that women eventually will take equally long education as men do, and that they will move into previously male-dominated studies more than before. When it comes to equality between geographical regions, it is acknowledged that education primarily has functioned as the instigator of a greater degree of centralization. The paradox is that even if it has been made formally possible for a higher number of people to take education, the content of education has strengthened other partly urban values.

A more liberal social philosophy both on the part of the powers-that-be and within less privileged groups, for example new immigrants, ensures that the equality issue is no longer seen as so important as suggested by the education policy programme notes. Moreover, as mentioned previously, formal education will most likely have less importance as the demand for non-formal learning and the more post-modern "competence that shows the difference" grows more popular. This will apply to both the philosopher in the café and for the enterprising businessman looking for a niche in business or industry.

- **The situation for primary school and upper secondary school**

Even if lifelong learning essentially comprises compulsory school, new and good connecting lines have not been created between the various education levels. Nor has an education system been developed that enables the realization of the visions of recurrent education. Young people must still stay in school for six to twenty years with few or no opportunities for other social contact. This will cause the problems currently experienced by school to increase, for example disciplinary problems will be on the rise as school becomes even more of a baby-sitting institution. In 2020 one finds far too frequently that the types of school intended to create motivation and inspiration for continued learning in actual fact "achieve" the opposite. For this reason we will see a growing interest in private schools. Growing numbers of parents rebel against comprehensive school understood as a place "where everybody should have the more or less same poor conditions". Primary school is particularly full of disillusioned teachers and encounters more and more problems recruiting teachers. Schooling for children and young persons will have about the same duration as today. The public authorities will, to some extent attempt to establish alternative programmes; but these will primarily be seen as stop-gap solutions for those who fall out of the system, not as genuine alternatives for everyone.

A number of large companies will establish their own upper secondary schools to recruit critical-factor labour for the company. This will most likely apply generally to vocational study branches with apprentice programmes.

Based on a lifelong learning perspective it is also probable that short and "custom-made" vocational education for adults will be established, where the competence the individual has acquired earlier will be credited.

Towards a future vision

Through brief glimpses we have hopefully offered some inspiration for reflections on the development of lifelong learning in the coming years. Our perspectives are generally based on the idea that there will be a continuous development in this field in the years to come without any major breaks or radical changes. Anything we cannot be sure about needless to say cannot be used as the foundation for our vision of the future. However, if, for example, a major environmental disaster occurred and had huge consequences for the Nordic countries, lifelong learning might take another direction entirely. Perhaps the financial rationales will be side-tracked, the state might become a more active instigator or society and the environment might receive greater priority at the expense of lifelong learning.

To guide our further discussion and research work on various aspects of the probable future development for lifelong learning in the Nordic countries, we will invite our respondents to offer more comments, questions and new ideas on this theme. Through more rounds of analysis of the existing material and new insight from our co-players we hope to broaden some of the perspectives within this theme.

References

Bell, D. (1973). *The Coming of Post-Industrial Society – A Venture in Social Forecasting.* New York: Basic Books Inc.

Giddens, A. (1991). *Modernity and Self-Identity – Self and Society in the Late Modern Age.* Oxford: Polity Press.

Grepperud, G. (1999). *Samarbeid mellom høgre utdanning og folkeuniversitetet. Omfang, aktivitet og relasjon- (Cooperation between the Norwegian Higher Education System and The Adult Education and Training Association).* Forskningsrapport 44. Høgskolen i Lillehammer.

Grepperud, G. (2000). *Økt kunnskap er også en utfordring- The Challenge of the Knowledge Society.* Under arbeid.

Mellin-Olsen, S. (1996). *Samtalen som forskningsmetode: Tekster om kvalitativ forskningsmetode som del av pedagogisk virksomhet (The conversation as research method).* Caspar forlag: Bergen.

The Ministry of Education, Research and Church Affairs (1997). NOU 1997:25 *Ny kompetanse* (*New competence*).

The Ministry of Labour and Local Government (1998). *Norge 2030 – en forvaltningspolitisk visjon for det neste årtusen [Norway 2030 – An administrative policy vision for the next millennium].* Memo: Oslo.

The Nordic Council of Ministers. (1998). *Pamphlet on popular enlightenment and working life in the Nordic countries.*

Torney-Purta, J. et al. (1999). *Civic Education Across Countries: Twenty-four Nation Case Studies from the IEA Civic Education Project.* The International Association for Evaluation of Educational Achievement. Amsterdam.

Contributors

Leena Ahteenmäki-Pelkonen
EdD, Department of Education, University of Helsinki, Finland
Research interests: Self-directed learning, open learning, distance education, supervision (arbetshandledning), critical theory, transformation theory
Address: Department of Education, P.O. Box 39, FIN - 00014 University of Helsinki.
Telephone: + 358 9 191 28007 or + 358 400 403 467
Fax: + 358 9 191 28073
E-mail: leena.ahteenmaki-pelkonen@helsinki.fi

Heidi Engesbak
Cand. pol. (sociology), researcher at the Norwegian Institute of Adult Education, Trondheim. Fields of research: Reform 94, social mobility, social reproduction, work values, cultural consumption.
Address: Norwegian Institute of Adult Education, Nedre Bakklandet 60, N-7014 Trondheim.
Telephone: + 47 73 99 08 40
Fax: + 47 73 99 08 50
E-mail: Heidi.Engesbak@nvi.no

Karin Filander
LicEd, Researcher in the Research Institute for Social Sciences, Work Research Centre at the University of Tampere.
Filander has worked as a co-ordinator of continuing education in the Institute of Extension Studies at the University of Tampere. She is now participating in a multidisciplinary research project in the Work Research Centre. The project is studying the modernization process of the Finnish public sector from the viewpoint of human resources and work organizations. Filander's study contributes to an analysis of changes in agency, subjectivity and identity in the Finnish public sector.
Address: Work Research Centre, University of Tampere, FIN-33014 University of Tampere.
Telephone: + 358 3 215 7259
Fax: + 358 3 215 7265
E-mail: ttkafi@uta.fi

Gunnar Grepperud
Professor in distance education at the University of Tromsø.
Address: UNIKOM, University of Tromsø, 9037 Tromsø.
Telephone: + 47 776 45963
Fax: + 47 776 44554
E-mail: Gunnarg@unikom.uit.no

Anja Heikkinen
PhD, Professor of adult education at the Department of Education, University of Jyväskylä, Finland.
Heikkinen has initiating the network vocational education and culture since 1993 which will be found on http://www.uta.fi/~hoanhe/vetcult.
Address; University of Jyväskylä, P.O. Box 35, 40 351 Jyväskylä
Telephone: + 358 14 260 1670
Fax: + 358 14 260 1661
E-mail: hoanhe@edu.jyu.fi

Marianne Horsdal
Mag. art. in Literature, Associate Research Professor at the Department for Contemporary Cultural Studies, University of Southern Denmark, Odense Denmark
Horsdal is taking part in the Research Project on Adult Education and Democracy, and she has completed a report for a pilot project under the program Democracy 2000 ,«The sites of liberal education as a basis for citizenship» which is a comparative investigation based on life-stories from Norway, Finland, and Denmark
Research interests: Narratives, identity, citizenship, life-long learning, intercultural learning, and democracy.
Address: Nørrebystrand 27, 5400 Bogense, Denmark
Telephone: + 45 64 86 14 01
E-mail: horsdal@litcul.sdu.dk

Odd Einar Johansen
Fil. mag. in Social science/international pedagogy, former secretary-general of The Norwegian Folk University and now Director of Public affairs, The Norwegian directorate of Labour Inspection, Oslo.
Fields of research: Adult education, international education and competence.
E-mail: Odd.Einar.Johansen@arbeidstilsynet.dep.no

Juha Kettunen
PhD, D.Sc, Director of Vantaa Institute for Continuing Education, University of Helsinki, Lummetie 2 A, FIN-01300 Vantaa, Finland.
Telephone: +358 9 19129001 (office)
+ 358 50 5512280 (mobile)
Fax: + 358 9 19129000
E-mail: Juha.Kettunen@helsinki.fi
Main fields of research: Management education, continuing education, and labour markets.

Ove Korsgaard
Phd, Associate Professor at the former Royal Danish School of Educational Studies, from July 1, 2000 The Danish National Institute for Educational Research, Hermods gade 28, DK 2200 Copenhagen N, Denmark.
Field of research: Adult Education, democracy, globalization.
Telephone: + 45 35 81 01 40
Fax: + 45 35 81 45 51
E-mail: ove@dlh.dk

Kristiina Laiho
Researcher at the Department of Education, University of Jyväskylä, Finland.
Address; University of Jyväskylä, P.O. Box 35, 40 351 Jyväskylä
Telephone: + 358 14 260 1670
Fax: + 358 14 260 1661
E-mail: kristiina.laiho@saunalahti.fi

Vanttaja, Markku
Master of Education, researcher in the Department of Education, University of Turku. Fields of research: Sociology of Education and Adult Education.
Address: Department of Education, University of Turku, Lemminkäisenkatu 1, 20520 Turku, Finland.
Telephone: + 358 2 333 8584
Fax: + 358 2 333 8830
E-mail: markku.vanttaja@utu.fi

Torstein Rekkedal
Cand. ped., Director of Research and Development, NKI, Norway.
Rekkedal has published a lot of books, research reports, articles and papers on media, methods, student support and counselling in distance education and he

has chaired the research committees of the International Council for Distance Education and the Association of European Correspondence Schools.
Address: P.O. Box. 111, N-1341 Bekkestua, Norway.
Telephone: + 67 58 88 00
Fax: +67 53 05 00
E-mail: Torstein.Rekkedal@adm.nki.no

Risto Rinne
PhD., Professor in Adult Education in the Department of Education, University of Turku. Visiting Professor in Aalborg University. Fields of research: Sociology of Education, History of Education, Comparative Research.
Address: Department of Education, University of Turku, Lemminkäisenkatu 1, 20520 Turku, Finland
Telephone: + 358 2 333 8818
Fax: + 358 2 333 8830
E-mail: Rinne@utu.fi

Hannele Salminen
Licentiate in Science of Education (Lis. Sc. of Ed.). Development Manager at the Department for Education and Science Policy in the Division for Adult Education and Training, Ministry of Education, Finland.
Main field of research: Education reforms, education policy and policy planning.
Address: Meritullinkatu 10, 00170 Helsinki, Finland.
Telephone: +358 9 1341 7264
Fax: +358 9 13416984
E-mail: hannele.salminen@minedu.fi

Per-Olof Thång
PhD, Associate Professor at the Department of Education, Göteborg University, Box 300, S- 405 30 Göteborg, Sweden.
Main fields of research: Adult education, mainly municipal adult education, labour market training and also learning in working life with a focus on short educated people in industry.
Telephone: + 46 31 773 2239
Fax + 46 31 773 2089
E-mail: Per-Olof.Thang@ped.gu.se

Tarja Tikkanen
PhD. associate professor at the Norwegian Institute of Adult Education, Trondheim.

Fields of research: Learning, training of older workers, competence development, participation in adult education, lifelong learning.
Address: Norwegian Institute of Adult Education, Nedre Bakklandet 60, N-7014 Trondheim.
Telephone: + 47 73 99 08 40
Fax: + 47 73 99 08 50
E-mail: tarja.tikkanen@nvi.no

Sigvart Tøsse
Cand. phil., associate professor at the Norwegian Institute of Adult Education, Trondheim. Fields of research: History of adult and popular education, workers' education and adult education policy.
Address: Norwegian Institute of Adult Education, Nedre Bakklandet 60, N-7014 Trondheim.
Telephone: + 47 73 99 08 40
Fax: + 47 73 99 08 50
E-mail: sigvart.tosse@nvi.no

Bjarne Wahlgren
PhD, professor of Adult Education at the former Royal Danish School of Education Studies, Copenhagen, and director of Danish Research Centre for Adult Education. Fields of research: Learning in the workplace end the developing work, the relation between non-formal education (folkeoplysning) and the working life, qualifications of teachers and education policy.
Address: The Danish National Institute for Educational Research, Hermods gade 28, DK 2200 Copenhagen N, Denmark.
Telephone: + 45 39 69 66 33
Fax: + 45 39 66 32 32
E-mail: wahlgren@dlh1.dlh.dk

Gun-Britt Wärwik
PhD student at the Department of Education, Göteborg University, Box 300, S-405 30 Göteborg, Sweden.
Main field of research: Adult education with a main focus on learning in working life.
Telephone: + 46 31 773 2266
Fax + 46 31 773 2089
E-mail: Gun-Britt.Warvik@ped.gu.se